CONTENTS

Raoul Millais: *Study of a Grey Hunter*.

MILLAIS:

THREE GENERATIONS IN NATURE, ART AND SPORT

MILLAIS

Three Generations in Nature, Art & Sport

J N P WATSON

THE
SPORTSMAN'S
PRESS
LONDON

Published by The Sportsman's Press 1988

Watson, J.N.P. (John N.P.)
  Millais: three generations in nature art and sport.
  1. English paintings (Family). Millais
  I. Title
  759.2

ISBN 0-948253-28-2

Photoset and printed in Great Britain
BAS Printers Limited, Over Wallop, Hampshire

PREFACE

This is the saga about an unusual inheritance of family talents and interests. Since much has already been written on that great 'Renaissance' figure, John Everett Millais, I have confined myself to a general survey of his career and his affection for history and music as well as art – while emphasising a side of his character to which little attention has so far been given. That was his close and abiding dialogue with wild Nature and his passion for field sports – particularly flyfishing, deerstalking, gameshooting and hunting (riding to hounds) – and which he probably loved in that order. I do not believe it would be an exaggeration to say that he devoted one-quarter of his active life to those pursuits.

Effie, his wife, combined her communion with music and art and her considerable sense of history with a deep interest in wild life and a wholehearted approval of the countryside sports. There was little that John and Effie Millais did not share.

However, it seems that although they did all they could to encourage in their children an interest in natural history and everything to do with the countryside, they did little to arouse any dormant gifts there may have been in the artistic sphere. Perhaps they had seen too much of what was described in Victorian times as 'the long-haired, velvet-coated tribe!' – too many of whom at worst pretended, or best aspired, but too few of whom attained. The boy who became one of Britain's great portrayers of wildlife, their son John Guille (who represents the middle generation in this book) received virtually no formal art training, and was persuaded to make the army his career.

Throughout his six years service in the Seaforth Highlanders, however – in Edinburgh, Glasgow and Dublin – he contrived continuously to ply his natural history research, his sport and his drawing and painting of mammals and birds, all of which interests had begun in early childhood. And the evidence is that, notwithstanding those preoccupations, he proved an entirely dedicated and successful soldier, although his commanding officers must have found his many applications for leave rather tiresome at times. John Guille, like his father, joined his talent with an extraordinary questing mind and adventurous spirit. As nothing substantial has appeared in print regarding this towering Victorian/ Edwardian hunter – apart from his own writings (of which I am happy to admit to making the most extensive use) – I have given him a considerably larger part of the book than his more celebrated father.

It must be extremely rare for men in three consecutive generations to share a similar genius, interests and recreational motivations; but I can think of no better example of it than Sir John, John Guille and the latter's son, Raoul. For Raoul, who emerged from the Byam Shaw and Royal Academy Schools as a highly accomplished animal artist, went on, as a professional equestrian painter, to draw anything he chose with consummate skill. He is, too, as I shall show, like his father and grandfather an irrepressible field sports-man, a traditionalist and a conservative in the best sense of those terms, and a person of colossal energy.

There are, perhaps, those armchair psychologists who will interpret the mutual zest for shooting and fishing in these three generations of artists as a necessary Philistine counterbalance in their characters. On the contrary, readers of this book who are hunters – hunters in the widest sense, from rough shooters and fishers with float-and-worm to big-game hunters and riders to hounds – understand that the pursuit of animal by man, done wisely and sympathetically, can endow the closest possible involvement with Nature. And that if those sports are 'cruel' they save hundreds of worse cruelties.

The paradox is that the more the true and devoted hunter pursues, the more his knowledge grows and the more he loves that which he kills. No breed of men is more conscious of that phenomenon than the Millais clan. I do not believe that John Guille Millais, for example, could have achieved anything like the scope of animal pictures that came from his pencils and brushes had he not been motivated by his ever-prevailing hunter-adventurer instinct. Since his day mankind has become increasingly aware that sport, of that idealistic nature, and wildlife conservation are closely linked.

Without the help and continuous cooperation of Mr Raoul Millais I could scarcely have attempted to piece these three generations together comprehensively. He not only lent me copious family notes, papers, books, paintings and sketches, but spent many hours, over a period of some ten months, talking about his father and grandfather's work as well as that of his own. I am profusely grateful to him, too, for checking all my typescripts. My thanks are also due to his son, Hugh, who took similar trouble reading through my chapters and making many useful suggestions.

The photograph of Lady Millais is reproduced by Gracious permission of Her Majesty the Queen. In addition I would like to record my warmest appreciation to the following: Mr and Mrs John Lees-Millais who lent me family photographs and showed me their collection of Millais paintings; Mr Nicholas Fitzherbert for permission to reproduce Raoul Millais' painting of his father, Major Cuthbert Fitzherbert; Mr Jeremy Maas for allowing me to reproduce Frank Baden-Powell's monochrome portrait of Sir John Millais at his last visit to the Royal Academy; Major Nicholas Collin for the portrait of his champion greyhound, Holystone Fairy; the Hon. Mrs Simon Maxwell for *Stallions Fighting;* the Garrick Club for Charles Holroyd's portrait of Sir John Millais; the Countess of Feversham for permission to reproduce Raoul Millais' equestrian portrait of her; the National Portrait Gallery for Sir John Millais' portrait of John Leech, Thomas Woolner's portrait of William Holman Hunt and the photograph of J. E. Millais posing as Dante; Mr Hamish Wallace for lending me the photograph of his father, Frank Wallace; Mr John Wylie for *Summer Morning*; Lord Ashcombe for permission to reproduce Raoul Millais' painting of the Cubitt boys and Major Bruce Shand and Mrs Simon Elliott for the photograph of it; my neighbours, Mr Peter Stephen Hornung and Mrs Peter Duncanson for the loan of several first edition books by J.G. Millais; the Tate Gallery for *The Order of Release*; Merseyside County Art Galleries for *St Isumbras at the Ford*; Glasgow Art Gallery and Museum for *The Ruling Passion*; Manchester City Art Gallery for *Glen Birnam*; the staffs of the British Library, London Library and Westminster City Library for their helpful cooperation; Mrs Audrey Guy, who typed the text; and to my wife, Lavinia who handled the plethora of correspondence connected with that and the illustrations.

J.N.P.W.
Pannett's Shipley
Horsham
Sussex

1

CHILD MEDALLIST

Enter John Everett, born 1829

'Roselle . . . proved an endless source of interest and amusement to the juvenile artist. He could fish when he liked in ponds well stocked with perch and tench, and in the park was a fine herd of fallow deer, in which he took great delight. A drawing of his – perhaps his best at that date – represents the tragic end of one of those beautiful creatures that he happened to witness. The circumstance impressed him deeply and, as he often remarked in after life, aroused in him the spirit of the chase, even in those early days and in such calm surroundings . . .'

That is John Guille Millais – popularly known as Johnny – writing of his father, John Everett Millais. The period is the mid-1830s, when John Everett Millais was a boy of six or seven years old and the setting the island of Jersey where the Millais' had made and kept their home since the time of the Norman Conquest.

I begin the saga there, because taken as a whole, the family motivation concerns sport; it is as much about the pursuit of game, fur, feather and fin, with rod, gun and horse as it is about art. The mutual drive of these three successive generations of men, John Everett, Johnny and Raoul, is a devotion to Nature, animals, plant and human nature, expressed in an endless seeking to know Mother Nature's truths, through interpreting her graphically, accurately by pencil, pen and brush, in her every aspect. But man is also a predatory animal and not necessarily less an artist for that. The good predator retains a deep affection for that which he hunts; he is thrilled by the chase. The colour, the smell, the composition of the landscape, the creatures' habitats, take on a fresh excitement for him, whether with hound, gun or rod, when the hunt is on. So it was neither contradiction nor paradox that John Everett Millais, the aesthete, who was co-founder of the Pre-Raphaelite Brotherhood and eventually President of the Royal Academy, should have 'the spirit of the chase aroused in him' by the beautiful sight of that dead fallow deer, or that he should become a passionately keen rider to hounds and spend two or three months of every year of the majority of his adult life shooting and fishing in the Highlands.

John Everett Millais, though a delicate child, was an infant prodigy. 'When he was only four,' said a contemporary cousin, 'he was continually at work with pencil and paper, and generally lay on the floor covering sheets with all sorts of figures . . . when he did anything on a larger scale he used to come to my father throwing his arms round his neck in an affectionate manner, saying "Uncle, you do not always praise me as the others do; you show me the faults".'[1] A conventional education was not in the boy's scheme of things. He saw it as stultifying, inhibiting, an impediment to his moral and emotional growth. After only two days at school, when a master tried to beat him for disobedience, he bit the man's hand and was immediately expelled. His mother – born Emily Mary

Evamy, the widow of a Mr Hodgkinson when she married John William Millais – a woman of forceful personality and one with a great love of painting and music, became his tutor and a most successful one, too. 'I owe everything to my mother,' declared John Everett when he grew up. But he was duly thankful to his father, a fine man, a musician and artist, too, and, incidentally, one who held the reputation of being 'the handsomest man on Jersey'. Good looks are a Millais trait.

'Better make the boy a chimney-sweep than a artist,' said the Millais' friend, the President of the Royal Academy, Sir Martin Archer Shee. But when he saw some of John Everett's drawings – many done when the boy was with his parents in Brittany for two years in the mid-1830s – he was astonished, 'hardly believing they were the production of so childish a hand.'[2] When the boy was nine a place was secured for him in Mr Sass's preparatory school of art in Bloomsbury and, while there, he secured the Society of Art's silver medal. Young Millais related how, the day following the presentation, three jealous bullies, one of whom had also competed for the medal, overpowered him and hung him, head downwards, out of the window, tying his ankles to the window-guards with scarves and cords. He was unconscious by the time some passers-by rushed to the doorbell and obtained his release.

HRH The Duke of Sussex who presided at the prize-giving 'patted my brother's head,' recalled William Millais, 'kindly begging him to remember that if at any time he could be of service to him he must not hesitate to write and say so . . . We had been in the habit of fishing every year in the Serpentine and Round Pond by means of tickets given to us by Sir Frederick Pollock, then Chief Baron; but a day came when this permission was withheld from everyone. Then my brother wrote to the Duke's private secretary, and we were again allowed to fish there . . .

'In those days the Round Pond at Kensington was a favourite resort of ours. The shores were fringed with flags and rushes. There was plenty of English mud, too, in which the juvenile angler could wade and had to do so in order to get his line clear of the surrounding reeds. We used to tramp to and from the neighbourhood of Bedford Square buying our fresh bait at the Golden Perch, in Oxford Street, on the way. We were keen sportsmen, and probably the pleasure we took in it was not lessened by the envy of other little boys to whom the privilege was denied. As a result of these expeditions many fine carp, perch and roach were captured.'[3]

When he was still only ten John Everett was admitted to the Royal Academy Schools, the youngest pupil ever to find a place there. Archer Shee was now even readier to propose him to the keeper of the Royal Academy Schools: 'Not having any of the printed forms used on this occasion I beg leave to recommend the bearer John Everett Millais as a candidate to become a probationer in the Royal Academy. His age and aspect will, I think, justify me in bearing favourable testimony to his *moral* character, and combined with his talents will, I am sure, interest you in his favour . . .'[4]

But the honour and the rigour of that did nothing to reduce young Millais' passion for the outdoors, the countryside and sport. He and his brother William were enthusiastic cricketers, going to Lords every Saturday in the season to study the game; and, during the summer holidays, they often walked all the way to Hornsey and back for a day's fishing in the New River. The brothers also delighted in adopting a vantage point by Buckingham Palace to watch the Queen and the Prince Consort take their daily drive up Constitution Hill. Their father was with them the day a lunatic fired a pistol at the Queen; and, says William, 'my father immediately rushed away from us and seized the man, who was just inside the railings of the park, and held him till some of the mounted escort came to his assistance.'

John Everett often stayed with his half-brother, Henry Hodgkinson, at Oxford, and while there made the acquaintance of the owner of nearby Shotover Park, Mr Drury, who took a great liking to him and gave him a gun with complete liberty to shoot over his property. William went once, too, 'And we boys had the run of the place to our hearts' content, fishing and shooting wherever we liked.'

The seed of Pre-Raphaelitism, the school of art with which the name of Millais is, above all, associated, began around 1843 when William Holman Hunt and John Everett first met in boyhood, when Millais was in the Academy Schools and Holman Hunt had failed in his first attempt to draw there. 'Suddenly the doors opened and a curly-haired lad came in and began skipping about the room,' Hunt remembers. 'By-and-by he danced round until he was behind me, looked at my drawing for a minute, then skipped off again. About a week later I found the same boy drawing from a cast in another room, and returned the compliment by staring at *his* drawing. Millais, who of course it was, turned round suddenly and said, "Oh, I say you're the chap that was working in Number 12 the other day. You ought to be in the Academy". This led to a long talk at which Millais said that he was much struck by the drawing which he had seen me working at . . . and that if a drawing or two like that were shown for probationship, I should be admitted at once.' He soon was.

Later, the two boys shared a studio and even contributed to one another's paintings, their styles being remarkably similar. They also held the mutual opinion that true art implies an unswerving faithfulness to Nature and that the Renaissance artist, Raphael, who was then the great idol of the art world, was, in fact, an imperfect craftsman, even

A sketch by John Everett Millais from 1841, when he was twelve years old.

(*left*) John Everett Millais in his twenties.

(*below*) Close friends of the artist: (*left*) William Holman Hunt by Thomas Woolner, 1853 and (*right*) John Leech in 1852 by Millais.

an imposter. 'His cartoons, in particular, show this,' the two youthful geniuses agreed, 'and his *Transfiguration* still further betrays the falsity of his methods. We must go back to earlier times for examples of sound and satisfactory work.'

In old age, Holman Hunt wrote to Millais' son, Johnny, telling him that 'it was in the year 1848 that your father and I determined to adopt a style of absolute independence as to art-dogma and convention: this we called "Pre-Raphaelitism". Dante Gabriel Rossetti was already my pupil, and it seemed certain that he also, in time, would work on the same principles . . . he added to our title of "Pre-Raphaelite" the word "Brotherhood" . . . shortly afterwards William Rossetti, F. G. Stephens and James Collinson joined . . .'[5] Their motto was: 'Truth and the Free Field of Unadulterated Nature'. They published their own magazine *The Germ*: they vowed not to smoke, drink or swear; they made a point of keeping aloof from the Academy, whose establishment condemned the style and hated the mutual signature to be found in the corner of Pre-Raphaelite Brotherhood pictures. Nevertheless, Millais was proposed and seconded, in 1850, as a candidate to be an Associate of the Royal Academy and was only refused on account of his age.

D. G. Rossetti's membership of the Brotherhood was shortlived. 'It turned out that he was never a Pre-Raphaelite at heart,' said Holman Hunt (who taught him practically all the technique he ever knew). 'Only two years after he first joined the Brotherhood, I got him to come down to Knole to paint a background straight from Nature which I overlooked and helped him with. After two days, however, Rossetti was heartily sick of Nature, and bolted back to London and its artificial life.' Millais, as Johnny points out, was a quite different character. 'My father hated humbug . . . It was the poetry of Nature that appealed to him – the love, hope, sweetness and purity that he found there – and it was the passionate desire to express what he felt so deeply that spurred him on from the beginning to the end of his life.' (Much later Beatrix Potter was to give witness to Millais' contempt for Rossetti's work. 'Papa asked Mr Millais yesterday what he thought of the Rossetti pictures', she wrote in her journal for 5 March 1883. 'He said they were all rubbish, that the people had goitres – that Rossetti never learnt drawing and could not draw. A funny accusation for one P.R.B. to make at another.')[6]

Millais loved people much more than things; he was fascinated by personality and human motivations. Deeply preoccupied, too, with the romantic side of history and literature, he favoured the big canvas, on which he could distil life-size, dramatic, poignant and beautiful scenes from the past, with every character, every point of clothing, every artefact, drawn and painted with the minutest accuracy. The first of his Royal Academy exhibits, painted when he was seventeen, was *Pizzaro Seizing the Inca of Peru* and then, said Spielmann (who was one day to write the introduction to the catalogue of Millais' posthumous exhibition) '. . . he was recognised as a marvel and all stood astonished at his work.'[7] The loathed Pre-Raphaelite Brotherhood signature first appeared from his hand in the corner of *Isabella*, the subject for which Millais took from Keats's paraphrase of Giovanni Boccaccio's fourteenth-century narrative verse. Holman Hunt described the picture as 'the most wonderful in the world for a lad of twenty'.

That was followed by *Christ in the Carpenter's Shop*, portraying the boy Jesus with his parents, *The Return of the Dove to the Ark*, and, in 1850, what was described as 'the most Pre-Raphaelite', *The Woodman's Daughter*, an analogy, a study of the tentative yet affectionate childhood meeting between aristocracy and peasantry in which, as a Pre-Raphaelite supporter remarked, 'Every blade of grass, every leaf and branch and every shadow that they cast in the sunny wood is presented here with unflinching realism and infinite delicacy of detail,' while Millais' brother William, records that 'every touch in the fretwork tracery, all about it has been caressed by a true lover of his art. I think, perhaps, the most beautiful background ever painted by my brother is to be found in *The Woodman's Daughter* . . .

In these his glorious early days, one can see that not an iota was slurred over, but that every beauty in Nature met with its due appreciation at his hands.' In 1852 came *Ophelia*, over which the botanists expressed themselves amazed at the minute accuracy of every leaf and flower.

That devotion reflected Millais' strong dislike of London and yearning for the country, a prejudice which he frequently expressed. He was over six feet tall and very strong, though exceptionally slim. When he was unable to get away rambling and sporting in the country he practised all sorts of feats of agility in his Gower Street studio. The Pre-Raphaelite, F. G. Stephens – who was the model, in 1849, for Ferdinand in Millais' *Ferdinand Lured by Ariel* – recalled that 'it was in the Gower Street studio that Millais was wont, when time did not allow for outdoor exercises, to perform surprising feats of agility and strength. He had . . . so greatly developed in tallness, bulk and manliness that no one was surprised at his progress in these respects. He was great in leaping, and I well remember how, in the studio, he was wont to clear my arm outstretched from the shoulder, that is about five feet from the ground, at one spring. The studio measures nineteen feet six inches by twenty feet thus giving him not more than fourteen feet run. Many similar feats attested the strength and energy of the artist.'[8]

Millais hated dirt and smoke, ugliness and vulgarity of every kind. Here he is in a letter written from Gower Street at the time of the Great Exhibition of 1851: 'such a quantity of loathsome foreigners stroll about the principal streets that they incline one to take up residence in Sweden outside of the fumes of their tobacco. I expect all respectable families will leave London after the first month of the Exhibition, it will be so crowded with the lowest rabble of all the countries in Europe.' He also had little time for pomp and circumstance. 'Do you intend coming to town to see the funeral of the Duke [of Wellington]?' he was asking Mr Combe on 23 October 1852. 'I do not generally care for such things, But I shall make a little struggle for that. It will be worth seeing.'[9]

He soon found a new outlet for his superabundant energy, his sporting instincts and desire for country air. He became a close friend of John Leech, *Punch*'s chief cartoonist, the original illustrator of the Surtees novels and a great many other books, and an ardent devotee of the hunting field. (Leech was in like mind with the old ostler he drew in *Punch* and had him saying 'the 'orses like it, the 'ounds like it, the men like it, and even the fox likes it!') He introduced Millais to foxhunting and at the end of 1853 Millais was writing: 'Every Saturday I accompany Leech, the *Punch* draughtsman, into Hertfordshire, where good horses await us, and we stay overnight at a friend's, and set off in the morning. I have been four times out and have only had one spill, which did not hurt me in the least. I should not follow the chase, but that I enjoy it above all other recreation, and find myself quite fitted for such exercise. The first time I ever rode over a fence gave me confidence from the comparatively easy way in which I kept my seat. Since then I have ridden over pretty nearly every kind of hedge and ditch.' Leech took him along to an Oxford Street bootmaker, who observing that Millais' calves and ankles were what Johnny describes as 'in the embryo state so mortifying to young manhood', exclaimed politely, 'Ah, Sir, what a fine leg for a boot.' But he quickly took the wind out of Millais' sails by adding 'same size all the way up!' Leech was so amused he immortalised the scene in *Punch*.

Johnny recounts his father's further hunting career. 'By the end of the first season he had acquired a firm seat on horseback, and was known as a bold rider across country; and except when in later years Scotland claimed his presence, he followed the hounds with ardour year by year, visiting alternately, Hertfordshire, Bedfordshire and Leicester, where he and Leech and Mike Halliday [friend and pupil of Millais] kept their hunters . . .'[10]

A painting by John Everett Millais, aged twenty: *The Woodman's Daughter*. It was described as 'his most Pre-Raphaelite'.

John Everett Millais in the hunting field, by Leech.

In 1855 Millais introduced Leech to salmon fishing. Leech was fascinated with the sport and within a month was writing excitedly to Millais that 'last week I went out pike fishing at a most beautiful place called Fillgate with one Jolliffe . . . he was in the 4th Light Dragoons and was in the ever memorable Balaclava charge. He gave me a vivid description of the dreadful business. Altogether I have rarely had a more pleasant day . . . Let me hear from you sometimes, for cannot your time be much more agreeably employed than writing to yours always, my dear fellow, John Leech.'[11]

By that time Millais was married to Effie, formerly the wife of John Ruskin, champion of the Pre-Raphaelites. Millais and Effie's dramatic romance began just as the Crimean war, referred to in Leech's letter, was brewing.

PLATE 1   John Everett Millais: *The Order of Release, 1746*, 1852–3.
Effie Ruskin, the artist's future wife, stood for the
woman in the painting.

PLATE 2   John Everett Millais: *Glen Birnam*, 1891.

2

EFFIE

John Ruskin's fame as an art critic dated from 1843, when he was only twenty-four, and the first volume of his *Modern Painters* was published. By 1851, when he began to praise the work of the hitherto scorned Pre-Raphaelites, there were few who disputed his taste and judgement. 'Mr Millais and Mr Holman Hunt are endeavouring to paint, with the highest possible degree of completion, what they see in Nature,' he enthused, 'without reference to conventional or established rules; but by no means to imitate the style of any past epoch. Their works are, in finish of drawing and in splendour of colour, the best in the Royal Academy, and I have great hope that they may become the foundation of a more earnest and able school of art than we have seen here for centuries . . .' The Brotherhood could not have asked for a more valuable or authoritative supporter; Ruskin added that he 'could not compliment them in the choice of a *nom de guerre*, as the principles are neither Pre-Raphaelite, nor Post-Raphaelite, but everlasting.'[1]

Through that association Millais was soon a friend of the Ruskins, who were 'captivated by his natural charm, his exuberant interest in human experience and childlike impulsiveness in conversation.'[2] In the spring of 1853 Effie Ruskin – the daughter of George and Sophia Gray of Bowerswell, Perth – stood as the model for the wife of the young rebel Scottish clansman in Millais' eighteenth-century scene, *The Order of Release, 1746*. The setting is a prison waiting-room in which the Highlander is shown ushered by the gaoler to his wife who carries their child, while proffering the certificate of pardon. The family collie – a delightful example of Millais' loving skill as an animal artist – has its forefeet on the prisoner's kilt. 'As a piece of realistic painting it may challenge comparison with anything else in the world,' was Andrew Lang's verdict. 'The work is saved by expression and colour from the realism of a photograph.' *The Order of Release* turned out in its way to be a most prophetic picture for Millais and Effie.

That summer Ruskin was invited to give a series of lectures in Edinburgh. Resolving to combine that expedition with a tour of the Highlands for himself and his wife, he invited Holman Hunt and Millais and Millais' brother, William, to accompany them. Hunt, who was planning to sail to Palestine to paint, declined, but the Millais brothers readily accepted. The Ruskins' servant, Crawley, completed the party. They had no sooner finished the first leg of their journey, in Northumberland, than Millais in a letter to Hunt was declaring himself enthralled with Effie. 'Today I have been drawing Mrs Ruskin, who is the sweetest creature that ever lived; she is the most pleasant companion one could wish . . . Ruskin is benign and kind. I wish you were here with us. You would like it.'

Ruskin led them on via Edinburgh, Stirling and Callandar, to Brig o' Turk by Loch Venarchar, a place that particularly appealed to him for its associations with Scott's novels. They would have stayed there at the New Trossachs Inn only a night or two, had not Ruskin decided to commission Millais to paint a pair of portraits locally, one of Effie at the ruins of Doune castle, the other of himself by a stream. ('Than Ruskin no author has written of hurrying water more eloquently, or loved it more consumingly,' in the words of his biographer; 'from the Tay to the sources of the Rhone, from mighty and powerful rivers to sparkling country streamlets.')[3] The spot Millais chose, for what was to become one of his most celebrated studies, was the river at Glenfinlas. 'A lovely piece of worn rock, with foaming water, and weeds and moss and a noble overhanging bank of dark crag,' Ruskin wrote to his parents, 'and I am to be looking quietly down the stream. I think you will be proud of the picture.'[4]

Ruskin liked the feel of Brig o' Turk; he found it a congenial place in which to compile his 86-page index for his *Stones of Venice* and to prepare his Edinburgh lectures; and he did not wish Millais to hurry over the portraits. Moreover he was confined with a sprained ankle for part of the four months they were there. While William Millais spent most of his time fishing and sketching, John Everett and Effie were increasingly together. It rained most of the time. 'Wet weather again,' Ruskin was telling his parents on 14 July, 'but Millais has painted a beautiful study of Effie with foxgloves in her hair, and I think he will do the castle of Doune superbly.' After a few days they moved from the inn, to cheaper accommodation in the village schoolmaster's house. Millais' pupil and fellow-sportsman, Mike Halliday, came to stay with them for a few days and much fun was had by all.

When it was wet Effie and Millais played battledore and shuttlecock or read to one another or blew bubbles, and she cut his hair for him and recounted episodes from Scottish history of which she had a great knowledge. When it was fine they went for long walks on the heather moors and he taught her drawing and painting, and Effie wrote to her mother that she 'never saw such a kind dear man as Mr Millais.' Hearing a servant refer to her as 'the Countess' that was Millais' nickname for her ever after. He drew numerous sketches of the party's activities, such as *Highland Shelter*, showing himself and Effie closely covered by a plaid against the rain, and *Awey – yegoo!*, a local injunction for sending people on their way or seeing them off on an outing, which was a favourite expression of Effie's. She and Everett, as she called him (to distinguish him from the other John, her husband), had a great deal in common, a mutual sense of humour, a deep feeling for history and a great love of wild life and the beauties of Nature, among many other things. Her appreciation of art was approaching the level of his own.

Millais was now growing a little disenchanted with Ruskin. 'Having the acquaintance of Mrs Ruskin is a blessing,' he informed Hunt; 'her husband is a good fellow, but not of our kind, his soul is always with the clouds and out of reach of ordinary mortals – I mean that he theorises about the vastness of space and looks at a lovely little stream in practical contempt.' Ruskin, for his part, posted a letter to his father saying 'I don't know how to manage Millais, his mind is so *terribly* active, so full of invention that he can hardly stay quiet a moment without sketching ideas or reminiscences, and keeps himself awake all night planning pictures.'[5]

Millais was saddened at this time by the news of the departure of his close friend, Hunt, for the Holy Land. 'You can't go abroad before the Turkish Question is settled,' he pleaded, but Hunt's heart was set on the idea and he braved the potentially dangerous Mediterranean voyage all the same. Millais was not only depressed, too, about being in love with another man's wife, but also in the knowledge that Effie was trapped in a desperately sad marriage. By now he had seen for himself what he called Ruskin's 'hopeless apathy in everything regarding her happiness.' She told him a good deal more.

This is how she was soon to describe her position, at the beginning of her marriage, to her father. 'I do not think I am John Ruskin's wife at all . . . I had never been told the duties of married persons to each other and knew little or nothing about their relations in the closest union on earth. For days John talked about this relation to me, but avowed no intention of making me his Wife. He alleged various reasons, hatred of children, reli-

Effie – Euphemia Chalmers Ruskin (née Gray) – in 1853, by John Everett Millais.

(*below*) John Everett Millais: Millais offering Effie Ruskin a dish of water during their Highland romance. 'How well your brother and my wife get on together,' Ruskin told Millais' brother, William.

Effie and Millais, who entitled his sketch *The Countess as barber*.

gious motives, a desire to preserve my beauty and, finally, this last year told me his true reason (and this to me is as villainous as all the rest) that he had imagined women were quite different to what I was, and the reason he did not make me his Wife was because he was disgusted with my person the first evening 10th April [1848]. After I began to see things better I argued with him and took the Bible, but he soon silenced me . . . Then he said, after six years, he would marry me when I was twenty-five. This last year we spoke about it . . . He then said, as I professed quite a dislike to him that it would be SINFUL to enter into such a connexion as, if I was not very *wicked*, I was at least insane and the responsibility that I might have children was too great, as I was quite unfit to bring them up. . . .'6

When the Ruskins married in 1848, she was a very pretty and vivacious twenty-year-old, he was a tall, handsome man of twenty-eight, with beautiful manners, great eloquence and charm, a writer of glorious prose and already famous in his field. It was true there was a sinister omen to their union. By a twist of fate the Grays' house had once belonged to the Ruskins and the room in which Effie was born was the room in which John Ruskin's grandfather had committed suicide. Yet, on the surface, there seemed to be no good reason why this imposing couple could not make a happy marriage. It was clear from the start, however, that, for Ruskin, the married state was a romantic ideal rather than a passionate union of two bodies. To begin with he loved the virginal, remote, pretty, childlike, some-what unreal Effie. For him she would be a decorative social asset rather than a wife in the full sense.

Ruskin was impotent. Many years later, when the possibility of his marrying a second time arose, he said to his confidante, Mrs Cowper Temple, 'have I not often told you I was another Rousseau?' He was referring to Rousseau's confessions of masochistic fantasy and masturbation, 'of which I was not able to break myself.'7 Ruskin's earlier life was by no means conducive to a warmly loving orientation in manhood. He was an only child

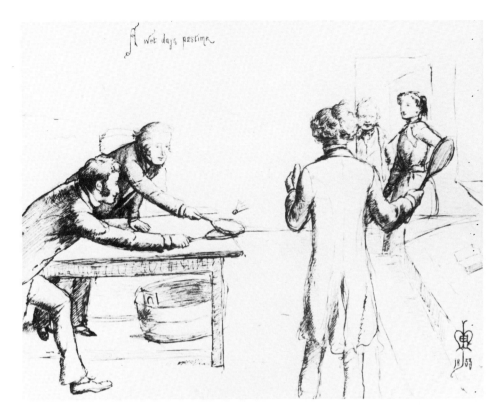

A *Wet Day's Pastime* by John Everett Millais. Playing battledore and shuttlecock are (*left to right*) William Millais, Ruskin and John Everett Millais. Effie is looking on.

brought up by parents who doted on him, but who taught him from infancy that their affection was dependent upon his total submission to their will. He was a lonely, emotionally deprived boy. His mother was a self-centred emasculating type of woman, possessive but incapable of true motherly love; his hard-working father was mean, miserly, rather malevolent and remorselessly strict. 'As a child,' Ruskin declared, 'I had nothing to love.' But he did grow up to love things, beautiful things – paintings, sculptures, buildings, flowers, rivers, woodlands – and abstract things, mathematics and philosophy – with some of the passion with which, had his early environmental circumstances been different, he might have been able to love a woman.

Effie brought no dowry to the marriage; John's books had not yet begun to make much money, so the young Ruskins were largely dependent upon his father's allowance. They had gone, in August 1851, to Venice, where John worked incessantly and Effie was pleasantly distracted by the smart social whirl. When they returned in June 1852 they went to live in London at Denmark Hill with his parents, who, wanting their son to themselves, displayed increasing resentment of Effie's presence, while Ruskin showed himself to be much more interested in them than in her. Such a situation was guaranteed to bring frustration, bitterness and hatred in its wake.

There were many who believed that the old Ruskins persuaded their son to invite Millais to Scotland – or that he himself planned it – with the deliberate aim of compromising Effie with adultery. Among those was his friend, Miss Douglas-Boswell: 'I never doubted the taking of John Millais to the Highlands was a regular deep-laid scheme, which doubtless JR imagined could not fail, judging the world by his own wicked self. But a good God, watching over the unsuspecting victims and putting grace into their hearts, prevented his malicious designs.'[8]

It did not seem at Brig o' Turk that Ruskin was aware of Millais' love-sickness, although on 16 October he was writing to his father that 'Millais paints till his limbs are numb

. . . he won't take exercise in the regular way, but sometimes starts and takes races of seven or eight miles if he is in the humour; sometimes won't or can't eat any breakfast or dinner, sometimes eats enormously without seeming to enjoy anything. Sometimes he is all excitement, sometimes sick and faint as a woman, always restless and unhappy. I think I never saw such a miserable person on the whole.'

Ten days later the Ruskins moved on to stay with Effie's friend, William Stirling, Perth's MP, at Dunblane. Millais remained a few more days at Brig o' Turk working on the Glenfinlas portrait before travelling on to Edinburgh (where he awaited the Ruskins and John Ruskin's lectures)[9] and then returning to London just in time to hear he had been elected an Associate of the Royal Academy, the youngest ever.

At Denmark Hill, during the months following Effie's Highland idyll, the bitterness of her situation was accentuated. She was neglected, threatened and insulted by both her husband and her in-laws. Her anger and frustration, spurred on by love for Millais, led to a fierce loathing of 'the Ruskin tribe' as she called them. For his part Ruskin was all injured innocence. 'Imagine every question asked in a kind tone,' he was to write to a friend, 'every answer given with a snap, and that continuing the whole day . . . and utter ingratitude for *all* that was done for her by myself, my father and my mother . . . She hated me as only those hate who have injured.'[10] Millais, not seriously believing that he could ever marry Effie, but determined to alleviate her misery, implored her mother to send one of her other daughters, Sophia, to keep her company.

Sophia went, and was made to listen to a catalogue of slander against Effie, who, said the Ruskins, was '. . . a poor silly creature simply raised into respectability by John's talents . . . She thinks herself very clever and people make much of her, but she owes that to John's great abilities and is merely a Scotch girl with bad manners . . . She is bold and impudent, and made such advances to John that she threw her snares over him in the same way as she has done over Millais. She is the cause of Millais' present unhappiness and is so in love with him that she thinks of nothing but him, and is, with the exception of her mother, the most intriguing woman John has ever known and he will write a book about her conduct and get a divorce from her tomorrow.'[11]

By March 1854 Effie was ill and on the verge of a nervous breakdown. She wrote to her father explaining all, and, in the following month, begged her mother to come to London and take her home. On 25 April she left by train for Perth, never to return to Denmark Hill.

Meanwhile the Grays had been consulting their solicitors, and Ruskin was duly cited. He pleaded Effie's 'insanity' and that he could prove his 'virility'. Doubtless he was capable of the latter, but it did him no good. Supplied with a certificate signed by two doctors, Effie gave evidence that the marriage had not been consummated, and by mid-July had procured an annulment. 'The judge has signed a sentence declaring the pretended marriage a nullity,' Effie's proctor wrote to Mrs Gray; 'and Miss Gray is free from all bonds of matrimony.'

Millais, notwithstanding his hearty dislike of Ruskin, stuck to his promise by completing and delivering the Glenfinlas portrait. A furious old Mr Ruskin took a knife, threatening to rip the canvas, but his son intervened and rushed the painting to Rossetti's studio.

It was to Rossetti that Millais now wrote, triumphantly, about his own and his parents' move out of Gower Street: 'We are leaving this old house and have taken a splendid little crib at Kingston, overlooking the Thames and on the other side Hampton Court and deer – I am to have the upper part of the stabling turned into a first-rate painting room . . . My good fellow, I am so thoroughly disgusted with London life and Society (which is as false as hell) that I am longing for the country. I wish old Daddy Hunt would return and that we could the three of us go off and paint together . . .'[12]

John Everett Millais: *Fishing in Loch Achray*. Opposite Millais is his brother William, talking to Effie. Ruskin's servant, Crawley, is in the back of the boat.

Millais, who had denied himself the pleasure of contacting Effie again for fear of compromising them both, at last burst forth – from a Derbyshire inn, from which he was fishing with John Leech – on 29 July with his congratulations on her escape: 'It is the best news I have ever received in my life . . . You may always feel happy in having done your duty, for you have done John Ruskin an even greater service than yourself. You were nothing to him but an awful encumbrance, and I believe the source of all his sullen irritability. Love was out of the question in such a nature . . . Now, dear Countess, do not be distressed with any more backward thoughts but pray to God that the future may be as happy as the past has been otherwise. . . . I must see you before returning to London, *if you will invite me*. Oh! Countess how glad I shall be to see you again . . . Since the time of my first hearing of your intention to separate from Ruskin I have been in a constant state of anxiety, so much so that I am now quite dull in my head . . . I should think you find it rather difficult to return to your old signature, "Effie Gray". You must now grow so fat that cabmen will refuse to take you as a single fare.'[13]

Another eight months were to elapse, however, before he saw her. Her health was slow to return; she would not, for the time being, contemplate a second marriage. But at last, in May 1855, Millais was exulting to Holman Hunt that 'I should tell you first that next Month please God I shall be a *married man* . . . I am very anxious about this change in my life as you may imagine. Since I last wrote I have been in Perth to see her, which was indeed a strange meeting. I was only there a few days as I was backward with my work, and had to return in haste. However, I saw enough of her to arrange matters to this end . . . Ruskin I have long since finished with, a few letters passed between us, and in his last, in answer to my saying that I must of necessity cease to continue on terms of friendship, through circumstances he must be aware of, he replied in an abruptly angry manner, commencing "Sir" and ending "Yr Obedt Servt" . . . I hear of him of course continually, that is one thing that disturbs me, as She will never escape hearing his name mentioned – Well it is certainly a strangely tragic tale, and I hope the last scene will be a happy one for her, poor body . . .'[14]

It was indeed. Of her new wedding day, 3 August, Effie wrote in her diary: 'I said to myself this is no time for anything but happiness and comfort while I look back and see what wonderful things have happened to myself, my family and Everett, how much cause I have to bless God for this day . . . Mr Anderson [the minister of Kinnoull] having arrived . . . Papa came to take me down and said "Come away, my dear lassie, this time I feel happy in putting you into good hands". My bridesmaids, very youthful ones, were standing at my door . . . In the dining room was William Millais, Mr Anderson, Everett, and myself with Papa to sign the contract. I felt very happy. The last time I had signed any paper or document was a little more than a year before when in Doctors Common I was sitting in a lawyer's room and signed my signature Euphemia Chalmers Gray . . . to get free of a hateful and loathsome contract.'[15]

John Everett and Effie Millais enjoyed a glorious fortnight's honeymoon in Argyllshire, Bute and Arran, where deep-sea fishing provided their chief diversion and for the first two years of their married life they lived in a rented house, Annat Lodge, adjacent to her parents' home, Bowerswell, Perth.

Effie brought four sons and five daughters into the world. First came Everett (who became a widely acknowledged expert on the breeding of domestic animals), then George (who, with Everett, became the boys in Millais' world-famous *The Boyhood of Raleigh*). Geoffroy was next, then Effie (afterwards Mrs James, whose son was the model for *Bubbles*). Effie sat for a great many of her father's paintings. In 1865, John Guille, Johnny, with whom this book is later principally concerned, followed Effie. And lastly there were Sophie, Carrie, Alice (Mrs Stuart Wortley) and Mary (Mrs McEwen), all of whom also feature in Millias' pictures.

And their mother lived happily ever after, except that she never fully recovered from the emotional scars of her first marriage; and that Queen Victoria who scarcely recognised annulment any more than divorce – and had also been informed that Effie had more or less thrown herself at Millais – refused to receive her until forty-one years later, when she did so at the special request of the dying artist.

'During the forty-one years of their married life,' said Johnny, 'my mother took the keenest interest in his work . . . taking upon herself not only the care of the household and the management of the family affairs, but the great bulk of his correspondence . . . Possessed in a considerable degree of the artistic sense, she was happily free from the artistic temperament, whilst her knowledge of history proved also a valuable acquisition. When an historical picture was in contemplation she delighted to study anew the circumstances and the characters to be depicted, and to gather for her husband's use all particulars as to the scene and the costumes of the period. Her musical accomplishments (for she was an excellent pianiste) were also turned to good account in hours of leisure, and not infrequently as a soothing antidote to the worries that too often beset the artist in the exercise of his craft.'[16]

For the next four decades Effie takes a central place on the Millais stage. But she never really got over her Ruskin ordeal. Fifteen years after her second marriage she was writing that she 'had nearly died of all those years of distress and suffering', which 'still hurt . . . dreadfully' and that her nervous system was 'so shaken' that she would 'never recover again.' For the rest of her life she was plagued by acute insomnia. As for Millais, his initially forgiving attitude to Ruskin soon transformed into a hatred almost as strong as Effie's. 'I can scarcely trust myself to speak of Ruskin,' he wrote to Hunt within a year of his marriage. 'He certainly appears to me (now that I know *all* about his treatment of my wife) to be the most wicked man I have known in my life.'[17]

3

'A GREATER BREADTH OF TREATMENT'

Johnny Millais who states that, next to his family and his art, his father valued his fishing above all, also emphasises John Everett Millais' outstanding capacity for human affection (another characteristic with which he may be sharply contrasted with Ruskin), and mentions his numerous lifelong friendships. Those companions were nearly all very talented men, starting with his artist brother, William, and proceeding with, among others, Holman Hunt and the Rossettis, Walter Deverell, another ardent support of the Pre-Raphaelite Brotherhood; Rupert Potter, barrister, skilled amateur photographer and father of Beatrix; Mike Halliday; the poet Robert Browning; Charles Collins and his brother, Wilkie, who wrote *The Woman in White*; and other novelists, like Charles Dickens, Anthony Trollope, (several of whose works he illustrated), George Du Maurier, W. M. Thackeray, and Charles Reade, the author of such fiction as *The Cloister and the Hearth*, *It's Never too late to Mend* and *Peg Woffington*.

And – probably valued most dearly of all, after Hunt – John Leech. When Millais fell in love with Effie he fell in love, too, with the Highlands, where Leech was his frequent guest. Fishing and shooting were essential therapies for both – for Leech regular foxhunting was even more important – and neither could abide anyone talking shop when they were intent upon their sporting activities. Leech satirised himself in *Punch* as 'Mr Briggs', the sportsman, so, of course, Millais featured in the same series.

This is one of the bizarre stories Millais told his son about 'Mr Briggs'. Based on Millais' home and walking in the hills near Blair one day in 1856, Leech found himself unwittingly in the middle of a deer drive and, suddenly, face to face with a furious Duke of Atholl, who called the trespasser an outlaw, a 'Rhoderic Dhu' and 'vile Sassenach'. Leech beat a hasty retreat, but had his revenge a little later when all Britain was laughing at the skit he made of it in *Punch*. Atholl, having seen this caricature of himself, invited both Millais and Leech to a series of deer drives. The Duke enjoyed a return joke at Leech's expense when the two of them shared a butt, without Leech knowing that his host had seen the *Punch* issue, or even identified him as the trespasser. Atholl produced a pistol, pointed it at Leech's head and shouted 'Now I am Rhoderic Dhu on my native heath and you, vile Sassenach, are in my power!' That, apparently, nearly gave the highly sensitive and nervous Leech a heart attack.[1]

Although Millais had no more resolute and staunch supporters of his work than his many literary and artistic friends, Thackeray, returning from Italy in 1855, rather put him in his place. The famous author strode up to him in the Garrick Club smoking room with: 'Millais, my boy, you must look to your laurels! I have met a wonderfully gifted young artist in Rome, about your own age, who some day will be the President of the Royal Academy before you.'[2] That was prophetic. Thackeray was referring to Frederick

John Everett Millais in his thirties, posing as Dante. Photograph by David Wilkie Wynfield.

Leighton, who forty-one years later, as Lord Leighton, died in the office of PRA – to be succeeded by Millais.

The years immediately following Millais' marriage, the late 1850s, were at once his most prolific and his most critical. Having learned the art of copper engraving he produced most of the etchings for Tennyson's collected verse, that being his principal work during the two years he and Effie lived at Annat Lodge. But there were, too, the great canvases to be conveyed for exhibition at the Royal Academy and elsewhere in London, and occasionally in Paris. The summer of 1855 found them in rented accommodation in London, but the following year, with Effie expecting her first child (Everett), Millais went alone to his studio in Langham Chambers which he shared for a time with his friend, Captain Luard. 1856 was the year of *The Random Shot, Autumn Leaves, The Blind Girl* (for which Effie was the model) and *Peace Concluded,* another typical Millais subject in which a wounded officer, returned from the Crimean campaign, lies on a couch with an Irish wolfhound at his feet, while his wife sits alongside.

The model for the wolfhound was the Millais' dog, Roswell, which had been bred in the Queen's kennels and was given to Effie by a Mr Debas. The Millais' were greatly attached to Roswell. However, he became such a terrible poacher that they decided to send him out to Effie's brother, George, in Australia. George Gray used Roswell to great effect as a kangaroo hunter, until one sad day he ate some poisoned meat put out to destroy dingoes, and died.

Millais' first letters to Effie from Langham Chambers sounded happy enough: '*April 7th.* We have just had breakfast. Luard is smoking a first pipe, and has prepared a palette for me to paint the little child's white dress. I found everything so nicely packed, my darling, that Luard has been noticing it and envying me . . . Luard and Robert Malcolm [the model for *Peace Concluded*] get on admirably together. They are at this moment talking about the Crimea, and we have just been looking at L's sketches from Sebastopol. Halliday has just appeared, so I am writing this in a howl of conversation and much smoke. I dine with Leech at six . . . *April 18th*. Yesterday I went with Luard to the Garrick and afterwards to the Olympic Theatre to see *Still Waters Run Deep*, a most admirable play . . . This afternoon I go with Leech and his madam to choose bonnets. He says there is but one really good place – not a shop – so I daresay I shall be able to get something pretty for you . . . *April 29th*. Dearest Countess, yesterday I went to the Royal Academy and made Luard write to you as you would be anxious to know how my pictures were placed . . . I saw Landseer there, and Grant, who was most civil, and both expressed great admiration for my work. *May 1st*. Last night Martineau, Halliday and I dined with Luard at the Garrick, after which we adjourned to the Victoria Theatre for the fun of the thing, to see a regular out-and-out melodrama, and were not disappointed. We got a box for 5s, and laughed so immoderately at the pathetic parts that we were nearly turned out . . .'[3]

Notwithstanding all his carefree attitude and apparent insouciance, from the summer of 1856 for the next three years Millais was irked by increasing attacks from other Academicians and critics, many of whom were generally more spiteful than constructive. On 1 May he is writing home: 'On the whole the critics are rather worse than ever . . . I have found out the name of *The Times* critic. It is F. . . ., an artist. I don't expect any better treatment from the press in my lifetime, as the critics are too intimately tied up with the profession.' And on 2 May: 'Every day I meet with the Academicians I perceive new horrors. So determined are they to insult every man, who chooses to purchase my works, that this year they have done the same with Miller as they did with Arden when he bought *The Order of Release*. For the first time they have not sent him an invitation to the dinner, at which he smiles knowing the reason. Anyhow, it is rather a triumph for us, as these wretched, ungentlemanly dealings tend to reveal the truth.'

Towards the end of 1856 Millais painted another huge picture entitled *A Dream of the Past, Sir Isumbras at the Ford*, the last of his in the truly pre-Raphaelite style. The subject

John Everett Millais: *Roswell*, 1856. 'He was bred in the Queen's kennels and given to Effie by a Mr Debas.'

is a veteran knight dressed in armour and riding a thick-set charger while helping the two children of a woodcutter by giving them a lift on his saddle across a stream. The setting sun symbolises the nearly spent life of the old warrior. It is a fine and noble scene, if a little ponderous with Victorian sentimentality. Exhibited in 1857 it was, says the artist's son, 'greeted with howls of execration, the lion's roar of Mr Ruskin being heard high above the jackal's yelp of his followers. The great critic could see in it no single point for admiration, only faults of fact, of sentiment and of art.'[4] The picture was satirised by an artist called Sandys which prompted Beatrix Potter to commit the following wry comment to her journal. 'I believe Mr Millais thinks very little of Sandys' work. He caricatured Millais' *Sir Isumbras at the Ford*, putting Millais for the Knight, with Rossetti and Holman Hunt. I wonder if that had anything to do with his dislike.'[5]

During the eighteen months following Effie's marriage to Millais, her former husband did not raise a word of criticism against the artist's work. In his *Academy Notes* of 1856 Ruskin describes *Autumn Leaves* as 'by much the most poetical work the painter has yet conceived; and also, so far as I know, the first instance of a perfectly painted twilight.' But in 1857, he was saying of *Sir Isumbras*, 'this is not a fiasco, but a catastrophe'. And so the situation remained for the next two years at least. That summer of '57 Ruskin, viewing Millais' *Mariana*, declared that 'he has gone to the dogs and is hopelessly fallen.' In 1859 Millais' three principal exhibits were *The Vale of Rest, The Love of James I of Scotland* and *Spring Apple Blossoms*. He wrote to Effie that April that 'if he [Ruskin] abuses them he will ruin himself as an art critic'. But abuse them Ruskin did and was duly condemned by Millais: 'He does not understand my work, which is now too broad for him to appreciate, and I think his eye is only fit to judge the portraits of insects. But then I think he has lost all influence as a critic.'[6]

All that was after Millais had fathered Effie's first child. So one cannot help wondering whether Ruskin's condemnation at that time in the face of the acclaim Millais' paintings received from most of the other respected authorities was due to bitterness and jealousy because Millais had proved a successful husband where Ruskin had shamefully failed.

'Ruskin will be disgusted this year', Millais goes on to inform Effie 'for all the rubbish he has been praising, before being sent to the Royal Academy, has now bad places. There is a wretched work like a photograph of some place in Switzerland, evidently painted under his guidance, for he seems to have lauded it up sky-high; and that is just where it is . . . in the miniature room!' And there were the 'jackals'. '*April 29th*. I have just come from the private view. To tell you the truth I think it likely I shall not sell one of the pictures. The clique has been most successful against me this year, and few people look at my work . . . The fact of the matter is I am out of fashion . . . What will become of Art, I don't know. I am sorry I have no good news for you, my dear, but the look out is anything but refreshing . . . *May 10th*. No words can express the curious envy and hatred [my] works have brought to light. Some of the papers, I believe, have been so violent that, for two days together, they have poured forth such abuse as was never equalled in the annals of criticism. My works are not understood by the men who set themselves up as judges. Only when I am dead will they know their worth.'[7] But further revealing his underlying self-confidence, he told her a few months later that 'my position is as good as any except Landseer's; and this they, too, will know.'[8]

There was one group, however, who appreciated his work above all and that was the great authors. He was a prodigious illustrator and perhaps the most highly popular one. 'I am fond of *Orley Farm*', (published in 1862), commented Trollope, 'and I am especially fond of its illustrations by Millais which are the best I have seen in any novel in any language.'[9]

Millais never failed to spend the autumn in Scotland, whose moors and rivers, in their

John Everett Millais: *A Dream of the Past, St Isumbras at the Ford*, 1856.

turn, never failed to soothe him. In 1860 he took the shooting at Kincraig, Invernesshire, with his friend Colonel Aitkin. In August 1861 he was sporting with Mike Halliday in Sutherland and writing home to Effie that 'yesterday Mike and I shot all day, but the ground is very inferior . . . Poor little man, he couldn't walk the hillsides and was done up so completely that he only shot three brace which made in all $17\frac{1}{2}$ . . . I send a box away to you . . . I am almost sorry I sent you the grilse yesterday, for I killed a fine salmon this morning, 10 lb weight. I hooked it far away from anyone and had the fish on for more than half an hour without being able to make anybody hear by shouting. At last Mike caught sight of me waving my bonnet and came up to my assistance with the gaff, and after playing the fish until it was quite done, he succeeded in securing it. It was a beautiful clean salmon (not grilse) just up from the salt water. It struggled awfully and took me down the river in the most gallant way . . . Poor little man [Halliday], he hasn't even risen a fish at all yet, except trout.'

The following August found Millais fishing in Sutherland, at Helmsdale, where his host was Colonel Reginald Cholmondeley. He then moved on, with Halliday to Inveran Inn, Tain, in the Highlands, where he spent most of the month of September casting his line on the Shin; but the shooting was better than the fishing which, he tells Effie, 'is very bad this year, but . . . Brandreth gave me a *magnificent* salmon-rod – *insisted* on my taking it – and supplied us with a lot of lights and tobacco. Leech is not here yet. Have you heard of him? The river is too low here now, strange to say, and last year it was too high.'[10]

A season or two later Millais and Reggie Cholmondeley were guests of the leader of the Liberal party, Sir William Harcourt, in Argyllshire, in the hills around Inveraray. 'Harcourt and I shot twenty-three brace yesterday in a frightful sun, and enjoyed the day very much ... The cuisine is like that of a good club. His [Harcourt's] cook is here and manservant and the comfort is great, altogether delightful ... the Duke and Duchess of Sutherland left yesterday. She looked so pretty at luncheon on Sunday. We have a great deal of laughing. Today we are going to fish in Loch Fyne for *Lythe*, which afford good sport; and tomorrow we shoot again. Cholmondeley has his keeper and dogs with him. Harcourt has a kilted keeper of his own, besides the ponies for the hill with saddlebags. We are going to visit the islands in a yacht as the rivers are too dry for fishing salmon ... I will return directly the fortnight is out, but not before as Harcourt looks on me as the mainstay of the shooting ... I like to hear from some of you every day, that you are all well; and, after this fling, I will return and work like a Trojan before going South ...'

Before leaving Harcourt's party, Millais dined several times with the Argylls at Inveraray Castle where Dr Livingstone, the African explorer, was a guest. 'On Friday we returned to Loch Awe, and near Inveraray found Lord Archibald Campbell and another younger brother catching salmon for the amusement of Dr Livingstone, who is at the Castle. We were introduced and I had a chat with the Doctor. They caught salmon in a poaching way with lead and hooks attached, which sank among the imprisoned fish who are in pools from which they cannot get out. The same afternoon the Duchess called with a carriage full of pretty children and asked us to dine again which we did after killing twenty-eight brace on the hill. There was no one staying at the castle but Livingstone, but the party was large enough, as there are sons and tutors in abundance. In the evening we played billiards, and at tea drew out the African traveller who is shy and not very communicative. Tomorrow we shoot again and I think of returning on Wednesday. The black game shooting commenced yesterday, and I killed two, and this week we shall beat the low hills for them ... I am anxious to return and get on with my work.'[11]

He was only at his easel at Bowerswell for a month, however, before he and Effie and Sir William Harcourt were off to the Continent, travelling through Switzerland to Florence where they were conducted on a tour of the galleries by Sir Henry Layard, the archaeologist. On Layard's advice Millais bought Michaelangelo's statute, *The Leda and the Swan* from the Galli family, in whose possession it had been for 300 years. (This was said to be almost the last occasion on which a Michaelangelo work was allowed for sale outside the country, as the Italian government were then about to put in force an Act prohibiting the removal from their shores of great works of art.) In Rome, Harcourt and the Millais' were taken by their friend, Lord Arthur Russell, for an audience with Pope Pius IX, whom Effie described as 'a very nice benevolent looking old gentleman.'[12]

On Christmas Day 1863, their friend Thackerary had died, and, within a couple of months of that, while Millais was working in his Gower Street studio, John Leech's housemaid rushed in breathless, saying her employer had just had 'another bad attack' and was crying 'Millais! Millais!' Leech's old friend and brother-artist dropped his palette, sprinted through the streets of Kensington and dashed up the stairs, to find Leech in the death-throes just as he arrived. Leech was only forty-six. Wilkie Collins was another intimate friend lost to Millais in 1864.

Six years later, Charles Dickens was another. After Millais had drawn a portrait of Dickens on his death-bed, the novelist's daughter, Katie, wrote to him: 'No one but your-self, I think, could have so perfectly understood the beauty and pathos of his dear face

John Everett Millais: *Effie Deans*, 1877.

John Everett Millais: *Miss Nina Lehmann*, 1869. 'The picture which struck me most,'
said Beatrix Potter, 'was Mr Millais' portrait of Miss Lehmann as a child. I think
it is the most powerful in technical qualities I have ever seen by him.'

PLATE 3   *Lieutenant J.G. Millais, Seaforth Highlanders,*
painted by his father, John Everett Millais, in 1890.

PLATE 4   Two paintings by John Guille Millais:
Hagenbeck's Pheasant, 1908 (top) and *Walrus*.

as it lay on that little bed in the dining room, and no one but a man with genius bright as his own could have so reproduced that face to make us feel now when we look at it, that he is still with us in the house. Thank you, dear Mr Millais, for giving it to me. There is nothing in the world that I have, or can ever have, that I shall value half as much . . .'[13]

Among the many colourful occasions in Effie's and John Everett's social life, standing out from the 1860s and '70s is a ball given by the Duke of Sutherland for General Garibaldi. 'The great soldier, wearing, as in Italy, the red shirt ever since associated with his name, entered the ballroom with the Duchess on his arm and was greeted by all present with the homage due to Royalty as he passed down the room . . . Very striking was the expression on his face, at once so earnest and so genial; and still more conspicuous was the contrast between his simple dress and the gorgeous array of all the rest of the company . . .'[14] Some time later they were presented, at a Foreign Office reception, to Czar Alexander II, whose life was to be ended by an assassin. 'A very sad and distinguished-looking man,' said Effie.

She also comments on the State ball they attended in honour of Nasir ud-Din, the Shah of Persia, a monarch who was also to be assassinated. 'The Shah, as is well known, has a grand collection of jewels . . . but even he must have been astonished by the wondrous display of diamonds that met his eyes that night. About 800 tiaras were worn by the ladies present, who were perhaps not unwilling to show him what old England could do in that way . . .'[15]

In the winter of 1867–68 Rubenstein, the great pianist, visited the Millais'. 'My father and mother were both passionately fond of music,' says Johnny, 'and on the second visit he was good enough to play the whole evening to the great delight of themselves and their friends.'[16]

1868 found Millais with W. P. Frith RA (celebrated for *Derby Day*, *Ramsgate Sands*, etc.) at the Great Exhibition in Paris, and – accompanied by the picture dealer, Gambert – they went on to the Forest of Fontainebleau and the chateau of Rosa Bonheur, the animal artist. They were met at the station by the 'coachman' looking like 'an abbé . . . with a black, broad-brimmed hat, and black cloak, long white hair, with a cheery, rosy face.' Frith noting the 'coachman's' red ribbon asked Gambert, 'do priests wear the Legion of Honour?' To which Gambert replied 'What priest? That is Mademoiselle Bonheur!'[17]

To return to Millais' career, an 1859 picture of nuns, entitled *The Vale of Rest* – a title taken from the lines of a Mendelssohn song, *the vale of rest, where the weary find repose* – marks the first sharp turning-point in the artist's professional life. There, for the first time, the critics noted the merging of his old Pre-Raphaelite concern with detail into what Johnny calls 'a greater breadth of treatment', but without losing his careful attention to every accessory. By the mid-1860s Millais had won a name in the British art world as the one who, above all, could produce on canvas the most moving and striking atmospheric effects. Three of his finest examples were *The Eve of St Agnes*, a scene inspired by a poem by Keats, with Effie again as model; *The Black Brunswicker*, showing a young officer of that regiment bidding farewell to his betrothed (for whom Dicken's daughter, Kate, stood as model) on the eve of Waterloo; and *The Romans leaving Britain*, a portrait of a Roman soldier clasping his native love for the last time before joining the ships seen on the shore below.

Two outstandingly expressive pictures from Millais' brushes in 1867, *Rosalind in the Forest*, a scene from *As You Like It*, and *Jephthah's Daughter*, in which the Israelite leader is shown holding the daughter he is pledged to sacrifice, display a further move away from his preoccupation with minute detail, another example of his 'greater breadth of treatment'. And, in 1870, came the charming *The Boyhood of Raleigh*, with young Walter and his brother

John Everett Millais as game-shot, photographed by Rupert Potter.

(the Millais boys, Everett and George, posing) listening eagerly to a tanned veteran Genoese sailor's accounts of his adventures on the Spanish Main.

That year Millais managed to get away for three months in the Highlands and was able to paint his first full autumnal Scottish landscape. Entitled *Chill October,* it was of a backwater of the River Tay, five miles from Perth, a very wild, lonely place, the haunt of duck and coot and moorhen. 'The scene, simple as it is, had impressed me for years before I painted it,' he wrote. 'I made no sketch for it, but painted every touch from Nature, on the canvas itself, under irritating trials of wind and rain.'

Lord Justice James, amateur critic, was one who in particular appreciated how perfectly in that picture Millais had captured the spirit of wild autumn. 'Every true painter is a poet,' was his appraisal. 'A good landscape is especially a descriptive poem, and in this landscape the artist has shown us how well he has seen, how thoroughly he has felt, and how truly he has followed Nature.' There were neither grasses, mosses, lichens nor indeed any foliage that a botanist would not instantly recognise. 'Millais', insisted Spielmann, 'could paint the time of day; he could moreover, draw a tree, as few of his contemporaries could do it; and sky and grass and dew-drenched heather, luminous screen of cloud and tangled undergrowth – he painted them all, not only with love, but with an enthusiasm which he had the happy faculty of imparting to the spectator.'[18]

But, returning to *Chill October,* there was another man who, though a faithful help-mate, could by no means see the worth of the picture. That was the porter at the local railway station, who morning and evening, helped Millais to-and-fro with his canvas and easel. 'A dinna ken how the man cud dae it, it was that cauld,' he said. And after the sale, in 1871: 'Is it true, as a' was sein i' the papers, that Mr Mullus had got a thousand pounds for yon picture, he painted here? Weel, it's a verra funny thing but a' wudna hae gien half-a-croon for it mysel'!'[19]

Following *Chill October* came other landscapes, again showing Millais' deep knowledge of the shape and form of trees and flowers and water reflections, and his successful search for what Johnny describes as 'the Soul of Nature' – pictures such as *Over the Hills and Far Away*, *Murthly Moss*, *The Old Garden*, *Lingering Autumn*, and *The Deserted Garden*. While painting he loved to listen to, and distinguish birdsong, but for game birds he was invariably ready with his gun. Once, when he noticed a big pack of blackgame approaching, without moving from his painting-stool, he threw down his palette, picked up his gun and killed a 'cock as it flew over his head.

Millais had now become a very enthusiastic deerstalker and between 1867 and 1871, besides many other stags, five 'royals' fell to his rifle. His most exciting stalk – the one of which he was afterwards most fond of relating – was in pursuit of a 10-pointer near Loch Luichart. He and his host stalked it for three days without getting a shot. At last, on the fourth day, they found him in company with a herd of some fifty other deer and among them an eight-pointer, nearly as good as the principal quarry. The animals were feeding at the head of a big corrie. A puff of wind sent the deer scampering along a pass. 'A sharp piece of manoeuvering and a quick run', however, enabled the stalkers to cut them off, and Millais brought both stags down as they came by at full gallop.[20]

Millais' reputation as a rifle shot was now well known, and his friend Joe Jopling, a member of the English eight, frequently urged him to enter competitions. But neither target shooting, nor public display of any kind for that matter, had any appeal for him. So far as Millais was concerned being a crack shot could only be put to only one useful purpose – field sports.

'He was a true sportsman, a good shot and an ardent fisherman,' says Johnny. 'To

John Everett Millais: *The Deserted Garden*, 1875.

John Everett Millais: *Miss Diana Vernon*, 1880.
Since she was posing as Prince Charles
Edward of '45 Rebellion fame, the painting
came to be known as 'Charlie is my Darling'.

the latter pursuit he brought the same power of concentration remarked by the great man in his studio, and he could have killed anyone who began to talk to him of pictures when his mind was running on salmon or grouse. He often said how many times he had wished to paint a grouse-drive, and, for fear of comparisons, it is perhaps, the only thing I am glad he did not paint . . .[21]

'Our tenancy of Murthly (Perthshire) commenced in 1881, and for ten consecutive years my father held it to his great delight. He knew by heart . . . every bit of the ground and every turn of the river and his love of the place increased year by year . . . Except deer-stalking – and for this, as time went on, he felt himself getting a bit too old – Murthly had everything that a sportsman could desire. Though big bags were not to be made, there was ample sport for two or three guns from August 1st to the end of January . . . Besides pheasants, of which about a thousand were reared every year, from 300 to 600 brace of partridges were brought to bag each season. There was also first-rate wood shoot-ing, including blackgame, woodcock, capercailzie, rabbits and roe deer. But what pleased us most of all was "the bog", situated in the middle of one of the grouse moors, about three-quarters of a mile long, with another small bog some eight hundred yards away where the duck . . . could take refuge on being disturbed . . .'[22]

The author of that enthusiastic note was sixteen years old when his father took Murthly. Encouraged by such a man as John Everett Millais, and the like-minded Effie, it is scarcely surprising that Johnny Millais grew up to make his name, too, as an artist, naturalist and hunter – and as an explorer.

He would be the only one of the Millais children to win a measure of fame in his own right.

4

'JOHNNY-WITH-THE-
LONG-GUN'

Enter John Guille (Johnny), born 1865

Just as the great John Everett Millais is on record as being 'continuously at work with paper and pencil from the age of four', so, from about the same point of childhood, his son Johnny was preoccupied with a desire to be deeply involved with wild Nature. And, only a little later, with other high aspirations.

'From the time I was a little schoolboy of eight I had always longed to be an artist and a naturalist, and to hunt and explore in new lands.'[1] As soon as he was large enough and strong enough to hold a gun these aims were accelerated by shooting, skinning and studying different species of birds and adding each to a rapidly expanding and meticulously stored collection. And by drawing and painting the plumage, too.

He began 'shooting seriously', he says, when he was nine, relying on any old weapon he could borrow or hire. One day, in 1879, when firing at an oystercatcher on the Tay with a hired muzzle-loading 12-bore, a piece of the gun sprung back and cut his cheek. Whereupon his horrified father, well knowing he would 'get a gun somehow or other', made him a present of a full-choked 20-bore and with it, Johnny claims, 'I shot the greater part of my collection.'[2]

That year, aged fourteen, he made the first of three solo shooting expeditions down Scotland's east coast, roaming from Dunbar in the south, to Loch Erreboll, in Sutherland. He would go by train to some point on the coast, send his bag, containing a change of clothes and spare cartridges, to a station thirty miles or so away, then work his way towards it, hunting the estuaries, sandbanks, inlets, mudflats and stream beds as he travelled. Very often, when he was in tantalising reach of a rare migrant, he did not retrieve his bag for two or three consecutive days, in which case he usually slept in the open.

In 1880 he bought 'a pup collie-and-smooth-coated-retriever mongrel', which, he recalls, 'was the best and most courageous dog I have ever seen. She accompanied me wherever I went for fifteen years, and many a time in autumn we spent the night together lying in sandhills, sleeping where we could find a sheltered bank, or wakeful and watching for the dawn when it was too cold to sleep. There was never a sea too thunderous to enter or a bird fallen at a distance that was beyond Jet's powers, and being always with me I brought her education to a pitch of intelligence I do not see exhibited in field trial dogs of today, whose training is often calculated to destroy initiative and turn them into machines. (I can speak from experience, as I judged at many field trials) . . .'[3]

With the 20-bore in the crook of his elbow and Jet at heel he was frequently stopped on his coastal expeditions by angry gamekeepers, but when they knew of his errand, his quest for the skins of rare birds, being amateur naturalists themselves, they nearly always relented, and even led him to their cottages for tea and a night on the sofa. Johnny Millais claims to be acquainted in time 'with every fisherman and longshoreman between St Andrews and Arbroath, and I was known to them as "Johnny-with-the-Long-Gun" . . .

'It was rough work for one so young, but I loved the life as only a young naturalist can do, and when I shot a knot or a turnstone in summer plumage I did not envy any man in the world. Another good hunting-and-fishing-ground was Loch Leven where Sir Graham Montgomery used to let me have his private boat once or twice in the season every year, and here I got a fine series of ducks and other birds . . . My father and mother were always opposed to these constant absences on my part, but being good-natured and broad-minded people, and having regard to the fact that I always returned at some time or another, they got accustomed to my perpetual wanderings and ceased to wonder.'[4]

Notwithstanding the boy's gift for portraying birds and their plumage and other examples of artistic talent, the co-founder of the Pre-Raphaelite movement and Royal Academician, seeing no central future for Johnny-with-the-Long-Gun as an artist, set him on course for a conventional public school education with a view to an army career. At Marlborough Johnny was 'the boy with the catapult'.

There he soon became leader of the college gang, what the tutors called 'the undisciplined young reprobates, who spend their time fighting with town boys or wandering aimlessly in the forest.'[5] Devoting most of his spare time to the wonders of Savernake Forest, securing avian specimens for his collection, he was frequently caught out of bounds and birched or made to write out Milton's *Paradise Lost* twice over.

Retreating from his headmaster's house with his friend, Arthur Cayley, after their last dose of the birch – for leading a catapult fight against the town boys – a treat awaited Johnny Millais which would have delighted few but him. 'By this time I knew the call of nearly every small British land bird, and could stand in a wood or marsh and recognise all the different species. It was not surprising, therefore, that as we walked slowly along I was suddenly brought to a standstill by the cry of a bird I had never heard before. What was it? That I must discover at once. The cry was frequently repeated, and, passing through the shrubbery, there was the bird sitting on a willow tree. I had a secret pocket on the inside of my waistcoat in which reposed my favourite "catty" and a few shot. It was soon out and at the very first shot there was a welcome *plunk* and the rarity fell dead, a female cirl bunting . . . which I still treasure owing to the curious circumstances under which it was obtained.'[6]

Some of his happiest sojourns were during the school holidays at Andover Hall, Shropshire, the home of his parents' friend, Reggie Cholmondeley, who, to Johnny's ecstatic fascination, had turned his grounds into a private zoo. Mark Twain and his family were fellow-guests for a month and '. . . my sister Carrie and I used to hang onto his arm and he would tell me funny stories about Western days . . . With no hat on his shock head and a corn-cob pipe in his mouth, he would discourse for hours on any subject, and . . . in the evening would read to us chapters of *The Tramp Abroad*, which he had just completed.'[7]

Johnny never finished his last Marlborough term. Noticing one Sunday that a beehive hung from an apple tree close above the table around which his headmaster was holding a garden tea party, he could not resist a catapult shot, and was promptly expelled.

There is plenty of evidence of the fact that the older Millais was duly proud of his son's natural gift for drawing and that he found it useful, too. In 1878, for example, when Johnny was twelve and John Everett Millais was starting his picture *The Princes in the Tower*, he sent the boy on three successive days to make pencil sketches of the interior of the Bloody Tower where the Princes are alleged to have been murdered.

This copy of John Everett Millais' self-portrait was painted by Charles Holroyd and hangs at the Garrick Club, London. The original is in the Ufizzi Gallery, Florence.

(*below*) John Everett Millais with (*left*) John Bright, photographed by Rupert Potter in 1879.

John Everett Millais: *The Rt Hon. W.E. Gladstone MP*, 1879.

That year was a red-letter one for the family. John Everett, with several important works – notably *Chill October*, *The Yeoman of the Guard* and *The Bride of Lammermoor* – hanging in the International Exhibition in Paris, was created, along with Alma-Tadema, an officer of the *Légion d'Honneur*, and awarded the French Academy's top prize, the gold *Medaille d'Honneur*. With Frith and Gambert he visited the studios of Gérôme, Meissonier, and the actress, sculptor and painter, Sarah Bernhardt, who they found dressed as a boy and telling them that she 'hated acting and would rather succeed in painting or sculpture, or both, than in any other earthly calling.'[8]

Every painting of every sitter in every composition of J. E. Millais' turned out a true likeness of the model, as well as a brilliant evocation of the character intended, and by now he had assumed the role of Britain's leading portrait painter. In 1876 he received a commission from Manchester for a portrait of the Princess of Wales, who agreed to sit to him. Then the Manchester authorities changed their minds about the project; but he was soon busy with marvellous renderings of Thomas Carlyle, the Countess of Grosvenor, the Duchess of Westminster, John Bright, the Earl of Shaftesbury and the Viceroy of India, Lord Lytton. A later biographer-art critic hands down the opinion that Millais 'managed to secure invariably an atmosphere of distinction without losing either individuality or subtlety of characterisation . . . His preference for repose in representation did not lead the artist into a dry convention or with any disregard of the essential points of difference between people . . . Beneath their reserve there appears a wonderful variety of manner and superb power of interpretation.'[9]

Millais had just completed his portrait of the beautiful Lillie Langtry – 'the Jersey Lily', towering actress and intimate of the future Edward VII – in the summer of 1878 when his second son, Johnny's nineteen-year-old brother, George, then a Cambridge undergraduate, was taken seriously ill. He got soaked to the skin snipe shooting, (when, according to his doctor's orders, he should have been taking life much more easily), and died at Bowerswell that August. It was during the summer of 1878, too, that the family moved from Cromwell Place to the much larger house that Millais had built for them in Palace Gate, next to Kensington Gardens. In February 1882 Beatrix Potter recorded an amusing incident apropos the pride he took in it: 'Mr Millais is going to paint the portrait of one of the Duchess of Edinburgh's children. The Duchess is staying with Princess Mary, Kensington Palace. Mr Millais went to see her yesterday, doubtless very shy. She offended him greatly. She enquired where his "rooms" were, evidently doubtful whether a Princess might condescend to come to them. "My *rooms* m'am are in Palace Gate", and he told papa afterwards, with great indignation, he daresay they were much better than hers. He is right proud of his house.'[10]

'There are few parks in England more beautiful than these [Kensington] gardens,' he thought; 'I could paint some good landscapes here.' And he told Spielmann that he '. . . so delighted in painting landscapes, so much more than portraiture. You can so comfortably please yourself as to what you do in landscape. You have only yourself to satisfy. But in portraiture you have to please everybody . . .'[11]

1879 found Gladstone, the Liberal leader, then in Opposition, sitting to him and preoccupied with sympathy for the Bulgarians, (who were still suffering from Ottoman persecution) and busy condemning Benjamin Disraeli for his Turkish support. 'When Millais was painting this portrait,' said an intimate friend of the ex-Premier, 'Mr Gladstone was thinking what a terrible sin would be committed if England was to go to war for the Turks.'[12] Johnny remembered that, at lunch, Gladstone 'discussed with an insignificant boy like myself the relations of birds and their influence on human character . . .[13] and astonished us beyond measure by the extent of his learning . . . To my father he talked eagerly about the early Italian and Florentine painters . . . or we would be treated to a disquisition on fish and the art of capturing them; or, finding that my mother was interested in early Scottish history (a subject of which he had made a special study), he would pour forth to her from the founts of his knowledge, setting her right in the pleasantest manner . . . Music, sport, science, art, were all taken up in turn.'[14]

Gladstone sat for Millais twice more (in 1884 and 1886). Rupert Potter photographed the great statesman for the artist's reference, an event graphically described by Beatrix. 'Papa has been photographing old Gladstone this morning at Mr Millais'. The old person is evidently a great talker if once started. Papa said he talked in a set manner as if he were making a speech, but without affection. They kept off politics of course, and talked about photography. Mr Gladstone talked of it on a large scale, but not technically. What would it come to, how far would the art be carried, did papa think people would ever be able to photograph in colours?

'He told several long stories of which the point was exceedingly difficult to find, including one about a photographer at Aberystwyth thirty years ago, how the working classes enjoyed looking at the photos in his window, and it occurred to them to get ones of their friends, but at this point, Mr Millais broke in with the request that Mr Gladstone would sit still for a moment . . .

'He was very inclined to talk, but it interrupted the painting. He did not seem conceited, nor yet difficult to manage like Mr Bright is when being taken. He was sitting in a gorgeous arm chair which was taken by Captain James [Millais' son-in-law] from Arabi's tent at the battle of Tel-el-Kebir. How that surprising person Captain James managed in the confusion of conflict to carry off a heavy, Belgian, highly-ornamented arm-chair, is as extraordinary as the manner in which he won the Victoria Cross at the same battle.'[15]

Many years later Gladstone wrote to Johnny: 'The result of your father's practice was that, of all the painters I have ever sat to, he took the fewest sittings. This, as well as his success, was due, I think, to the extraordinary concentration with which he laboured. He had no energies to spare; and no wonder when we see what energies he put into his pictures.'[16] Gladstone told Spielmann that 'it was most enjoyable to sit to Mr Millais . . . to see him at work is a delight, for the way he throws his heart and soul into it.'[17] The French artist, Benjamin Constant gave the opinion that 'Millais' portrait of Gladstone is a page of history . . . This painting can hold its own as a work of art by the side of the greatest masters of the past. Rembrandt himself could not improve it by juxtaposition.'[18]

1881 was Millais' best vintage year for portraiture. '. . . I have two pretty ladies to paint and Cardinal Manning immediately, so I have enough to do,' he was writing to Effie on 31 March. 'Letters are pouring in and I am beside myself to answer them.'[19]

Disraeli, by then Earl of Beaconsfield, Cardinal Newman, Tennyson and half-a-dozen more sat for him that year. Disraeli had met the artist in 1875 as a fellow-guest of the Duke of Rutland, with whom the Premier was breaking his journey on the way north to Balmoral. He remarked to the Duke that he had 'never come across anyone with such a refreshing and continuous flow of original observations' as Millais.[20] Disraeli was dying in the spring of 1881. He missed his final sitting, but the picture made the Royal Academy that summer all the same.

Queen Victoria immediately commissioned a small replica of it in October and duly wrote her gratitude: 'The Queen wishes herself to express to Mr Millais her warm thanks for the beautiful picture of dear Lord Beaconsfield. It . . . has for her a peculiar and melancholy interest from being the last portrait her dear and ever-lamented friend and great Minister ever sat for, and when, as it were the shadow of death was already upon him, Mr Millais has given the peculiar, intellectual and gentle expression of his face.'[21]

For Millais the happiest stroke of 1881 was his securing the tenancy of Murthly, in Perthshire, with all the variety of sport it offered, though Johnny relates an occasion when

Two portraits by John Everett Millais from 1881:
Alfred, Lord Tennyson (left), and *Cardinal Newman*.

the Royal Academician was not so happy. 'My father was in one of the forward butts to the left, and I in one at the extreme end of the bog. I was getting most of the shooting and, as the drive was nearing the end, my father, seeing some snipe slipping away between us, moved down behind the bushes to a butt exactly opposite me, without telling me he had done so. By-and-by a snipe came along low, and I killed it when, to my horror, an incensed parent suddenly rose from behind a big whin bush in the line of my fire, and let go some red-hot words . . . Happily only two pellets had struck him, one on the forehead, and the other on the chin . . . A word of explanation satisfied him that the accident was due to himself alone; and, for the rest, what can you not forgive a man who has just tasted part of an ounce of No. 6? The only unpardonable thing was the flippancy of a wretched punster who persisted in calling me "Bag-dad" for the rest of the day!'[22]

The one recorded occasion that Millais was really angry with his son in his pursuits with a gun occurred in 1882 when Johnny was down from his first term at Trinity College, Cambridge, and this dialogue took place:

'"Hallo, young fellow, you seem unusually flush of money; that is a bit unusual, is it not?"

'"Well," I answered, with a certain amount of youthful pride, "I won eighty pounds the other day pigeon shooting, and I expect to make some more by and by."

'"Now look here, Johnny," said my irate parent, "I will give you anything you like in reason for your sport or your Natural History, but I draw the line at pigeon shooting. It is not a clean game and I won't have you mixed up with that crowd; so give me your promise you will not shoot pigeons again." '[23]

About that time Johnny's grandfather, George Gray, asked him to name a present he wished to give him. The young man's somewhat predictable reply was 'a first-class pair of ejector guns, please'. The weapons he bought, made by Reilly, had been exhibited at the Paris Exhibition and were, Johnny thought, 'perhaps the first pair of good ejector guns ever made, and cost £120 . . . the subsequent bill rather startled the old man, but he paid it with a good grace.'[24]

Johnny served in a territorial battalion of the Somerset Light Infantry for three years from 1883. He was drawing and painting in earnest, too, and, in 1886 sold some pictures to *The Graphic*. He also provided drawings for a number of books, the best commission coming from Henry Seebohm, the naturalist, whose monograph on the *Charadriidae* he illustrated. On the strength of those fees and his savings from his militia pay he went on a naturalist's tour of western America – based on his brother Geoffroy's ranch in Wyoming – which, he says, 'fostered a spirit of restlessness and roving that has never left me.'[25] But while he yearned to travel, explore, hunt, research and depict, his father was still bent on him going for a regular army commission, so sent him to a crammer run by a Mr James, otherwise known as 'Jimmy'.

' "Jimmy" disliked me,' Johnny recalls, 'because I was always drawing wapiti or grizzly bears in books on fortification, or taking French leave to go off and shoot or fish.' Although the wayward young candidate was given the sack from the crammer for going absent for a week just before the army final exams, he sat them, passed, and, through the influence of Field-Marshal Sir Garnet Wolseley, a friend of his father's, was commissioned in the Scots Guards. Within a few days, however, for some unexplained reason, he was transferred to the second battalion of the Seaforth Highlanders, then quartered in Edinburgh.

During his five years in the Seaforths he appears to have devoted at least as much time at the lochside, on the moor or in punts, or stalking some rare wader along the shoreline, as he spent on parade or other military exercise. In 1887 he narrowly missed the chance of a posting to India, and 'about the same time, too,' he records, 'I met Col Cumberland, who was about to undertake a long journey across Europe and Asia through the Pamirs

John Everett Millais: *The Rt Hon. Benjamin Disraeli, Earl of Beaconsfield*, 1881.

Lieutenant J.G. Millais, Seaforth Highlanders. Dublin, 1889.

down to India . . . he asked me to accompany him. I applied to the War Office for permission, stating that I would make topographical maps of the whole route . . . They granted the permit, and I was in the seventh heaven of delight, but just at the last moment the colonel thought otherwise . . .'[26]

As restless Johnny's life quest was to 'seek, find and study the heart of nature', to have for himself and for the cause of the science of natural history representatives of the finest specimens of the world's fauna, he was forever applying to his commanding officer for sporting leave, a perquisite which, in those leisurely, privileged regimental days, was most generously handed out. To mention one of his more unusual shorter excursions, he was given special furlough to secure a head from a flock of wild goats that roamed the hills of Garve, near Strathpepper, in Invernesshire.[27] In 1889, he was granted much longer leave to go fishing, shooting and specimen collecting in Iceland, an adventure in which he was joined by his brother, Geoffroy, and sister Mary.

They arrived in Reykjavik on 18 June and wasted no time in booking a guide, Thorgrimmer Gudmansen, (who, incidentally, during the previous summer had acted in the same capacity for Rider Haggard when the author was researching for his book, *Eric Brighteyes*).[28] Here is Johnny, as though back at Marlborough, with a deadly catapult. 'Another very interesting bird whose acquaintance I made for the first time was Barrow's goldeneye, a larger and more handsome creature than our own goldeneye, but similar in its habits. In these northern wilds I found the catapult – not the clumsy round-elastic weapon of the country schoolboy, but the scientific and small square-elastic tweaker – a great aid in obtaining a few specimens where birds were numerous and fairly tame.

'In fact I never cared to disturb the whole place by firing off a gun unless absolutely necessary to procure some rare and shy species. With the little silent weapon I secured during this one trip one golden plover, one long-tailed drake, one Barrow's goldeneye, one ptarmigan, four purple sandpipers, three dunlins and four red-necked phalaropes . . .'[29] He wanted a reindeer head, but was persuaded by Gudmansen that the species was too rare to bother about, advice that was to rouse Johnny's acute frustration. 'Like a fool I listened to him and left my rifle at Akuyreri, so my feelings as a keen hunter may be realised when, next morning, as we rode off in a sandstorm to the waterfall at Dettifoss, we came plump up against two reindeer bucks, lying on a little mound within seventy yards! At first they absolutely refused to run away and tried to stare us out of countenance. One was a fine fellow with a really splendid head and I watched him trotting slowly away with disgust than can be more easily imagined than described.'[30]

The party rode over 1,000 miles round the island, greatly enjoying themselves. 'Iceland is one of the few European countries where the traveller can wander at will', noted Johnny nearly thirty years later, 'and live with a small additional cost on the produce of his gun and rod amongst charming people. The trail of the serpent made by the tourist's dollar had not yet contaminated the peasantry as it has done in Norway, and there is yet room for a few sportsmen in their northern wilds.'[31] Inheriting as he did a cogent sense of history and local custom from both his parents, his Icelandic narrative includes a brief but lyrical account of the island people's story and their character. He, Mary and Geoffroy sailed home via the Faroes, where he took a close interest in the whaling industry.[32]

Meanwhile, in London his parents were enjoying the social life they relished (especially Effie). In midsummer, 1884, they were entertaining in a big way, as noted by Beatrix Potter: 'Papa and mamma went to a Ball at the Millais' a week or two since. There was an extraordinary mixture of actors, rich Jews, nobility, literary, etc. Du Maurier had been to the Ball the week before, and Carrie Millais said they thought they had seen him taking sketches on the sly. Oscar Wilde was there. I thought he was a long lanky melancholy man, but he is fat and merry. His only peculiarity was a black choker instead of a shirt-collar, and his hair in a mop. He was not wearing a lily in his button hole, but to make up for it, his wife had her front covered with great water-lilies.

'Lord Kinnaird was the greatest object. A little crooked old man with shirt-collars up to his eyes, and one black glove on, about an inch too long in the fingers.'[33]

John Everett Millais' career was closely approaching its zenith. He had been created a baronet in 1885, the year of his picture, *The Ruling Passion*, (also known as *The Ornithologist*), a portrait of the naturalist, John Gould, surrounded by his daughters and grand-children and a number of his exotic bird specimens, all of which, says Johnny proudly, 'were taken from my collection.' 1885 was the year, too, of the celebrated *Bubbles*, for which the artist's four-year-old grandson, Willie James, sat, and which was bought by the *Illustrated London News*, who when they had done with it, sold it to Pears the soap manufacturers. 'Next to Reynold's,' in Fish's estimation, 'it is Millais to whom we turn among English painters for the true rendering of the child in art.'[34]

He got Rupert Potter to photograph the *Bubbles* scene, the circumstances of which are recorded by Beatrix, who adds another note or two about him. 'Mr Millais came here 15th in the evening to get papa to photograph next morning. He seemed in good health and high spirits. "I just want you to photograph that little boy of Effie's. I've got him you know, he's (cocking up his chin at the ceiling), he's like this, with a bowl and soap suds, and all that, a pipe, it's called *A Child's World*, he's looking up and there's a beautiful soap bubble; I can't paint you know, not a bit, (with his head on one side and eyes twinkling) not a bit! I want just to compare it, I get this little thing (the photo of the picture) and I hold it in my hand and compare it with the life, and I can see where the drawing's wrong."

' "How are you getting on with your drawing?" Mr Millais asked me. My certes, I was rather alarmed, but he went to another subject in a second. He is a simple person in worldy affairs, he said to papa about the election, "I supposed we're all obliged to vote aren't we?"

'He addressed some most embarrassingly personal remarks to me, but compliments from him would take longer to turn my head than from any other source. If he sees a tolerably comely girl, he cannot keep his tongue still, and I am perfectly certain that when I was a child he used to tease me in order to see me blush.'[35]

Travelling by train from Perth to Dunkeld one day Millais overheard the conversation of two young men as the train stopped at Murthly station. 'Oh Murthly,' said one, 'that's where Millais the artist lives. Seen his pictures this year?' 'Yaas', drawled the other, 'but I don't think much of him since he's taken to advertising soap . . .'[36] But Millais himself was, of course, perfectly horrified when *Bubbles* was used as an advertisement. (Within ten years, incidentally, the child who was Bubbles was Midshipman James, one day to be an admiral.)

'Millais was,' said Spielmann, 'accused of some quarters of playing to the crowd when he composed his little dramas and devised the pictures of pretty children, which the public so loudly applauded. To which Millais angrily retorted, 'If I wanted to paint a "popular" picture I should paint an old man in spectacles reading the Bible by the fireside; and the fire would be reflected in his spectacles. And I should paint a tear running down his nose and the fire would be reflected in the tear; that would be a "popular" picture I can tell you!'[37]

Spielmann goes on to claim Millais' preeminence as a portrait painter. 'He had the noble power of making his sitters live and breathe . . . other portraitists there were, Watts, Ouless, Herkomer, Holl, but Millais . . . never surrendered his premier position . . .'[38] How well Millais himself was aware of the development of his artistic power is reflected in this

John Everett Millais: *The Ruling Passion* (sometimes known as *The Ornithologist*), 1885.

little memoir of Spielmann's. In 1886 after seeing some of his much earlier pictures exhibited at the Grosvenor Gallery '... he arrived at Lady Leighton's for dinner. "Quick," he exclaimed, in an exhausted tone, "give me some champagne, I'm quite ill!" Then, after a draught, he added, "I've been seeing all my old work – all my past misdeeds have been rising up against me. Oh, the vulgarity of some of them, my dear fellow, the vulgarity! ... I would like half my pictures to go to the bottom of the Atlantic if I could choose the half to go." '[39] But, along with many other critics, Beatrix Potter thought the earlier work was better. 'Millais will doubtless paint some noble pictures yet', she said after attending the exhibition, 'but on the whole his work seems to have passed its prime.'[40]

Although he was more interested in people than anything else and happier, on his own admission, painting landscapes, he was also a brilliant portrayer of animals, as the vivacity and litheness of his cat in *Puss in Boots* and the authentic character of his kittens in *A Flood* show. Then there are the delightfully realistic mice in *Mariana* and lizards in *Ferdinand Lured by Ariel*. Also the greyhound in *Isabella*, the collies in *The Order of Release* and *Effie Deans*, the deerhounds in *The Twin Daughters of T. R. Hoare Esq.* and the bloodhound in *The Ransom* all testify to his accomplishment. Spielmann claimed for him that 'had he given his attention to the lower, instead of the higher animals, there is little doubt that he would have been a far greater animal painter than Landseer, though not so pop-

John Everett Millais
photographed at Dalguise
by Rupert Potter in 1879.

ular; for he never sought to humanise them as Landseer did, to the delight of an animal-loving, but somewhat unthinking public. For Millais a dog was a dog, to be loved as such and not half apotheosised into a human being . . . In the execution of dogs he has never been excelled.'[41]

Millais was, like Sir Thomas More, a man for all seasons; and he was a Renaissance man, at once literary, sporting, musical and witty as well as a genius in visual art creativeness; and a practical, orderly man, too, who disliked pretentiousness as much as he disliked unpunctuality and untidiness, as Johnny has shown us. 'He hated the affectation of the long-haired and velvet-coated tribe . . . and just dressed like other men according to circumstances of time and place, only too happy to escape the observations of strangers as he moved about the world . . . In early life my father was devoted to chess, at which he became so expert that, at the age of twelve, he was frequently pitted against Harvitz, one of the finest players of the day, and in later years . . . he loved to work out the problems in the *Illustrated London News*, and every Saturday night he would take the paper up to his bedroom for this purpose . . . Another pastime of his was writing nonsense verses for the amusement of his friends.'[42]

The early 1890s produced their share of disaster as well as triumph. In 1891, when Millais lost the tenancy of his beloved Murthly, he took the shooting and fishing leases of another Perthshire property and rented a house called Newmill, which, in January 1892, was burned down while Millais and Effie were there. Johnny's soldier-servant, Private Whiteford, was in residence, too, looking after a water-spaniel, the property of a brother officer to which, said Johnny, 'I had promised to give a couple of months training at home during my long leave.' The dog, first to smell the smoke, raised the alarm, but nearly everything was lost, including that valuable pair of hammerless ejectors, George Gray's present. 'One thing of mine, however, was saved,' Johnny records. 'Whiteford, who knew I valued extremely a case of drawings I had done in western America, pluckily broke through the window from the outside and, fighting his way through smoke and flames, just managed to reach the case and stagger out with it, though nearly suffocating in the attempt.'[43]

In 1892 Sir John Millais suffered the disappointment of seeing Johnny resign his army commission. The young Seaforth Highlander, having been left some money by his uncle, Everett Gray, decided to spend it on a long South African trek and to earn his living with the hunter's gun, the artist's pencil and brushes and the author's pen.

After the death of Sir John Millais four years later, Beatrix Potter entered a nice memoir of him in her journal and went on to say a little about her own and Johnny's incipient artistic gifts: 'I shall always have a most affectionate remembrance of Sir John Millais, though unmercifully afraid of him as a child, on account of what the papers call "his schoolboy manner". I had a brilliant colour as a little girl, which he used to provoke on purpose and remark upon at times. If a great portrait painter's criticism is of any interest this is it, delivered with due consideration, turning me round under a window, that I was a little like his daughter Carrie, at that time a fine handsome girl, but my face was spoiled by the length of my nose and upper lip.

'He gave me the kindest encouragement with my drawings (to be sure he did to everybody!), vide, a visit he paid to an awful country Exhibition at Perth, in the shop of Stewart the framemaker (who invited him), but he really paid me a compliment for he said that "plenty of people can *draw*, but you and my son John have observation". Now "my son Johnny" at that date couldn't draw at all, but I know exactly what he meant.'[44]

The next chapter shows how well Johnny came on.

5

ADVENTURES ON THE VELDT

Although Johnny loved the Highland regiment that had been his master since 1886 his decision to retire, at twenty-seven, only a few months before his captaincy was due, was long premeditated. Perhaps the only consideration that held him back, during the last two or three years, was the wish not to disappoint his father. Johnny was not only a well qualified naturalist and hardened traveller, possessed of an insatiable wanderlust and yearning for adventure and sport, but he was one, too, who had proved he could earn his living as a writer and illustrator. His *Game Birds and Shooting Sketches* – a broad and heavy tome, as all his scientific and fully illustrated works would be – was published in the year he resigned from the Seaforths.

The book contains the most brilliant essays on, and paintings of, grouse, capercailzie, blackgame and ptarmigan, while its Scottish shooting anecdotes and drawings reflect that adoration of the wild Highlands which he shared so abundantly with both parents. Fittingly, his father provided the frontispiece to the book – with a fanciful drawing of the eighteenth-century naturalist, Thomas Bewick.

As for his own artistic talent he commented, sarcastically, that 'had it been my good fortune to have any art education whatsoever . . . who knows that I might not have blossomed into a great artist, like Mr Aubrey Beardsley, for instance?'[1] On the other hand he made an unusual claim to have been an art *tutor* as a child. 'As a little boy . . . I once sat on Landseer's knee, and armed with pencil and paper, devoted half an hour of my valuable time to teaching him how to draw deer!' In other words even at that age he was claiming to be a more profound student of the anatomy of deer than the man who was held up as the greatest animal artist of his day. Johnny thought that 'only one man towers above the heads of all other artists of wild beasts and birds of this or any other time – Joseph Wolf.'

There is a passage in a later book of his, describing a Highland stalk he enjoyed a few weeks before leaving the army, a deerstalking experience nicely demonstrating his preoccupation with prize specimens and his ardent desire to secure the best trophies. '. . . Now when a stag lies down it may be from one hour to three before he moves again; so, after waiting for more than two hours, we came to the conclusion that these, at any rate, intended to take their maximum of repose; and during this long and somewhat chilly wait, we overhauled the merits of the herd. There were certainly six good 10-pointers amongst them and at least one royal, but the stag that had engrossed our attention from the first had by far the best head amongst them, though in point of size he looked rather small in comparison with his comrades. The more I looked at him the more I longed to call him mine. I told Grant [his ghillie] quite seriously I would give half-a-year's pay to get a good chance at this particular stag, upon which he opened his eyes in amazement at such wild extravagance, his idea being no doubt that a subaltern in Her Majesty's service must needs be right handsomely remunerated.'[2]

As Johnny turned his thoughts to South Africa, heads were his priority again, prize specimen horns of the great antelope species of the veldt, heads and the skins of the veldt birds for his collection and for the British Museum. And as he relished the prospect of his forthcoming adventure he must have experienced a glorious sense of liberation, of spreading his wings, like a hawk that is no longer subject to the will of his falconer-owner, but has broken free to join his kith and kin in the wild. For his recent travels, to Iceland, the Orkneys and remote regions of the Highlands, had been restricted by commanding officers who had ordered him back to the 'lure', so to speak, back to barracks by pre-ordained dates. Now he was his own master.

On board the *Norham Castle* he read or re-read Baldwin's *African Hunting* along with *A Hunter's Wanderings in Africa* and *Travel and Adventure in South-East Africa,* by that greatest of nineteenth-century hunter-naturalists, Frederick Selous, who, though fourteen years his senior, was to become his fellow-traveller and closest friend, as well as his mentor. Johnny would be Selous' biographer, too.

After two and a half weeks with 'excellent cuisine, great comfort and a good band to play every evening on deck', the *Norham Castle* was being steered her last few miles into Cape Town bay, 'the brightest gem in the South African scenery', as he calls it. 'Round the majestic monument of Table Mountain still soar the eagle, the buzzard and the white-necked raven; while, in the surf, regardless of boats and boatmen, groups of little green cormorants may be seen any day pursuing their finny prey to the very verge of the beach

John Guille Millais: Satire – *South Africa – The Ideal,* 1894.

. . .' And out came his pencils, paintbox and brushes to sketch the scene. The drawing would become the first of more than 200 wildlife monochrome etchings for his book *A Breath from the Veldt*.

He took the train for six weeks' stay at Beaufort West, the attraction there being the hunting of the springbuck, 'the fleetest antelope in South Africa', and the blessbuck, 'the fastest in point of endurance'. In April he entrained for Johannesburg, a town already known as the 'Golden City', though only five years old.

'New as the town is,' Johnny reported, 'there still lives in it the wild spirit of the interior . . . This is most apparent in the morning market, when the Boers, with their transport waggons and splendid spans of magnificent oxen, come in to buy, sell, and be hired . . . There sits the old Boer on the top of his waggon, solemnly blinking in the sun as he puffs away at his magaliesburg and watches the manoeuvres of his native Zulu driving the dearly loved span with consummate skill; for these boys can drive and no mistake, merely using their voices as a scourge, where a less patient and weaker-lunged man would lose both his temper and his voice. There, too, may be seen Jews selling cheap wares; black boys waiting to be hired; Malays hawking bijouterie; sharp auctioneers yelling forth the manifold attractions of hungry-looking steeds, whose beauty no one seems to see but themselves; hard little Basuto ponies dashing hither and thither, mounted by every class and nationality under the sun; and, amongst the crowd, a big smattering of loafers and rascals ever on the look-out for doing a "softy" . . .'

He was particularly struck, in contrast, by a Salvation Army girl, 'whose personal charms not even the hideous costume of the "Hallelujah Lass" could hide. I saw her there selling the *War Cry*, and am bound to say a more lovely face and figure have seldom crossed my path. A right modest girl, too, to all appearances, with a sweet supplicating manner . . . It was amusing to watch her as she walked along the stoep of my hotel, and took one man after another captive . . . Nobody wanted her wares or cared tuppence about the "Army", but nobody, not even the hardest city man, could refrain from shelling out the "tickie" (threepenny bit) when once her eyes met his . . .'[3]

He met 'a good-looking well-mannered fellow of the better-class Dutch', Martinus ('Teenie') Landsberg, from whom he hired waggons and oxen for an eight months' trip into the interior, and arranged for them 'to start together the following Tuesday'. He then engaged the necessary native boys and ponies to complete his team and bought the rifles and ammunition, saddles and bridles, groceries and other stores, which he had ordered in advance.

'3 p.m. on 12th April saw us ascending the last of the range of hills leading eastwards from the "Golden City" – hills under which lie buried more riches than will be brought to light in this generation. Here the quartz-crushers are at work, filling the air with thunderous sounds; but one by one we leave them all behind, along with the recumbant forms of Kaffirs asleep or drunk. And now Johannesburg, with its poor, striving and sweating community, vanishes from our sight. With almost startling suddenness silence and solitude take the place of crash and boom and rush; the fine fresh air of the veldt blows in our faces . . .'[24] April found them at Teenie Landsberg's home, where they picked up Teenie's brother, Piet.

There being no mammals worth studying on the 'high veldt', Johnny took out his sketch-book and drew the birds, particularly the khooran and the bustard, the Bataleur eagle and the bone-breaking lammergeier of the high cliffs – until the blessbuck cropped up again and he stalked them under cover of a trained horse, and sketched that scene, too. All his drawings were to reflect not only a profound anatomical knowledge, but also a wonderful evocation of the animals' movements, habits and habitat.

He thought much about the gift of animal art. 'An artist may be a first-class performer as a draughtsman, composer and master of light and shade, and yet draw down upon himself the laughter of the experienced sportsman and naturalist when he attempts to show what birds and beasts are like in their wild state. And the reason is plain enough: he is neither a sportsman, nor a naturalist – very few artists are . . . We have got a bit sick now of these conventional lions, buffaloes and elephants in a chronic state of charge . . . a whole series of this same thing,' in his opinion, 'is as nauseating as the bulk of political speeches in these days of working-man worship.'

It was early May now and Johnny and his cavalcade were heading due north for Pietersburg, northern Transvaal's last village, and were hoping to cross the Limpopo by 1 June. 'On the 3rd [of May] we . . . had some difficulty crossing the Wilgah river, having to double-span – that is to fasten both spans of oxen, in all thirty-two, to each waggon separately – to get through the river, the sand being up to the axles, and the water pretty heavy. During the afternoon we crossed a nasty series of broken sand pits, and in one particularly bad place, which my waggon narrowly escaped, Teenie's waggon, following closely behind turned completely over, Piet and the whole of its contents being deposited on the veldt.' On the way they were joined by a highly experienced Dutch hunter, Oom Roelef van Staden and his two sons, Tace and Hert, together with their respective waggons.

'From the moment I saw him [van Staden],' says Johnny, 'I felt that here was the very man I wanted to complete my party . . . a fine manly fellow with a face so exceptionally handsome, so refined and so expressive, that I wished many a time that I could take him home to my father as a perfect model and type of an old African hunter . . . When I got to know him well and speak his language, as I presently did, I found him the most delightful and sympathetic of companions . . . there was an entire absence of that vulgar swagger and boorishness which are so often apparent in the talk and actions of inferior

John Guille Millais: *Oom Roelef van Staden.*

men, particularly among the Transvaal Boers . . . His travels had not been so varied or so widespread as Selous', but his hunting expeditions into all parts of the interior since he was eighteen years of age had given him a familiar knowledge of the country such as few other men possessed.'[4]

Van Staden advised Johnny to head for the 'fly' country on the south-east bank of the Limpopo, and on to eastern Mashonaland, in search of the white rhinoceros whose 'extreme rarity . . . made me anxious to obtain, if possible, a specimen for our national Museum.' The waggons and their crews followed the beaten track, while Johnny, accompanied by van Staden and his sons, rode on a parallel line on the rocky hills above, where – with the assistance of a good old pointer, rescued at starvation point from the streets of Johannesburg – they shot francolin, bush khoran and bustard ('the finest game bird in the world') for the pot. At the prior request of Mr Ogilvie Grant, of the British Museum, Johnny cured and preserved some of those birds' skins to take home.

Predictably, he suffered much from the anti-British attitude of the Boers, who, since their victory at Majuba Hill in 1881 and the proclaiming of the Transvaal a republic, had little but scorn for the Anglo-Saxon race. For Johnny the most open manifestation of that prejudice was the fact that they invariably named the laziest, most obdurate and least charming of their teams of oxen, 'Englishman'!

'Though possessing many good qualities', in his judgement, they 'lacked not only in humour but in that ready grasp of things in general that we are accustomed to look upon as amongst the essentials of an agreeable companion. An Englishman has hardly anything in common with them. Their fun is either forced, in the hope of showing themselves smarter than they really are, or is only such as may be found in mere coarseness and obscenity . . . the Dutchman keeps his shield arm up, and it is only after months of close association that you can see his character in its true light . . . [they are] the most credulous people in the world. Every day either Teenie, Piet, Tace or Hert came to me with some ghastly tale of what was going on up country . . . When I found they really believed [their grossly exaggerated alarms] I roared with laughter; for a Dutchman, though anxious to convey the idea that he is supremely smart, is in reality the most gullible creature under the sun.'

From his many conversations around camp fires Johnny gathered (from 'the more sensible-minded Dutch') that Boer rule was generally regarded as inept and insensitive and 'the people would heartily welcome an English administration of their affairs in exchange for the feeble and narrow-minded rule of their present Volksraad, whose ideas of politics are based on the Old Testament . . . and that in the Transvaal a renewal of the British Protectorate would be hailed with joy by the majority of the nation. On the other hand, as he conceded in another context, 'one cannot quite agree with the contemptuous aspersions that are cast by many on Dutch character and Dutch courage; for amongst these people, particularly the women, there has always been that indomitable spirit of self-reliance which, whatever their other failings may be, calls for the admiration of the world.[5]

'*14th May. Sunday.* It is a real pleasure to have a day's rest at the end of each week; for continuous trekking through uninteresting country becomes wearisome and monotonous in the extreme. Oom Roelef holds a service with his family and the Landsbergs in which the "Old Hundredth" figures conspicuously in the midst of the long Gregorian chants. I don't like it myself, so I generally spend the day sketching, writing and preserving specimens of game birds. Many Makatese come to trade mealies, fowls and kaffir corn for salt. As a rule the men and boys have pleasant, good-natured faces; but the women are simply hideous.'

The party reached the Limpopo on 2 June. 'We arrived just as some thirty transport

John Guille Millais: *Lion scaring vultures off a kill.*

waggons, all heavily laden with goods for Victoria and Salisbury were making the passage of the river; and a thoroughly inspiriting and truly South African scene it was: the yellow sandbanks glaring in the sun, the blue waters, the straining oxen dragging at their burdens with but their neck and shoulders above the water; while the Natal Zulus, immersed to their shoulders, swung their great ox-whips and yelled and swore prodigiously while driving their patient and willing teams to the further bank. The sand is deep in the bed of the Limpopo, and the river bank rises high out of the stream; the crossing is consequently a heavy pull for oxen; so double spanning (thirty-four to forty oxen to each waggon) is generally the order of the day.'[6]

Johnny exulted in the start of each day's hunting. 'Blessed Africa! it is always going to be a fine day there, sometimes too fine. You dress yourself quickly, see that your horse has his morning feed of mealies and kaffir corn, and swallow your own breakfast of tea and buck with a gusto such as only a hunter when the breath of the veldt is upon him knows anything of. Another ten minutes and you and your companion have lighted your pipes, seen to your rifle and cartridges, skinning-knife, etc. and are in the saddle and heading for the nearest bush. If you are in a "Thirst" country you take, of course, a water-bottle, and never go out without matches, as you never know when you will get back.

'Suppose now that you viewed a troop of buck, they will generally move a few steps forward on seeing you, and then you and your companion will have time to see if the head is any good. If it is, dismount quickly and take as steady a shot at him as you can – he is generally standing broadside on to you from fifty to a hundred yards off – and then, unless the animal is so hard hit that you can readily get up to him on foot, jump on to your horse as soon as possible, canter quickly after him, and try to find out the effect of your shot. By remounting at once you can see directly the line of the animal's retreat . . .'

He shot his first kudu bull on 6 June. 'Who can forget the happiness of a moment like that?' he asks, and goes on to describe how, with many a long ride and stalk, from many a patient wait, sable antelope, waterbuck, blessbuck, ostrich, eland, lion, warthog and

John Guille Millais: *Klipbucks descending a kopje*, 1894.

roan antelope fell to his rifle, while his waggon swelled with horns and tusks. Such meat as was not eaten for supper was cut into strips, 'biltong', and hung up for later consumption, while the hides were sold to passing traders.

His book is full of advice as to how each quarry species should be approached. Here he is, for example, on the reedbuck. 'He who desires to shoot a couple of heads of this buck will often have to work hard for days in the dry sluits, with both gun and rifle, even though the bucks be fairly numerous. If found in a very large water-course, the reedbuck will often not leave the open grass, but will run for half a mile or so and then stand and gaze at his pursuer. The sportsman should keep out of sight as much as possible, and then he may probably be rewarded by seeing his game again squat, when he can walk right up to him.'

The territory just north of that sector of Limpopo known as Mashonaland was ruled by the hostile Zulus of the Matabele tribe, and sinister messages now began to arrive at the hunters' laager, messages to the effect that all white men were to be duly warned that unless they withdrew into the Transvaal forthwith, they would be summarily slaughtered. The Matabele war had started; Fort Victoria was under siege. The Basadanotes, old friends of van Staden's and the Landsbergs', and now of Johnny's, too, friends who would not have received the *cave*, were in danger of being cut off. Johnny knowing, at that point in the journey, that only his Basuto ponies were up to the hectic trek involved – fifty miles there and back in the day – volunteered for the mission, riding one, leading the other. With both ponies slipping their knee-halters and bolting at the first resting-place, however, he was obliged to complete the journey on foot under a scorching sun.

He found the ponies at the Basadanotes' camp, where 'the Dutch hunters received me with that courtesy which I everywhere experienced from this class of men during my stay in South Africa. It will be a long time before the memory of that camp fades from my mind, with its koodoo heads leaning against the waggon, its suspicious Boer dogs, its stacks of biltong under the drying sheds, its white-capped Dutch women flitting about under the great trees, Zulus cleaning assegais or attending to the horses, and domesticated zebras that whisk their tails continuously in the blazing sun . . .

'The best refreshment their waggons afforded was brought out and, hearing my news, for which they were most grateful, they decided to trek out at once. I, too, dared not prolong my stay . . .' But there was a worse mishap awaiting him on the return journey. This time the ponies, terrified by the sudden rushing past of some wild animals, bolted again. Thrown on the rocky ground at a crazy gallop, Johnny lay unconscious for fifteen minutes. The ponies arrived at his own camp trembling and sweating. Two boys who were sent out 'with a lantern and a bottle of whiskey', found him on his feet but with a broken collar-bone, which two days later, was bound up at the police camp at Middle Drift. 'What hunter,' he wonders, 'cannot recall such a series of mishaps . . . However, koodoo marrow-bones and hot tea will dispel most men's cares, particularly when the flicker of the fire-light shines on a $45\frac{1}{4}$ inch sable head.'

There were many other disasters and anxious moments. Van Staden became very ill; and Johnny was obliged to put up, on frequent occasions, with the younger Boers' jealous sulks. His only dog, that mongrel pointer retrieved from the slums of Johannesburg, was killed while at grips with a wounded antelope; and several of his oxen died of tsetse-fly poisoning. Then a supposedly friendly chief called N'Dale turned up at the laager with forty warriors in readiness, he said, for a Matabele attack, but in reality to blackmail Johnny and his Dutch friends for rifles and ammunition and to pilfer what they could from the camp. They remained a menace for several days. On another occasion a pride of lions, mad with hunger, invaded the laager at night, killing and taking away three

precious donkeys. The men tied loaded rifles to trees overlooking one carcase remains, with cords connecting carcase and triggers and, by that device, revenged themselves on one of the lions.

Most animal-lovers in our late twentieth-century wildlife conservation mood and relative spirit of kindness, find it difficult to sympathise with the big-game hunters of old, who, killing by the hundred, saw themselves as bravely pitting their wits and strength against harsh nature. But, witnessing lions hamstringing buffaloes or zebras, Johnny and his friends had little sorrow to spare for a big cat succumbing in agony to bullet wounds. Or knowing how often and how slowly some of the ruminant animals died from accidents, or starvation, or predatory attack, they rarely felt guilty, from a humane point of view, if they maimed an animal and failed to finish it off. Treks were impossible without meat; a great many stalks, a great many shots, often at inordinately long ranges, were necessary; a wounding shot was 'just hunter's bad luck'.

Johnny, whose love of wildlife was as sincere as it was deep, perhaps came as close as any hunter in South Africa to feeling sorry for wild animals in distress and pain. The natives who had long known the devastating power of the *nux vomica* seed, made wide and fairly indiscriminate use of strychnine. But few Boers would have thought much about the consequences as Johnny did. 'The last night of our stay at Gong I went to bed early and tired after five hard days in pursuit of roan antelopes, without any result. About ten o'clock one of the hyaenas returned and began one of his awful howls within, I should guess, forty yards of the waggon. He had taken the poisoned bait, and never in my life have I heard anything more human and heart-rending than the cries he emitted some two or three minutes afterwards. Personally I did not much care for this barbarous method of killing animals, but really dangerous and offensive brutes like lions, leopards and hyaenas have, I suppose, to be got rid of anyhow as civilisation advances . . .'[7]

His dialogues with the boys in his employ brought out some intriguing native theories. 'One night, through Teenie, who speaks Zulu perfectly, I had a long talk with him ["Office", his Shangan boy] about his superstitions, beliefs and past life. His ideas about

Englishmen were interesting. They came, he said, from the bottom of the sea ten days to the eastward of Delagoa Bay. There they live entirely under water, with the salt waves splashing over them . . . The belief may possibly have originated with cannibal races of days gone by; for, apart from the dread with which the natives regard the white man, few of them care to kill him for food, his flesh being, it is said, so impregnated with salt as to be almost uneatable.

' "Office" thinks that the English came to Africa to get "biltong" and then go home and buy wives, while "Pompoon" affirms that they came over to keep dry, as in England it is always raining. They are certainly "dry" enough in one sense of the word, when they get there,' adds Johnny. 'In fact, I never saw so many thirsty Englishmen in all my life as in Johannesburg, where every second man who "has a few minutes to spare", seems to be afflicted with the hand-to-mouth disease.'[8]

It was August now. The time had come to return to Johannesburg and to say goodbye to Oom Roelef van Staden. 'Together had we tasted the hopes and fears, the sweets and disappointments of the happy hunting-grounds, and under these influences our comradeship had ripened into the affection of brothers; for no form of existence brings men closer together than the wild free life of the hunter . . . The longer one knew him the more one's interest and affection were enlisted by the simplicity and unaffected earnestness of the man's whole nature . . . in my mind old Oom will ever stand out as a model of what a hunter and a true gentleman should be . . . [His] old Frau and the girls were in tears as we kissed all round; and I must confess I was deeply moved.'[9]

John Guille Millais: *Clas, a Shangan Hunter*, 1893.

Johnny's most important task in the 'Golden City' was to commission 'Mr Duffus, an enterprising Scotchman from Aberdeen' to photograph his waggon and heads. That done he set about organising his final commitment in South Africa, which was to secure some white-tailed gnu, or black wildebeest heads. To his mind 'this extraordinary looking creature' was 'the most interesting animal in the world.' And, although his principal original quest in South Africa was for sable antelope and kudu, it was the half buffalo-half antelope black wildebeest – with its belligerent antics, great speed, strange feeding habits, long peregrinations and herd rituals – that fascinated him most in the end.

The black wildebeest seemed to be rapidly approaching a state of extinction. Whereas there were once tens of thousands scattered in troops all over southern Transvaal and the Free State high veldt, by the 1890s there were probably fewer than 550, most of them fenced in on private land. The only substantial numbers running wild were to be found near Kronstad, on an estate owned by a difficult and extremely anti-British septuagenarian called Piet Terblans, whose acquaintance Johnny now sought. Having secured an introduction he 'made for him a few days later, traversing in a Cape cart the grassy uplands of the Orange Free State.'

'You are an Englishman,' Terblans said in disgust. 'You cannot shoot wildebeest! My son will shoot one for you.'[10]

Though Johnny insisted that he himself must be the stalker, the old Boer duly arranged for his son, Jan, to bring round a dead animal in the morning. 'I went to him at once,' says Johnny, 'and told him that I did not wish for the wildebeest, and should certainly not pay for it; upon which he seemed much annoyed – marvelled, too, that any man should care to be at the trouble of shooting one himself when here was what he wanted lying, as it were, at his feet.' Eventually, Terblans agreed for him to go hunting provided he bought the carcase.

Having the greatest difficulty in getting within range of a herd unnoticed, it was not until the fourth day on the farm that Johnny managed to get in a successful shot at a wildebeest bull. For his next attempt he persuaded Jan to drive a herd towards him. 'Having flattened myself out behind the largest ant-hill I could find, I lay and watched the tactics of my companion as he proceeded to head the troop about half a mile away. It was one of the prettiest and most exciting experiences with wild animals that has ever fallen to my lot. Without it, I could never have known what a wild thrill of joy – not unmixed with fear that they will alter their course – the sight of a herd of these wild-looking creatures can cause as their black forms advance towards one, now cantering, now walking slowly and glancing distrustfully back at any object from which danger is suspected.

'Closer and closer they came, like a regiment of black horses advancing . . . Will they ever stop cantering? . . . Now do I bless that foremost cow as she swings round towards me, immediately followed by the rest of the troop at open order. Now is the moment of supreme excitement. I lie glued flat to the ground, not daring to move. On they come, and I see that it will be quite safe to drop the 200 yard flag and prepare for a close shot. However, eighty yards is quite near enough, as both rest and position are good, and the animals would stampede if they came a yard nearer.

'The rifle creeps up the side of the ant-heap . . . All one's physical forces are strained to the utmost to subdue the tumultuous beating of the heart and concentrate one's mind on the need of perfect steadiness at this critical moment, and it is with intense satisfaction that one finds that all is well immediately the trigger is pressed . . . The wound is a mortal one.'[11]

In addition to that triumph Johnny made a close friend of the hitherto forbidding Piet Terblans. 'My host and his good vroo [wife] became more and more loquacious, till by the end of a week I found the man whom I had heard everywhere stigmatised as a grasping ogre, an honest old farmer, who was actually asking me to prolong by visit – without paying for my board!'

And so, in November, he entrained for Cape Town and his ship, saying '. . . farewell to Africa with its sunshine, its dust, its hardships and the many attractions – attractions now unhappily on the wane, for every day that passes brings with it a growing throng of fortune-seekers and adventurers who, obliterating the landmarks of the past, gradually drive the children of Nature farther and farther afield, and will probably continue to do so till the whole country is bereft of the romance and the glories of days gone by . . .'

During his first sojourn in Cape Town, nine months before, he had paused for rueful reflection on what he had been told of the general depletion of South Africa's wildlife, especially the larger antelope species. And close to the beginning of *A Breath from the Veldt* he calls for 'the formation of a national game preserve on the lines of Yellowstone Park, in western America . . . Here is where our American cousin has shown his foresight and good sense. Let us not therefore be behindhand in foreseeing the inevitable destruction of the truly magnificent fauna – a fauna no other country possesses in such variety and all-round beauty.

'Let Mr Cecil Rhodes do a popular thing, which will receive the unanimous support of all lovers of nature, and cause the British South Africa Company to assign a district for the sole preservation of the wild game. This will in no wise inter-fere with the advance of civilisation, but will retain for South Africa some of the

Piet Terblans, a scraperboard drawing by John Guille Millais.

63

John Guille Millais: *Black Wildebeests at Play*, 1893.

beauties of creation for which she is justly considered so famous. How easily the animals indigenous to the country can be preserved, and their decrease stopped, can be seen here and there, where far-sighted farmers, having suitable lands have adopted such a policy . . .'[12]

In a footnote he comments that, two years having elapsed between this exhortation and his book going to press, Rhodes's plans for a national reserve at Cape Town and Captain Gibbons's for a game farm in Mashonaland were already well in hand before the time of publication. It was too early for him to foresee the Sabie National Park – founded in 1898 in northern Transvaal – which was to become the Kruger National Park.

He was to return to Africa – less than a year later, to north Africa – and in very different circumstances. He married Frances (Fanny) Margaret, the high-spirited daughter of a Lincolnshire landowner and barrister, P. G. Skipwith. Their romance began at a hunt ball and continued with a honeymoon in Morocco. She was soon to be made starkly aware of how it felt to be married to a wanderlust naturalist-explorer.

6

THE PRESIDENT'S LAST TREK

Within weeks of sailing home from Cape Town Johnny began researching for *British Deer and Their Horns*, the project that would now keep him busy until 1896. It was a subject that had preoccupied him, as much if not more, than any other since childhood. The book, which is interlaced with numerous stalking anecdotes, drawings of heads and incidents depicted from personal observation, involved him in two years of busy travel, albeit travel of a considerably more comfortable nature than the trek of 1893. To name a few of his visits, in Scotland, where both roe deer and the red have been present since prehistoric times, he was the guest of the Earl of Cawdor in Nairnshire, and of Lord Lovat at Beaufort Castle in Invernesshire. In Devon he stayed with Lord Fortescue to make his notes on the red deer of Exmoor; and in Dorset with the Earl of Ilchester at Melbury House, Dorchester, whence he crossed to Brownsea to study the island's imported Japanese Sika deer.

That great falconer and naturalist, his friend, the Hon. Gerald Lascelles, Deputy Surveyor of the New Forest, put him up at the Queen's House, Lyndhurst, to learn the history and natural history of the Forest's fallow; and the Duke of Bedford gave him the free run of his estates and its famous herds at Woburn.

Johnny and Fanny rented a house near Horsham, in West Sussex, during the early years of their marriage, where their neighbour, Charles Lucas, of Warnham Park, invited him to study the fallow and red deer that were established there during the previous generation.

The following memoir illustrates how well informed he kept himself on any unusual specimens that were reported. 'An adult buck, which was said to be pure white was well known in the woods of Kinross in 1894, and a friend who hunts with the Fifeshire hounds told me that the pack got onto this buck one day and ran him to Ladybank, where he was left and the hounds whipped off. I do not think he has been killed or I should have heard of it.'[1]

Throughout all that research he kept half an eye on his father's health. Sir John Millais' life, though rising to its zenith in terms of fame and public honour, had clearly been ebbing from about the time Johnny returned from South Africa, and a spirit of pessimism set in. Towards the end of 1893 the great artist had the satisfaction of receiving the Order of Merit, but a few months later while working on two of his finest paintings, *St Stephen* and *Speak! Speak!* he was brought down by severe attacks of lumbago and rheumatism and contracted a throat infection. Feeling very low, he told his fellow Academician, Briton Rivière that he was '. . . dreadfully despondent at times, overwhelmed by a recurring conviction that the game is played out – no more pictures wanted. As long as our work looks fresh and new it is called garish, and must be so to a certain extent, not being fairly

John Everett Millais photographed in his studio by Rupert Potter in 1886. Millais'
portrait of Lord Rosebery is on the right.

gauged with the old masters, through the ignorance of critics who are not able to see
the extraordinary amount of good form in the moderns – notably in the illustrations to
magazines.'[2]

A little later, in an essay entitled 'Thoughts on our Art Today' for *The Magazine of
Art,* he expanded on these sentiments. 'The only way to judge of the treasures which the
old Masters of whatever age have left us, whether in architecture, sculpture or painting,
with any hope of sound deduction is to look at the work and ask oneself "what was that
like when it was new?" . . . Imagine the Parthenon as it must have looked . . . in all its
pristine beauty and splendour . . . a white marble building blinding in the dazzling bright-
ness of a southern sun . . . and many of us, I venture to think, would cry at once, "How
excessively crude!" No: Time and varnish are two of the greatest of Old Masters and
their merits and virtues are all too often attributed by critics to the painters of the pictures
they have toned and mellowed.'[3]

He championed the contemporary animal artists when he told his Perth friend, Dr
Urquhart, that 'many men draw and paint domestic animals better than the old masters –
notably Henry Davis. A fine old Velasquez with a hero on horseback, looking as if he
would eat you up, is mounted on a poor horse, poorly drawn – an impossible creature.
A far higher standard in this respect is required now. None of the old masters can touch
Meissonier in this respect.'[4]

The summer of 1894 saw a general improvement in his health but his throat got worse –
he had, all his life, been a hardened and perpetual pipe-smoker – and, with it, his voice
became low and almost whispering. Although his last fatal illness was upon him, he set

Effie in middle age.

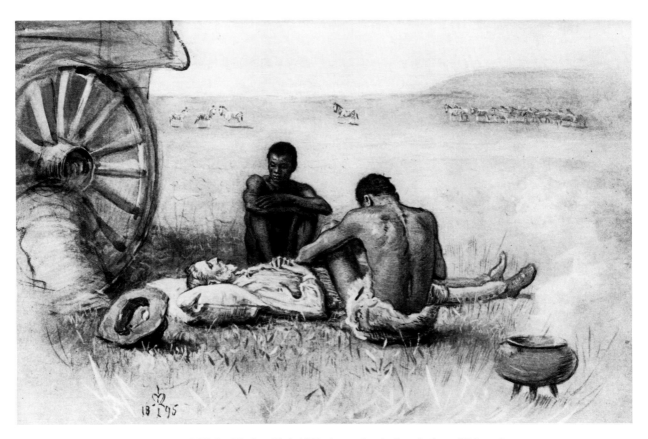

John Everett Millais: *The Last Trek*, 1895, drawn for the frontispiece of Johnny's
A Breath from the Veldt.

about drawing *The Last Trek*, the frontispiece for *A Breath from the Veldt*, with a relish.

Johnny, who wanted him to compose a fuller developed painting from it, knew that
'. . . the subject appealed strongly to his feelings. It was that of a scene I had myself witnessed in South Africa,' he tells us, 'a white hunter dying in the wilderness attended by
his faithful Zulus. The title, *The Last Trek*, too, seemed to please him (perchance as having
some relation to his thoughts about himself); and after talking some time on various
points – such as the atmosphere of the Southern plains and the appearance of the parched
and sun-cracked soil – he suddenly paused in his walk about the room, and putting his
hand to his forehead, said solemnly and slowly, "This is going to kill me! I feel it, I feel
it!"

'The idea seemed to be but momentary. In another minute, he was quite calm again,
and throwing down his palette, which was already prepared, he pulled out his cards and
quietly commenced a game of "patience". An hour later he felt so extremely unwell that
he retired to his own room downstairs, closing the studio door behind him, for the last
time. He had commenced, though he knew it not, "The Last Trek".'[5]

Lord Leighton, the President of the Royal Academy, being too ill to preside at the
Academy dinner in May 1895, Millais rallied sufficiently to speak in his place. Nor did
he miss that opportunity of expressing something of his devotion and gratitude to the
Academy. 'I entered the antique school as a probationer when I was eleven years of age,
then became a student in the life school,' he told them, his husky nostalgic voice barely
audible. 'And I have risen from stage to stage until I reached the position I now hold
of Royal Academician, so that, man and boy, I have been intimately connected with

this Academy for more than half a century. I have received here as free an education as any artist – an advantage any lad may enjoy who can pass a qualifying examination – and I owe the Academy a debt of gratitude I can never repay. I love everything belonging to it – the casts I have drawn from as a boy, the books I have consulted in our library, the very benches I have sat on, not forgetting my own dear good brother-members who surround me at this table . . .'

And the voice became increasingly faint and wheezy, prompting the Archbishop of Canterbury to remark afterwards that 'Sir John fulfilled the duties of President with such geniality and such eloquence when we could hear him and such perfect dumbshow when we could not!' Sir George Reid RA recalls Millais on the same occasion 'patting Lord Rosebery on the back . . . and the thought crossed my mind – how many artists would have ventured to pat a Prime Minister of England on the back?'[6]

Leighton died of heart disease in January 1896, and the following month Millais was unanimously elected to succeed him as President. (His own vote went to Philip Calderon.) 'Did you hear of Lear's pun?' Holman Hunt was asking in his congratulatory letter. 'It was that the *Millais-nium* of Art had come: You have gone a letter higher – from P-RB to PRA.'[7]

That summer the *Daily News* gives us a picture of the ailing President in the galleries of the Academy during the last days before the opening. 'He was in the rooms on the Saturday before the private view . . . shaking hands with old friends and saying in a hoarse whisper, which told its tale tragically enough, that he was better . . . The galleries were full of painters, young and old, hard at work, much to do and little time to do it in – when someone said "Millais is in the next room". Young men and old, they all looked in, mournfully realising it might be their last chance to see the greatest of their brethren. There he was leaning on the secretary, and slowly going his round. One young painter perched upon a ladder, varnishing his canvas, felt his leg touched, but was too busy to turn round. Again he was interrupted. It was the President, who, in a scarcely audible whisper, wished to congratulate him on his work . . . There was a discussion amongst a few of the members about a picture that in the hanging had not so good a place as it deserved. "Take one of my places," he said; and he meant it. It was not the first time he had offered to make way, giving up his own position for an outsider.'[8] He remained, if less energetic, less communicative, quite a busy man. He was a principal adviser in the building of the Tate Gallery; in 1895–96 he painted *A Disciple*, *The Forerunner*, prophetically, *Time the Reaper* and half-a-dozen portraits.

The ageing Effie was now, as wife of the PRA, basking in reflected glory, as intimated in this little vignette of 25 February that year by Beatrix Potter. 'Met Lady Millais in Gloucester Road. She was being bullied by a lady in a velvet mantle, so I merely insinuated the remark that I was sure that she must be receiving more congratulations than she could attend to, whereupon she seized my arm to cross the street, expressing a wish to die together, there being a procession of female bicycles. I thought it a characteristic mixture of graciousness and astute utility, she walking with a black crutch-stick, but most amusingly elated.'[9]

As Johnny's manuscript for *British Deer and Their Horns* was ready for the publishers by the early summer of 1896, he was hoping for another frontispiece from his father's genius hand. But although Sir John's creative life was over, his son did manage to involve him tenuously in the book. 'As any little distraction was a relief to him I brought him every day a few drawings of deer and deer-stalking on which I was then engaged. They interested him greatly, and after careful examination he would write on his slate a short criticism of each and his advice as to which to use for my book and which to discard, together with other hints and suggestions that I need hardly say were most valuable. The

A portrait by Frank Baden Powell: *Sir John Millais PRA on the arm of the Academy's secretary, on varnishing day before the opening of the 1896 exhibition.*
The artist stands on the ladder to the left of the picture to varnish his painting *The Admiral's Daughter: Outward Bound.*
The woman, thought to be Emily May, is waiting to varnish her portrait of General Clarke (hanging above Millais' head).
Other identified paintings are Seymour Lucas's *The Story of the Spanish Main* (bottom row, to Millais' right) and Peter Graham's *Beetling Sea Crags where the Gannet builds* (in front of Miss May).

last I showed him was a little drawing of a stag lying in the sunshine on a hillside, which reminded him so strongly of a famous stalk he once enjoyed that he began a long account of it on his slate and worked away until he was quite exhausted. In the end he wrote, "Don't show me any more, it makes me think of Scotland, which I shall never see again."[10]

'Henceforward he was a prisoner in his own apartment. Everything that the highest medical skill could suggest was done to prolong his life; but there was no arresting the decline that now set in. Even a whisper became a great exertion for him; he suffered, however, but little pain, and the presence of his wife and family, who were about him night and day, added greatly to his comfort.'[11]

By command of the Queen bulletins of the patient's health were sent to Windsor; and Millais, when Princess Louise arrived on her behalf to ask whether he had a special request, enquired if the Queen would give his wife an audience, and, Johnny records, 'my mother was most graciously received by Her Majesty, who expressed in the kindest way her sympathy with the dying man and his family.

'He has now sunk into a comatose state, significant of the coming end, and in the afternoon of August 13th, in the presence of his wife, my brother, Everett, and two of my sisters, he breathed his last.'[12] Organised by the Royal Academy staff, Millais' funeral took place in St Paul's Cathedral five days later. His pall bearers were Holman Hunt, Philip Calderon, Sir Henry Irving, Sir George Reid, Field-Marshal Viscount Wolseley, the Earl of Rosebery (the former Prime Minister and Liberal leader), the Earl of Carlisle and the Marquis of Granby. He was buried in Painter's Corner, next to Leighton, and close to the graves of Sir Christopher Wren, Sir Joshua Reynolds and Sir Thomas Lawrence.

In Johnny's opinion Spielmann wrote the most fitting obituary. Here is the best of it. 'Such was Sir John Millais – heartiest, honestest, kindliest among all the English gentlemen of his day. He was a big man with a warm heart, which he wore upon his sleeve; plain spoken, straightforward, genial and affectionate, who rarely said a cruel thing and never did a harsh one; without a grain of affectation and without a touch of jealousy. Almost to the end of his life the moors seem to have kept him forever young, and their winds to have blown away the cobwebs of jealousy . . . So thoroughly did the greatness of the man match the greatness of the artist – such was his simplicity – that those who knew him mourned in him rather the friend whom they loved than the painter they honoured and admired.

'There is little need here to recall the splendid personality of the artist, the keen sportsman whose prowess with the gun, the rod and the long putting-cleek, and whose spirits, whether in the saddle or on foot, commanded the admiration of the many for whom the triumphs of art are a lesser achievement . . .

'As I write his figure seems to rise before me, shedding that magnetic pleasure round him that his presence always brought. He turns to look at me as he has done a score of times, from his round-backed chair before the great fireplace of the studio. He has discussed the pictures on the easels, ranged twice across the room in his half-halting, half-explosive, highly delightful way. His pipe is between his teeth, the beloved briar, more precious than the finest cigar Havana ever rolled. The travelling cap of tweed, at first raised once or twice as if to ventilate the head, then carelessly replaced, rakishly to one side, is finally thrown on to the table close at hand . . . the powerful kindly hand is placed with genial roughness on my shoulder; the smile so full of charm; the untutored, halting eloquence; the bright, happy, infectious roguery of the accentuated wink; the enthusiastic talk on Art, now optimistic, now denunciatory of fads and foolishness . . .

'I see him as he turns, Anglo-Saxon from skin to core; sixty and more by the almanac, but fifty by himself; vigorous and bluff, full of healthy power of body and mind . . . Once more I see him, forgetful of himself, striding off to the hospital to cheer a member of the Academy lying ill, for he is now the President and father of his flock. Then he vanishes from sight to his own room of sickness, agony and death . . .'[13]

Sir John was succeeded in the baronetcy by his son Everett, whose claim to renown was as an animal geneticist, and as the man who introduced the basset hound, as a hare-hunting species, into England. But he died within eleven months of his father, and by the end of 1897 Effie Millais – who for forty-seven years, with her striking personality and rich talents, had helped and encouraged her husband and managed all his business affairs, besides most successfully raising his large family – died, too.

There was only one member of that family to carry forward the torch of Art and that was his son, Johnny, who had already firmly established himself as a wildlife illustrator. The principal task he set himself during the next two years, however, was neither drawing nor painting, but biography. In two volumes – amounting to nearly a thousand pages, profusely illustrated – his *Life and Letters of Sir John Millais*, which remains the definitive account of his father's career, was published in 1899. While that was being knocked into shape at the printers he was busy with his next publication, *A Wildfowler in Scotland*.

Note the kingfisher in the bottom right of John Everett Millais' *Halcyon Weather*, 1892.

7

THE NATURALIST AT HOME

Johnny's *Game Birds and Shooting Sketches* (1892) and *A Breath from the Veldt* (1895) were still selling brilliantly. Theodore Roosevelt, in his book *African Game Trails*, described *A Breath* as 'one of the three most valuable books on African big game',[1] (the other two being Selous's *African Native Notes* and Schilling's *Flashlight and Rifle*). Johnny's publishers were to be delighted, too, with *British Deer and Their Horns* (1897) and his two-volume life of his father (1899). So that last couple of years of the century found him confidently ahead on his fifth work, *A Wildfowler in Scotland*, which was again at once a memoir and a textbook. Lovingly dedicated to his young wife, Fanny, it tells her, with many a nostalgic sigh, something more of his boyhood and early youth. The book portrays those happy expeditions along the Scottish coasts and the estuaries, especially the Eden and the Tay, in search of the rarer geese and duck, to skin for his steadily expanding collection. 'To the all-round sportsman . . . wildfowling and big-game hunting must,' he thinks, 'ever rank first in point of interest . . . and every true naturalist is a sportsman at heart . . .

'Ah, those early mornings by the sea, can one ever forget them? Those wonderful hours when Nature tremulously unfolds her charms to the new-born day and all the earth is gladdened at the sight . . . never in after years does one scent the briny odour of the ocean without recalling those days of perfect freedom, when all sense of hardship and solitude was swallowed up in the joy of the passing hour.'[2] He recounts the perils he endured when his punt was caught at sea in squalls, and over-turned; when he floundered on mudbanks, frozen to the marrow, or when a punt gun exploded by his head. He recalls the long pony rides to reconnoitre the estuaries for the waterfowl flocks, and he offers the would-be wildfowler a host of advice on dogs.

'In selecting a pup for wildfowling work the shooter cannot be too careful in his enquiries as to the cleverness, mouth, taste for the water, and other characteristics of the mother. Where possible he should ascertain this for himself, as the mental capacity and proclivities of the mother are generally transmitted to the pups. I think I am correct in saying that a dog gets from her most of his abilities, good, bad and indifferent, while his external form is due rather to the father. Good bench qualities will, of course, add to his value, as affording more pleasure to the eye, but otherwise they are of no importance.'[3]

He recommends a curly-coated retriever, or, alternatively, an Irish water spaniel and goes on to extol the virtues of his beloved Jet, the black retriever, bought from a publican in the Johnny-with-the-Long-Gun days – especially her near-suicidal heroism in retrieving birds from rough seas. She was 'equally reliable whether grouse driving, covert shooting or wildfowling . . . Every man becomes sentimental about something, and if I say too much about dear old Jet, who was my constant companion for sixteen years, the reader must forgive me . . . And now goodbye old Jet, fondest and faithfulest of companions! Stone deaf and stiff with rheumatism she quietly lay down and died in 1891 and I can hardly hope ever to see her like again.'[4]

By now Johnny had got to know his fellow naturalist, explorer and hunter, Frederick Selous, very well and a close correspondence had sprung up between them. In the autumn of 1898, Selous, hunting wapiti in the United States, was urging him 'to come here yourself as soon as you can. *Vous serez toujours le bienvenu*'. Within a year the Boer conflict was hotting up and he wrote: 'My dear Johnny, this war is a most deplorable business; but, of course, as you say, we must bring it to a successful conclusion now at whatever cost.' And on 1 January 1900: 'It is a bad business, justice is not on our side. There was a lot of work done by the capitalists to bring it about.'[5]

Having tried out Horsham from a rented house for a few years Johnny and Fanny decided it was a good vicinity in which to put down their roots. They had made many friends there, it offered fine opportunities for sport, and not least the town's railway station provided a quick service to London. So, just north of that quiet place they built Compton's Brow for themselves and their first two children, Yvonne Daphne, who was then five years old and Geoffroy, who was four. Their home was to have one most important adjunct, a methodically designed museum to house Johnny's ever growing collection of trophies. For Fanny life would be always one ruled by her husband's comings and goings and, often, very long absences.

Meanwhile, as ever, another book was on the way. 'About twenty years ago,' he wrote in 1901, 'a rare duck and a wader, both in immature plumage, fell to my gun, and, eager to identify the species I searched every known work on British birds . . . Birds galore were to be found there, *but not my duck*, and all those pictured and described were adults . . . Brooding over my disappointment I finally resolved to find out for myself all that was to be learned of these interesting creatures, their habits and modes of life, and every circumstance connected with their periodical changes of plumage; and then I decided I would some day embody this information in a book for the benefit of other students of natural history.'[6] The result, in 1902, was *The Natural History of British Surface-feeding Ducks*, with over 40 coloured plates, by Archibald Thorburn, and 25 black-and-white illustrations by Johnny.

Compton's Brow lay adjacent to St Leonard's Forest and close to several well-protected estates, excellent tracts in which to observe wild life. To observe, in particular, many of the creatures described – with his minute knowledge and experience as a field-naturalist and his expertise as a wildlife artist – in the monumental, three-volume classic, *The Mammals of Great Britain and Ireland*. Soon after publication, he tells how he had been 'grinding away' at the work for five years. 'It was a book that seemed at the time almost beyond my strength, owing to the quantity of material in the way of first-hand knowledge and illustration which I had to supply, to say nothing of the outdoor work and the books I had to consult. It was necessary to see, study, hunt and draw all the British species, including the waders, and this involved such constant work and travel that I feared a breakdown under the strain.'[7] Before putting pen to paper he consulted most of the leading specialists of the day on each species, carefully comparing their observations with his own.

But it was not all a hectic marathon. There were many leisurely outings from Compton's Brow, often involving members of his family. 'My garden abuts on the old forest of St Leonards and to all the hedgerows come the bank voles in the Spring . . . Two [voles] which I kept confined in a cage, which I considered unbreakable (and in which I had kept Orkney and Field Voles for months) escaped in ten minutes, and I had to catch more specimens . . . I used to keep them under a glass shade on my table, and it amused me to watch their pretty little ways as I wrote or painted. These became very tame, but . . . they were always fighting or chasing one another about, sitting up polishing their glossy coats, playing games of hide and seek in and out of the grass.'[8]

Following up sightings of water shrews on a stream bank in the summer of 1902, he

Johnny.

John Guille Millais: *Black Grouse at the Playground*, from *The Natural History of British Game Birds*.

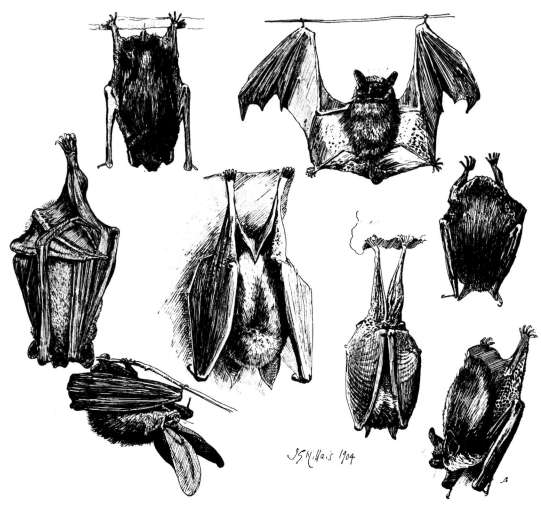

John Guille Millais: *Various Bats in Repose*, from *The Mammals of Great Britain and Ireland.*

returned to the same spot next day with Fanny, and, 'just as we reached it, we saw a water shrew skip across the stream and run into one of [its] surface tunnels. "Now I have you, Mr Water Baby", I thought, for I was anxious to catch a specimen and keep it alive. My wife guarded the exit to the water and I began at the other end and dug up the whole gallery . . .'[9] Then again, when studying common shrews in April 1904, he relates how 'my little boy, Geoffroy, who is an adept at catching small mammals, set a little nipper trap in the grass within thirty yards of my study window, where there is a large colony of field voles and shrews. The time was 10.30 a.m. At twelve he brought me a common shrew, quite warm . . . In the month of April he has captured ten shrews, all by day, for he takes the traps in at night as the heavy dews rust them.[10]

'I returned home one evening in May, 1904, to find my wife standing with blanched face, and the cook, the parlour maid and the nurse gathered together for mutual protection, and holding their skirts instinctively. "Do you know," said my wife, "that I've seen the most awful looking beast I ever set eyes on? He's in the potting shed now and I've shut him in. You must get your gun at once." Now potting sheds are not good places for practising with a 12-bore; so I took a candle instead and went to investigate. Yes, there he was, certainly. A perfectly bald rat with a transparent yellow skin, through which one could see the whole of his pink entrails working – I think he was about the most

76

uncanny beast I ever saw. The only hair about him was his whiskers, which stood out black and fierce and some fine whitish hair about the belly and limbs . . . I kept him alive for a day, then my little son managed to suffocate him through excessive kindness.'[11]

At Horsham, too, Johnny was able to make the most of the bat studies he needed. 'I have found one of the new electric torches very useful for searching crannies,' he tells us.[12] 'I have three times observed noctules on the wing in November at Warnham pond, near Horsham, once on the 1st [March] and twice on the 3rd, and the bat was on the wing during the whole of the middle of the day . . .'[13] Noctules, too, jog memories of his Cambridge days. 'Bell mentions that 185 noctules were taken from the roof of Queen's College. When I was a graduate there, in 1884, the species was exceedingly abundant about Queen's and Jesus Colleges, and at the "Backs"; I have seen noctules hawking above the King's Parade in the very centre of the town.[14]

'The Pipistrelle may be captured in many ways,' he advises. '. . . A net may be placed over the exit hole, or they may be taken in a butterfly net as they sally forth in the evening . . . I was advised to try a trout rod . . . and went forth one night and brought a pipistrelle down with the first stroke. About a month later I wanted another, and took my best rod out again; after three or four nights spent in swishing the air, with the expenditure of much 'golf' language and a serious accident to my best rod, I came to the conclusion that the efficiency of the method had been overrated.[15]

'Within a couple of miles of Compton's Brow there are two estates . . . where in June and July I go nearly every evening to stalk rabbits with a .22 rifle. While returning home about a quarter to eight I invariably find one or more hedgehogs out in the grass, commencing their evening meal and . . . I have lain down on the grass within a yard or so and closely watched their method of feeding . . . One particularly large male was always out and about the same place, a rough field close to a tangled "gill". I think he soon got to know me, as I have regularly stopped and watch him for three seasons. I have often had him walk between my legs and smell by boots after the first alarm . . .'[16] As for rabbit study Johnny had plenty of opportunity on '. . . a small rabbit shoot in St Leonard's Forest which I have managed for the last few years.'[17]

His chapter on the fox brings on another bout of university reverie. 'In 1884 I was a happy-go-lucky young fellow at Trinity College, Cambridge, where although by courtesy called a student, I fear the gun played a more important part in my education than the book. At this time, too, I was honoured with the friendship of the late Prince Albert Victor, whose shooting arrangements I used to manage, and with whom I enjoyed many a delightful day in the coverts and fields of the eastern counties . . .'

Johnny goes on to recount how the sporting Master of Downing College suggests taking

John Guille Millais: *Hedgehog Swimming*, from *The Mammals of Great Britain and Ireland*.

the prince for a day's shooting at a celebrated sporting estate, Borley Wood; how the Cambridge station master mistakes, in hilarious circumstances, Johnny for the prince; and how, at covertside, a short-sighted Master of Foxhounds shoots a fox. 'I ran towards my unfortunate friend, saying "do you know what you have done? You've killed a fox!" "Good heavens, is it possible? I thought it was a hare!" he exclaimed in anguish.' Johnny made a quick grave for the fox; but, after lunch it was dug up and carried out by a retriever. 'It was an awful moment, when even fibs of the most flagrant order were perhaps permissible. Such thoughts had just entered my mind, when C. [the MFH] like a noble fellow spoke up and made a clean breast of his sin, was humbled but forgiven after an inordinate amount of chaff. Of course the story got about, and he doubtless suffers for it to this day.'[18]

Just as the sacrilege of shooting a fox in the foxhunting Britain of the late Victorian era was taken so seriously, so the anti-foxhunting lobby was in a tiny minority. Those against otter hunting had rather more support. Johnny, an ardent student and lover of the otter, defended the sport. 'Otter hunting, in its legitimate sense, had been classed with bull baiting, bear baiting, cockfighting and badger-baiting and designated as "glorified ratting"; but those who have taken up the pen to condemn it evidently write in complete ignorance of the science, for there is no British sport, except salmon fishing, in which the purely natural pleasures of the chase are so predominant, or in which so little cruelty is practised.

'Added to this, in four cases out of six, the otter escapes and an exciting hunt without a kill is generally the order of the day ... The great charm of otter hunting consists in the beautiful surroundings into which it draws the follower and the pleasure of seeing hounds work out a line from start to finish.'[19] The modern field sportsman may remark on the lack of emphasis on wildlife conservation in Johnny Millais' writings, in this case the otter-hunter's contribution to the conservation of the rivers and streams. That a top-flight field naturalist should appear to be making such an omission only serves to remind us what relatively little impact the activities of mankind made on the rural environment until the twentieth century was well under way.

However, any activity that upset the balance of Nature distressed him and in a diatribe that still carries an echo he condemns the gamekeepers for their indiscriminate destruction of predatory species. 'The great mass of keepers, who pay no heed to advice, will go on doing the same stupid things their fathers did before them to the end of the chapter unless laws are made and enforced ... weasels are almost exterminated in my neighbourhood and the result is a never decreasing plague of rats assuming serious proportions, and in any season the rats do more damage to game, ducks and poultry than a plethora of weasels ... [weasels] should never be destroyed in the neighbourhood of ricks and farm buildings and even in woods frequented by game there are always a large number of rats and mice on which they subsist.'[20] He abhors the gin trap ('the cruellest invention of modern times ... this abominable engine of destruction is set often to inflict hours and even days of horrible suffering.'[21])

The red squirrel, the only British representative of the family *sciuridae* in his day, is shown to be something of a destructive menace. Little did he know that, within a few years of *The Mammals* publication, the even more harmful imported American grey would colonise almost the whole of England, replacing its pretty red cousin.

Having studied deer since boyhood and having already recorded most of the information on them in *British Deer and Their Horns*, he had little trouble in completing the chapters on those species. He was able to watch them by the hour at Warnham Park, a stone's throw from Compton's Brow. 'The best [red deer] fight I ever saw was in the park at Warnham, after the master stag, a 25-pointer, had been driven out by a young royal of great strength. It so happened that I moved the disinherited, and forced him into the

John Guille Millais: *Wild Cats*, from *The Mammals of Great Britain and Ireland*.

royal and his herd of nearly 100 hinds. This the new master resented. He at once dashed at the 28-pointer and the two became locked for a moment. Then ensued a battle of kings. Each stag fought with the utmost fury. Retreating to a distance of ten yards apart they charged at full speed for a period of twenty minutes.

'To give an idea of the strength of these charges, it is enough to say that several large pieces of horn were knocked clean off the antlers of the larger stag . . . The fight which I witnessed from a thirty-yard distance went on until at last both stags rolled to the ground and collapsed, but . . . the royal who had recovered his wind, suddenly sprang to his feet and galloped away to his hinds, where he heralded the victory in a paean of exultation . . . The 28-pointer seemed to be dead, but his heaving flanks showed he was very much alive . . . He staggered to his feet and with head down tottered slowly away to a big oak tree and lay down ... He lay, for two days without moving ... Next year he was a 32-pointer and was killed for his wonderful head, which I now possess.'[22]

Seals were his second delight. 'It was owing to my own want of knowledge as regards bats, mice and seals that first led me to study this subject [the whole range of British mammals], for in no work could I find accurate accounts of these animals. It took me four years and four separate expeditions to gain full knowledge of the grey seal alone, and I have endeavoured to acquire first-hand knowledge of all the creatures I write about and illustrate.'[23]

In fact he appears to have spent most of every August and September, between 1897 and 1904, studying and hunting the different seal species around the Scottish coasts, usually with a naturalist-sportsman companion. In the autumn of 1898, for example, it was with his brother-in-law, Philip Skipwith, in 1899 with his explorer and novelist friend, Hesketh Prichard, and Sidney Steele.

Prichard, incidentally, was a man very much after Johnny's heart, being possessed of a similar wanderlust, love of animals and fascination with other races of mankind. Johnny illustrated Prichard's *Through the Heart of Patagonia*, earning the author's most respectful gratitude for the pictures. ('I must record my indebtedness to Mr John Guille Millais for the pains he took with the illustrations for this book. Before I started my friend, Mr Millais, drew me some sketches of huemel guanaco and other Patagonian animals. These I showed to the Tehuelches and was once taken aback by being offered a commission to draw an Indian's dogs. He offered me a trained horse in payment. The praise of "the man who knows" is after all the great reward of art.'[24])

In May, 1903, Johnny was studying grey seals off the Scillies, as guest of the squire Dorrien Smith then holding sway on those islands beyond Land's End.

The Mammals includes minute statistics of the more interesting specimens he shot and ecstatic descriptions of both his observations and his stalks. 'I am exceedingly fond of lying with a telescope and watching seals on a sunny day. They are charming creatures and many of their little ways are very interesting.[25] ... It is almost a platitude to speak of their wonderful swimming powers, but the ease and grace of their turning movements under water are ever a delight to witness ... I have several times, when seated on the rocks, watched seals hunting in the crystalline depths beneath, and have once, in Orkney, seen one take a good-sized coal-fish and eat it under water ...'[26]

'In all forms of chase our pleasure is mostly due to the charm of the natural surroundings, and seal hunting is a fascinating sport ... Every man who has ever regarded the primitive isles of the north Atlantic with their barren coasts and sea-swept corries, their great precipices and foaming surges, must have felt the indescribable charms of a sport freed from the artificiality that often clogs the surroundings of deer forests and covert shoots. He can be alone with perhaps a trusted friend, and do all his own hunting amidst some of the grandest scenery in the world ...

'To the true hunter the rapture of pursuing depends but slightly on the name of the animal pursued. Under certain circumstances the boy in his teens may shoot a tiger or a stag, but little does he know of the delight of following, outmanoeuvring and finally securing, unaided, an animal difficult of approach, and it is in this that the essence of real sport lies ...'[27] Johnny's passion for the chase runs parallel, species for species, with his love for the mammal concerned. And he admits that his deepest affection is reserved – after deer – for seals.

Although for general interest, the quotes here are nearly all from the author's anecdotes, it must be emphasised again that these three volumes comprise an essentially scientific work, describing in detail where each animal was to be found, its habitat, its size and anatomy, diet, mating and family characteristics, defensive attributes and means of hunt-

PLATE 5   *Harlequin Duck*, by John Guille Millais, 1911.

PLATE 6   Deer studies by John Guille Millais:
Roe Deer, 1905 (top) and *Fallow Deer*.

ing or foraging. It deals not only with all the mammals then in existence, but all those, too, that ever inhabited the British Isles since the first glacial, or pleistocene, age – including the cave lion, sabre-toothed tiger, wolf, ox, hyaena, wild horse, 'three true elephants', which, his research told him, 'existed at least as far north as Yorkshire and . . . a hippopotamus identical with those now found in north, central and south Africa . . . was especially numerous in the Thames valley and ranged as far north as north Yorkshire.'[28]

He took Rudyard Kipling to task for writing in his poem *In the Neolithic Age* 'when the reindeer roared as Paris roars at night . . .' Johnny points out to the great novelist and poet that 'the reindeer does not roar during the rutting seasons, but emits a series of low grunts which are neither dignified nor awe-inspiring, as is the voice of the red deer stag. So I ventured to suggest that the poet should substitute the latter animal for the former.' Kipling replied: 'The change to red deer will be made for a new edition that's coming out soon . . . I have your big volumes of *The Mammals of Great Britain*, and I don't think that you anywhere state that the common hedgehog is extraordinarily proof against poisons – toxic for choice. He does not mind diphtheria or tetanus germs, and can also absorb mineral poison in large quantities. A learned professor told me so this year. Is it true?' Johnny's reply was crisp: 'It is very doubtful if hedgehogs are immune. They are easily poisoned by strychnine.' He also stated the opinion that 'many of his [Kipling's] wild beasts' conversations are distinctly as grotesque as they are imaginary,

John Guille Millais: *Common Seals ascending a Steep Rock*, from *The Mammals of Great Britain and Ireland*.

for animals do not judge things from the human standpoint, and the more we study them the more do we find that to do so is to take an . . . incorrect view of mammalian life.'[29]

His weighty volumes are adorned with charmingly accurate paintings by Archibald Thorburn, G.E. Lodge and himself, and with numerous sketches drawn from life by him, along with excellent photographs.

Ever since he returned from Iceland, via the Faroes, with his brother and sister, Geoffroy and Mary, in 1889, whales had fascinated him. Volume III contains a definitive chapter on each of the cetaceans. The rarest of the genus roaming British seas at that time was the blue whale, and, having no opportunity to study it locally, he went west. 'One mammal, the blue whale, it was absolutely necessary to examine in the flesh,' he explains; 'and this, owing to its comparative scarcity in British waters, I hoped to find on the Newfoundland coasts. Accordingly I set out at the end of July, 1905, with the intention of spending a month in quest of this, the greatest of all living creatures . . .'[30]

But the mammal that principally lured him to Newfoundland was not so much the blue whale as that magnificently antlered deer, the caribou. By the time he first embarked on a Newfoundland whaling ship he was already closely familiar with the history, the people, the fauna and the hinterland and he even penetrated parts of the island where no European had trod before. His first visit was in 1902.

Meanwhile his continuous role as dedicated field naturalist was much relieved by his life as a family man and as a field sportsman. Summers saw him flyfishing by the hour, winters game shooting. Three of his fellow sportsmen were fellow explorer-naturalists, too. Those were Abel Chapman, Fred Selous – and Arthur Neumann, who, besides being one of the greatest African hunters of his age, did much work for the colonial administration. Johnny was fascinated by this adventurer's career. Neumann acted as a liaison office for the East Africa Company, with the tribesmen, and a plotter of railway routes and roads. And during the Boer war, with his command of the Zulu and Boer-Dutch languages, he proved very useful as a mounted infantry officer. But, in contrast to Johnny, he was a loner, extremely shy and hypersensitive. 'In crowds he was like a hunted fox, and it was indeed strange to see a man who would cheerfully face a wounded lion or elephant thrown into a panic of nervousness by the traffic of Piccadilly.'

Having last seen Johnny as a fellow gun on covert shoots in England during the winter of 1901–02, Neumann wrote to him from Kenya the following summer saying 'I often think of our last meeting at Ward's shoot. It is curious how certain details, sometimes trifling, stand out in one's memory . . . Now the leading impressions left on my mind from that visit were: first the failure of that old brute of a butler to bring me an early cup of tea to my bedroom in the morning, by reason of which I (being an old crank and much addicted to my own habits) was more or less upset for the whole day; second, being dragged off for a beastly walk on the Sunday when I would much rather have pottered around with you and Selous; and third my envying Selous going off with you in the afternoon . . . Give my love to Selous when you see him again, Yours ever, Arthur Neumann. P.S. – Glancing through this production I notice what I say about that pleasant shooting-party at Ward's seems to imply that I did not enjoy it, and reads ungratefully to our kind host and hostess. That is not what I meant to suggest at all. I enjoyed myself very much there, and after you and Selous left I still had a most interesting and delightful companion in Abel Chapman, whose acquaintance it gave me the greatest pleasure to make. I only meant that it struck me as being so jolly you and Selous going about together from shoot to shoot.'[31]

Doubtless, in many respects, Johnny envied Neumann his life in Africa. But in 1902 Selous was the man he most wanted to emulate, and it was Selous's descriptions of Newfoundland, from expeditions in 1900 and 1901, that first lured him there.

8

NEWFOUNDLAND DISCOVERER

It was in August, 1902, that Johnny sailed for Newfoundland for the first time. The Victorian era was over; King Edward was on the throne. The almighty premiership of Lord Salisbury had come to an end, too; his nephew, Arthur Balfour was in that seat. Salisbury died as the sun was setting one evening in 1903. Historians have seen that as symbolic; contemporaries did not. Few believed that the Boer war had done much for Britain's reputation as a Colonial power, but fewer still believed that either empire, aristocratic government or peace were seriously threatened. Britain was still the strongest power on earth.

The white man had been settling on and securing the coasts of the oldest of England's colonies, Newfoundland, for nearly 400 years. But that territory had been waiting for an Englishman of science, integrity and adventure, a sportsman such as J.G. Millais, to strike into, and map, the hinterland, living off caribou meat and collecting the beasts' antlers to carry home.

'Mr Selous . . . told me he believed that, if I could get farther into the country to the west, which was quite unknown,' wrote Johnny, 'I should probably strike the main trails of a big southern [Caribou] herd.' He wasted no time in reading all he could find out about the colony, from Cabot's landing in 1497 to the first English traders, fishermen and whalers in the reign of the first Elizabeth, and the island's foundation as an English colony; from the white man's persecution of the indigenous Beothick Indians and W.E. Cormack's efforts to establish friendly relations with them, in the 1820s, to the influxes of the Micmac Indians from Labrador and to the rapid growth of the trading ports and stations. It was, he read, 'an island of forty-two thousand square miles, one sixth larger than Ireland.'

He sailed to St John's, where he quickly secured, from the president of the Marine and Fisheries Department, 'a permit to collect for scientific purposes such specimens as I required.'[1] Selous had booked two first-class guides and handymen for him, Bob Saunders (fifty-five years old, five feet six inches tall with 'eyes possessing the honest and sincere look of absolute truth') and Jack Wells ('handsome, amiable, good natured') each for two dollars a day. And with those native hunters and all his equipment – rifles and ammunition, trout rods, fishing tackle and landing nets, camping and cooking equipment, camera and films, reindeer sleeping bags and sou'westers, waterproof sheets and sailor bags, canoes, poles and paddles – Johnny took the overnight 'accommodation' train to Terra Nova station, whence he started his first trek through the wild Terra Nova country.

Heading first for Selous's old camp he soon had his diary out, recording the birds, '. . . belted kingfishers, goosanders, red-breasted mergansers, Canada geese and yellow-shank sandpipers were occasionally moored on the river; whilst on the lakes of Mollygojack and St John's I noticed a good many dusky ducks (*Anas obscuras*), the northern form of

Supper time in Johnny's camp. Jack Wells and (*right*) Bob Saunders.

our mallard. Grebes, probably sclavonians, interested me also, great northern divers, buzzards, peregrine falcons, merlins and, for the first time, the magnificent bald-headed eagle, or Bird of Washington, made its appearance. In the woods we heard the rattle of, and occasionally saw, the beautiful golden-winged and three-toed woodpeckers, whilst in camp at night the horned eagle-owl serenaded us with his melancholy hoots . . . As yet we had not met that delightfully cheeky fellow, the Canadian wood jay, moose-bird, or whisky jack, as he is variously named . . .'[2] Before the end of the month he provided himself and his assistants with their first fresh food when a caribou doe fell to his rifle.

His mission, as ever, was for prize heads. The deer around and beyond Selous's camp was forest-bound, giving little field of view, and he 'sighed for a place where I could wander about in the open and look for things with my telescope. From the north-west I could see with the glass an inviting-looking country where the white man had never been – so Saunders said, and Saunders had penetrated further than anyone in the swampy regions.'[3] Two weeks went by before he spotted a caribou with a head worth having.

' "A' don't believe there's a blessed stag outside the woods in Newfun'lan'," said Saunders, yawning as he lay on his back chewing blue-berries and, as he expressed it, "tired o' looking".

' "Well," I replied, "I believe that's one anyhow, Bob", for at that moment I had caught in the glass the white stern of a deer feeding about a mile below in a little marsh . . . At last! There he was right in the open and the wind perfect. Just the sight every hunter longs for!' Johnny stalked, stooping, then crawled and, '. . . getting a large rock between myself and the deer, found, on peeping round the edge of a stone that I was within ninety yards . . . I put the white foresight on his heart and fired . . .'[4] That provided his first good caribou head, the first of many.

He revelled in the venison-eating, pipe-smoking evenings around the camp fire when Bob, scion of a seal-hunting family, regaled him with the adventures of his childhood and youth. ' "A' got carried to the ice-huntin' myself when a' was no more than seven and a half years old . . ." Jack occasionally interposed with "You don't say? . . . Well, well, Bob!" or "Thet's what it is now."

'Bob went on: "Swoiles [seals] was much to us in the Spring, for it meant 'bout what we lived on whether the swoiles drove down in the Spring or not, and we struck 'em. So when a' was a little chap ma mother used to put me to bed and make me say prayers like this when swoiles was about. Lord God Almighty, send a swoile fer daddy, an' send a swile fer mamma, and a swile fer Uncle Jim, an' wan fer Uncle Jim's wife, an' a swile for little Tommy, and one each for Jarge an' Mary, and a swile each for cousin Will's family, not fergettin' a swile fer Aunt Jane what's a pore widder. An, oh Lord, don't let de ice blow off-shore when daddy's aboard an' bring 'un safe to hum. Amen. Then ma mother would call all over our relations to see a' 'adn't forgot none an' if a' hadn't remember 'em all she'd make me say de prayer all over again." '[5]

Then Jack suggested, ' "You tell Mr Millais o' that time, Bob, you had after ole Noah." ' And a long tale ensues concerning a septuagenarian who got lost rabbit shooting and went four days without food or bed. And, says Johnny, 'the men seemed quite merry and happy now, as long as they had a good fire of birch and plenty to eat. They had got over the idea that I wanted to shoot a big stag every day . . . altogether we had a very jolly time.'

Then they came upon the tracks of a phenomenally large stag, its hoof prints being nearly eight inches across, which a delighted Johnny photographed. And he shot another one 'with unusually fine double shovels in front, big bays and thirty-five tines.' He took out his fishing rod, too, and caught in one morning fourteen trout, char and ouananiche [land-locked salmon].

After a month in the wilds he hurried back to Terra Nova, because Indian guides awaited him in Canada. But that leg of the expedition never materialised, for he missed the steamer to Labrador which 'was disgusting, to say the least of it, as I had made my preparations carefully before leaving England and meant, if possible, to add the barren-land caribou, of the north-eastern corner of America, to my collection of hunting trophies. The loss of a month in the autumn means nothing in some countries, but in north Labrador winter closes down with a sudden snap about the beginning of October, and there you must remain with the Esquimaux till the next summer, if the last boat from the south fails to reach Nain and the north ports . . . Accordingly Bob Saunders and I retired to my lodgings and flattened our noses on the map of Newfoundland.'[6]

For his 1903 expedition Johnny chose to follow the Gander river, the source of which, beyond the Partridgeberry hills, he would eventually prove to be the discoverer. Spending a week in St John's, planning the trip, he stayed with his traveller and novelist friend, Hesketh Prichard, who was marking time on his way to Labrador, and while there made another friend of the colourful septuagenarian Judge Prowse. ('I think the reader would have laughed had he seen this judge of the Supreme Court and myself hunting for the problematical snipe . . . The Judge, with his hat on the back of his head and a pair of bedroom slippers on his feet – "Ye get wet anyhow, my boy" – jumped over the streams and fences like a two-year-old, working a somewhat wild pointer; and so whistling and prancing from marsh to marsh he covered the ground in a manner which quite astonished me. Nor will I forget his charming disregard for appearances when he came to see me off . . . bearing in one hand a bucket full of potatoes, and in the other – whisper it not in the Fly Fisher's Club, breathe it not in the gun-rooms of the north – a big bag of worms!'[7]

Signing up Bob Saunders again, this time in company with Saunders's friend, Sandy Butt, he headed on 7 September for the Glenwood timber mill, a place of frantic activity since Lord Northcliffe and his brothers had acquired 2,000 square miles of the island's best forest and were already exporting fifty million feet of lumber a year. From there he and his men took the steamboat across Gander lake and so to their canoes on the Gander river. Towards the end of the first day up river Johnny got a stag for the pot and '. . . we lost no time in taking the best of the haunch meat, fat and tongue, and in half-an-hour had continued our journey, feeling very happy as every hunter does when his camp is well supplied with the food on which his men alone can hunt.'[8]

His artist's eye was enraptured with the river scenery. 'The rocks in the foreground were of the most lovely colour, a rich blue grey. Over these poured masses of amber water of pellucid clearness. Little brooks and shining barrens, peeping out from amidst the dark forest on the right bank, led the eye away to distant hills of the most intense blue, whilst in the middle distance, away up the glistening river, were islands covered with the first "haps" [poplars] in Newfoundland, every leaf a-quiver in the blazing sun. On the left bank the land rose in rugged and distorted shapes, and was all covered with a medley of golden birch and scarlet rowan, and trees standing clear against a brown mass of tall "vars" and spruces in whose depths the glints of sunlight mixed with the purple shadows. Yet all this heterogeneus mass of colour seemed to blend, for Nature makes no mistake with her paints . . .'[9]

'It was delightful to sit and smoke and enjoy the charming *dolce far niente* laziness of basking in the sun, and wondering whether the good people of Sussex were still shivering under umbrellas and mackintoshes as they had been during May, June, July and August, in the year of grace 1903. One or two of my friends even cast eyes of pity upon me for coming to "those dreadful Arctic regions" as they fondly imagined Newfoundland to be. And yet how different it was. How nice to lie on the moss amidst the sun-warmed stones where thoughts were singing rivers and the dews of morning shone, and to listen for the bumping of the canoes round the bend . . .'[10]

He was reading Somerville's and Ross's *Experiences of an Irish RM*, when he heard a stick break 'two hundred yards away on the far bank.' It was a stag, which he promptly stalked and shot. ('The horns were not large, but very massive, and the head one of high quality, with thirty points'.) On 30 September he bagged another for the museum walls of Compton's Brow, and 'stood contemplating what is in some aspects the best head I ever shot.' It carried 49 points. Saunders told him that he had never seen a more perfect caribou head, being 'equal in quality to the head killed by Selous two years previously.'

On the 22nd, when the journey was brought to a halt by the strongest of the canoes being broken on the rocks, Johnny was again deep in a book – Rider Haggard's *She*, this time – when his hunter's ear caught an interesting sound. 'The remarkable woman "She" was about to drink again the fires of eternal life, and her speech at this exciting moment simply grips the reader, for it is the best thing in a remarkable work. Yet it was in no spirit of disappointment that I dropped the book softly on the stones at my side – for had I not heard some pebbles roll down the bank on the far side of the river? . . .'[11] It was a doe ('for a female she carried remarkable horns'), but she took fright and galloped away. Johnny had scarcely lifted his book again when he spotted a very large stag drinking

John Guille Millais: *Caribou on the east side of Millais Lake*, 1903.

a hundred yards away and immediately accounted for it. 'When the men came we took his entire skin and head, and as much meat as we could carry, and made camp.' Four days later they were back at the mouth of the Gander, and Johnny, the richer by "eight fine heads", prepared to return to Sussex.

As mentioned in the previous chapter, Johnny needed personal observations of the blue whale ('the greatest of all living creatures,' he says) to complete his *Mammals of Great Britain and Ireland*, and it was principally with that mission in mind that he went to New-foundland, via the Gulf of St Lawrence, in July 1905. Turning historian again he recounts Newfoundland's fishing trade since Cabot; he quotes Sir Humphrey Gilbert ('a place very populace and much frequented . . . the English command all there.'), and Sir Walter Raleigh ('if any misfortune happened to the Newfoundland fleet, it would be the greatest calamity that could befall England.'). Then he reminds his readers that that great adminis-trator, orator, philosopher and literary man, Chancellor Bacon, was the chief organiser of 'the London and Bristol Company for Colonising Newfoundland.' It was Bacon, too, who spoke of the 'Goldmine of the Newfoundland fishery, richer than all the treasures of Golconda and Peru.' Johnny read that it was the Spanish Basques who, in about 1550, inaugurated the whaling industry in the Newfoundland seas.

He goes on to eulogise about his days with the Norwegian whalers in pursuit of the finback and the humpback. 'To be in tow of a wild whale is something to experience and remember to one's dying day. You feel that you are alive, and that you are there with the sport of kings. No wonder the Norwegians are full of life, and the men from

John Guille Millais: *A Shot at a Finback*.

the captain to the cook, run to their several tasks with eyes and hearts aflame. This is a trade which will stir the blood of the dullest clod, and to the men who are one and all the finest seamen in the world, it is the very life and essence of the Viking nature.'[12]

August 15 found him at the St Lawrence whaling factory, about to board the whaler *St Lawrence*, with her Norwegian captain and crew, and contemplating the genius of the German-American scientist, Dr Rismuller, who, he says, 'has done more for whaling and the use of whale products than any other living man. To him is owed the utilisation of every part of the whale, including the flesh, the blood and liver and parts of the skin which were only regarded as wastage a few years ago.'[13]

The *St Lawrence* suffered a very stormy departure on the 17th, but next day the wind dropped and 'I was eating my breakfast and reading Dickens when at 9 a.m. I heard the engines slow down, and knew that meant whales, so I ran on deck . . .

'It was a moment of intense excitement when the two finbacks rose right in front of the bows and within easy shot, but the captain and I were gazing fixedly into the green and clear depths, looking for the blue whale, when far away down beneath the water I saw a great copper-grey form rising rapidly right underneath the ship. The captain signalled with his hand to the man at the wheel on the bridge, turning the vessel off a point just as the ghostly form of the whale growing larger and larger every moment until it seemed as big as the ship, burst on the surface beside us, and broke the water within ten yards. In a moment we were drenched in blinding spray as the whale spouted in our faces. I turned my arm to protect my camera and to click the shutter as the captain fired his gun. The latter planted the harpoon firmly in the great creature's lungs . . .'[14]

They put in with their kill at Little St Lawrence where 'our arrival was hailed with delight, for a "sulphur" had not been slain since May . . .' and where Johnny spent eight days in the company of the genius Dr Rismuller, studying the life cycle, anatomy and other characteristics of the blue whale for his definitive *Mammals*. Then he proceeded to Newfoundland for his third expedition to the island's interior.

'Nothing in the universe is so attractive as the unknown. To the man of imagination it is the great magnet which draws him away to seek fresh worlds to conquer. There is in the very sound of the word that hidden mystery that tinges the sober aspect of the present with colour of romance, and no one, however dull, is quite romance proof. In consequence, men rush wildly at the North Pole and after other unconquered fields . . .' Johnny goes on with the reasons why two-thirds of the 42,000 square miles of Newfoundland remained unexplored. The Newfoundlander was a fisherman, uninterested in creating farmland; the island was short of the tough wood needed to build the canoes that were the essential transport to strike at the centre of the island; besides which the White Newfoundlander, in contrast to the Indian, was an inept canoeist. As for overland journeys, horses could not go far because there was no grass, except on a few of the more slow-moving rivers, and men could only carry on their backs supplies for a short journey. No Europeans had made any serious attempt to explore and chart central Newfoundland since W.E. Cormack who reached what came to be known as Mount Cormack, approximately the middle point of the island, in 1822.

Now, early in September 1905, making elaborate arrangements for the longer and more arduous journey, Johnny put together a much stronger team than the tracker duo, which had previously sufficed. First there was a Sussex neighbour John McGaw ('a first rate comrade, excellent shot, a good hand at whatever he turned to, whether in the line of carpentry, mapping or photography'). Then there were Bob Saunders and Sandy Butt and a third White Newfoundlander, Frank Wells. Through the helpful telegraph operator at Conn river, Johnny also secured the services of an intelligent and enterprising Micmac Indian with a sound knowledge of Newfoundland's hinterland and its rivers, Joe Jeddore, two more Indians – and, to help lift the canoes and stores – six White packers.

From Long Pound the expeditionary party journeyed via Soulis Ann Lake, Baie d'Est,

John Guille Millais: *A Fighting Humpback.*

Brazil Lake and Little Burnt Lake, to Round Lake where 'the roaring camp fire crackled and shed its genial warmth . . . Out on the lake the water was like a sheet of glass, except in a little bay where a mother red-breasted merganser was teaching her young to dive. From the distance came the swan-like trump of the Canada geese, as they returned from berry-picking on the hills, and now and again we could hear the *who-eee* of the great northern divers as they settled for the night . . .

'Soon the golden ball sinks beneath the horizon, to be succeeded by a short-lived twilight. The querulous loon is uttering low-voiced calls to his mate, and grey phantoms rise cloud-like in the evening mists, drifting away with clanking voices into a land of silence. It is the day's departure and we turn to the incense of the larch smoke and the crackling blaze of the burning logs. Then one drops to sleep on a couch of scented vars amidst the lonely mountains of the northland, with the starlight overhead . . . It may seem strange to the town dwellers that there are many men so constituted that the luxuries of civilization have no attraction for them, but it is no mystery to those who have seen both sides of the picture. The outdoor man has by far the best of it, for he leads the life that God and Nature intended him to.'[15]

Beyond Pipestone Lake they were within an ace of bagging the great rarity of a jet black fox, but '. . . he saw us as quickly as we saw him and like a flash he whipped round and, erecting his magnificent brush of black and white, darted over the skyline and was lost to view. "There goes four hundred dollars" said Joe sadly. "Ah, if we had only been fifty yards to the right, we should have been out of sight and under the wind, and I could have 'tolled' [called, or whistled] him." '[16]

It was mid-September and they had reached the base of Mount Cormack. John McGaw climbed it, returning to inform Johnny that it was wrongly marked on Newfoundland's crude official map, by a distance of four or five miles. They found, too, a new mountain, south-west of Cormack, which they called Mount Frances (after Johnny's wife).

Having taken the heights of those and charted several hitherto unmentioned lakes, they came in for the fiercest rainstorm that Johnny had ever encountered on the island. Joe Jeddore, like most Indians, had a far greater aversion for wet weather than the Whites and on such occasions would go up to Johnny and McGaw with 'a face of extreme woe . . . "What's the matter, Joe?" we would say, "Ah, I have a lump like a lead ball just here," pressing his diaphragm. "I am very bad. John Hans at Conn river died of just such a thing last winter, and Joe Brazil, he – " "Let's look at your tongue," I would say, with my best Harley Street manner. "Yes, to be sure, a case of Asiatic cholera; don't you think so, Jack?" McGaw, thus appealed to, would at once ratify my diagnosis with a learned air, and go for the Burroughs and Wellcome case. Two azure globules of the most body-rending description were then inserted in Joe's mouth, and next day he would come up smiling.'[17]

Searching for the source of the Gander they pushed on to a totally unmapped and unknown tract between the Upper Gander and Dog Lake, involving a forty-mile walk away from the lakes. It was necessary to keep on the high ground to the south, so as to avoid the swamps. Here we have another glimpse of Johnny the team leader. 'Accordingly,' he says, 'I determined to divide the party. Taking the three Indians and Saunders and McGaw and myself we were to go right on to a spot where I knew there was good hunting on the upper Gander. Then McGaw and I would go into camp for a week or ten days and send the Indians and Saunders back towards Dog Lake to assist Sandy and Frank, who were meanwhile to get as far as possible.

'This theory seemed to be the best plan as not only could we survey the easiest route for the packers and canoes to follow, but we should probably kill some deer on the way. The meat of these could be eaten by the men, and their position pointed out by Joe,

Johnny's Indian guide, Joe Jeddore.

who was first of all to accompany us. We made an early start and after going a mile or two skirted round to the south-east to avoid swamps. Here we noticed a small brook flowing eastwards, and being the first water travelling in this direction, we decided to follow it up to its source, which was found in a small still pool, and which we knew must be the source of the Gander. This little brook emptied into a pretty lake about two miles long, which, having no name, I christened Lake McGaw ... After photographing our discovery we ascended rough ground through burnt timber and over rocks for two miles and then found ourselves on the shoulder of Partridgeberry hill.'[18]

Johnny went hunting and got a 27-point caribou while McGaw scored his first trophy. Then, guided by Jeddore, travelling back down river along the Gander, they took a detailed study of a beaver colony and Johnny made a plea for that mammal's preservation. 'In the time of Cormack (1822) beaver were numerous all over the central part of the island; but constant molestation, both by White men and Indians, made them so scarce that measures were taken for their protection a few years ago. This has done much good and the beavers have not been trapped or shot to any extent. The close time, however, ends in October, 1907, and it is certain that unless further restrictions are put on the killing of this interesting animal the whole stock in the island will be rapidly wiped out.'[19]

Johnny then shot another caribou ('Every eatable part of this deer, and the two others which we had previously killed, was eaten by ourselves and the men during the next eight days.') About twenty minutes later he recognised one of his old 1903 camp sites at the riverside. The fourth week of September found McGaw and himself stalking while waiting for the men coming down from Dog Lake with the canoes and the bulk of the camp equipment – and between them they secured all the nine deer they were allowed under their licence, including three fine specimen heads.

Johnny was still J.G. Millais, the discoverer. 'During the following eight days I experienced a great deal of hard walking to determine the course and position of Little Gull river, Great Rattling Brook and the lakes and hills adjacent to them. I found several new lakes in the valley between Serpentine Hills and Middle Ridge. I also found the correct trend of Great Gull river and its eventual convergence and course parallel to Little Gull river, and many other points which are of interest to geographers and surveyors . . . Joe and I must have walked over a hundred miles in the time, and I was somewhat weary when we reached Rolling Falls on the 9th of October . . .'[20]

When they got to the haven of Glenwood on the 14th it was time to say goodbye. Johnny and McGaw made Joe a present of a gun. 'See here, boss, next time you come to Newfoundland we'll go partners together. You can do all the shootin' and I will trap and we'll make lots of dollars . . . Goodbye, boss; you come again an' if I shoot a fifty-pointer I keep him for you.' Johnny watched him leave. 'The red man shouldered a seventy-pound pack, lifted his gun and drifted slowly out of sight.'

'In the year 1906 I resolved to continue my labours in the mapping of the central part of Newfoundland, which at that time,' said Johnny, in a memoir written after the First World War, 'was still uncharted owing to the difficulty of reaching the interior. No one seems to have been in the Mount Sylvester region since Cormack crossed the island in 1827, and the whole district, from the south at Long Harbor, to the Gander river in the centre at the east at Maelpeg to eighty miles to the west of Mount Sylvester was quite unknown. I was, too, resolved, to ascend the Long Harbor river, practically a long series of rapids and over-falls, because Howley, the Government surveyor, and an excellent traveller had failed to do so, and said it was impossible.'[21]

But it was not principally the discovery of the island itself that drew him back like a magnet, but the Newfoundland caribou, enticing him as no other quarry in the world could do with greater force – and also the people; for, like his father, Johnny loved good honest simple hunters and adventurers, in his own case especially those of Newfoundland. Having very carefully studied the habits and movements of the deer, he reckoned the great body of them moved southwards about the end of October with converging trails, and that those roads met around Mount Sylvester, where Joe Jeddore informed him that the country became high, rocky and open. This theory fitted in nicely with his other determination – to ascend and map the Long Harbor River, the largest unknown stream in the island. ('No white man has ever passed up its waters, so that it held some fascination for me.')

So 18 September 1906 saw him speeding across the Atlantic again for St John's. His previous assistants were all signed up on other jobs, but Joe Jeddore in cooperation with the keeper of the Long Harbor telegraph office and store, Philip Ryan, found him two other Micmac Indians called John Hinx (who had endured a very unpleasant experience of White employers' dishonest exploitation) and Steve Bernard. These two met him at the telegraph office on 3 October. Bernard arrived 'considerably the worse for wear,' says Johnny, 'as a result of one of the inevitable "sprees" which precedes such trips into the "country". But the walk of forty-five miles had sobered him, and he was in that frame of mind which brings a chastened spirit and a desire for work, having wasted all his money at the shrine of Bacchus.'[22] Two more Indians, Matty Burke and Johnny Benoit, agreed to help for the first week, which was to involve the worst of the rapids.

The bitterly cold night before starting the trek Johnny stayed at Philip Ryan's house, and was in for an eerie time. 'Immediately I entered [the bedroom],' he remembered, 'I felt a deadly chill and sense of depression. Being a man of sanguine temperament, the feeling was unusual . . .' After going to bed he noticed the shadow of a human figure

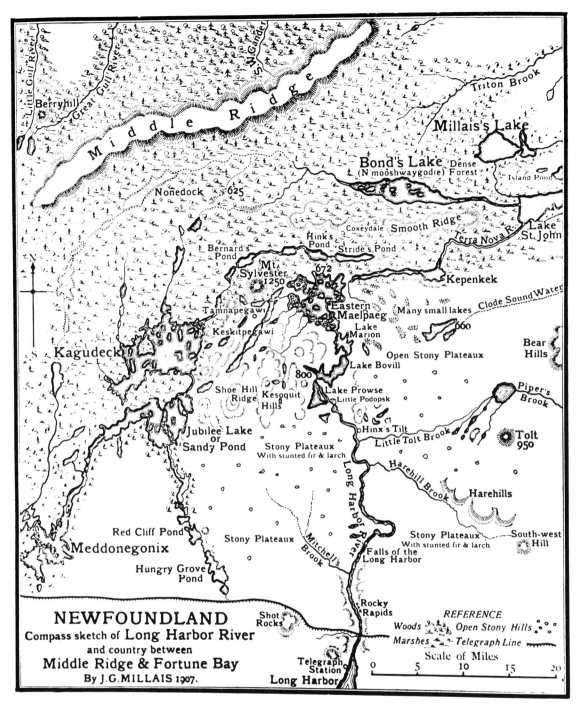

NEWFOUNDLAND
Compass sketch of Long Harbor River
and country between
Middle Ridge & Fortune Bay
By J.G.MILLAIS 1907.

REFERENCE
Woods   Open Stony Hills
Marshes   Telegraph Line
Scale of Miles
0   5   10   15   20

outlined on the counterpane, and, throughout the night, heard sounds of human life and movement and rustling skirts. He put his reindeer sleeping bag on top of the bed and climbed into that. He never slept a wink. 'The morning sun streamed in, and, as I lifted the reindeer bag from the bed, I saw plainly the central design on the counterpane. It was the perfect outline of a woman in black, whilst the stains around were blood red.' Two nights later, sitting at the camp fire, he retailed the experience to Steve Bernard. Bernard knew all about it. He told Johnny how Mrs Ryan had said repeatedly to the Indians that she could not endure the quietness and loneliness of the telegraph office.

93

John Guille Millais: *John Hinx and a thirty-five pointer.*

She committed suicide by putting a match to a barrel of gunpowder. She was carried to the room in which Johnny slept, and, concluded Bernard, 'no one has been in that room since.'[23]

On 5 October, when they were well up Long Harbor River, a quantity of willow grouse fell to Johnny's gun for the pot. But, less fortuitous, 'on this day the river became so impossible just above a large waterfall, that we had to resort to portage of one and a half miles to clear the worst of the rocks. In consequence our progress was very slow – sometimes not more than four or five miles *per diem* were made.'[24] That struggle was over on the 10th when they arrived at a fine lake, which, having no title, Johnny called Lake Prowse after his friend the judge. There Burke and Benoit left for their trapping-grounds, but 'promised to help us down the river at the beginning of November.'

Another week went by before Johnny encountered a really good caribou head. This was a stag with a harem which he 'dropped stone dead with a bullet in the side of the skull . . .' The horns were '. . . as massive as any that can be found on the island, and the whole head would have been an extraordinary one but for the hooky point that did

94

duty for the right brow.' Then they tramped on to Mount Sylvester (named after Cormack's faithful Indian follower, in 1822) at the prospect of which the Indians got very excited since 'both regarded the hill with a certain superstitious veneration.' The Indian belief was that whoever – visiting the summit for the first time – left a present in its prominent black cave would obtain his wish, whatever it might be. Steve Bernard wished for a new suit of clothes, Hinx for a new wife and Johnny Millais for a 50-pointer, which a few days later, he duly secured. 'What a head!' he whispered on sighting it. 'It must be the best in Newfoundland, such middle palms as neither I nor the Indians have ever seen before. I blessed the Sylvester spook, and . . . How we rushed up to survey our prize, what mutual congratulations passed, what enconiums were lavished on the Spirit of the Mountain!'

On 4 November he won the sixth of his '. . . six splended heads, four of which were of exceptional beauty. My collection of caribou was now complete, and this ended my hunting for the year, perhaps forever in Newfoundland . . . This season had surpassed all my previous expeditions, both in the way of success and in the enjoyment of finding and stalking deer in an open country where no White man had ever hunted before.' At Placentia he caught the train for St John's and, next day, the steamer for England.

He completed his Newfoundland comment, as usual, on a conservationist note, deploring the decimation of the deer by both White and Indian fortune-seekers and pot-hunters, but he ended in optimistic tones: 'At the present day there are probably more adult stags in Newfoundland than ever there were, but they take better care of themselves; this is the opinion of the Indians; and as long as the great central sanctuary is not invaded in summer, when the females are bringing forth their young, and no other railway is built to pierce their autumn trails to the south of the forest belt, Newfoundland will always keep her deer, one of her most valuable assets.'[25]

He made his own little contribution to the Newfoundland game. Sir Robert Bond, the governor of the province, asked him if he could procure some black grouse and capercailzie for colonisation in the island. Johnny found him forty from Norway and shipped them across in 1907.[26]

Millais lake, Mount McGaw, Lake Prowse, Mount Frances, Hinx's pond and Bernard's pond are some of the names the hunter-explorer and his friends were to be remembered by.

But a letter from Fred Selous serves as a reminder that 1906 was a year of tragedy for Johnny as well as triumph. The eldest of his four children, Yvonne Daphne, had just died of appendicitis at the age of eleven. 'Your letter awoke afresh all my sympathy for you and poor Mrs Millais for the loss of your dearly loved child,' he wrote. 'I suppose you can never hope to forget what you once possessed and can never have again . . . but time is merciful and whilst never forgetting the sweetness of dispositon of your dear child the sorrow of her loss will gradually hurt you less and less . . .'[27] Yvonne's younger brother Raoul was only five then, yet remembers her vividly as being ' "saint material" and very beautiful – people were always asking to paint her. We all loved her; she looked after us like a nanny. Her death was a terrible shock to me.'

Always kind and helpful to young people Johnny made a friend of Frank Wallace, then a budding animal artist. In his book *A Highland Gathering* Wallace tells how that began. 'Fired by his descriptions of roe stalking in *British Deer and Their Horns* . . . I wrote with the enthusiasm of youth and told him how much I had enjoyed it. He invited me to come and see him, and – after that first meeting – for many years I visited him every few months at his home near Horsham.'[28]

It was a friendship that would endure until Johnny's death.

9

FARAWAY PLACES AND
FAMILY LIFE

Enter Raoul, born 1901

One of the earliest memories of Johnny's artist-sportsman son, Raoul, is that of his father getting up from the dinner table at Compton's Brow in 1907, saying 'Well, that was very nice. Last good meal I'll have for six months, I daresay. Booked for Norway on Wednesday.' As usual it was the first the family had heard of it. Raoul, the Millais' third child, was then six years old.

'I wanted', declared Johnny with the true dedication of the founder of a grand-scale wildlife museum, 'a couple of good reindeer heads for my collection.' He had been to Norway first, mainly in pursuit of reindeer, in September 1900, when '. . . I tramped the stony hills there and plunged through the snow every day for ten or twenty miles in the hope of seeing a good stag . . .' Newfoundland intervening, it was not until the autumn of 1907 that he had another try. This time he was accompanied by P.B. Van der Byl and Fred Selous. 'It is, perhaps, unnecessary to detail the toil and discomfort we experienced during that fortnight. It snowed without cessation for ten days, and every reindeer had trekked far to the south-east. At night the temperature was freezing, the snow penetrated every chink of the wretched shelter, if it might be so called. Moreover, the cooking stove went wrong, and more often we went to bed after eating biscuits, cold tea and half-raw ptarmigan . . .'[1]

Johnny left Norway alone for the next three years, and, in 1908, turned west again. Following that first trip to Wyoming in 1886, aged nineteen, when, in his words, he and his brother Geoffroy 'tramped 350 miles over the prairies and the badlands and nearly died of thirst before reaching his [Geoffroy's] ranch,' the yearning to go back to the New World – and secure prize heads – never deserted him. From a Canadian trip, hunting moose in 1899, he leaves us this brief note. 'I found numbers of males were moving eastwards from Ontario into Quebec, all as if activated by some similar intention (migration in the rutting season) and for a whole week I followed trails of travelling males, passing directly east towards the three rivers . . . By making a fresh expedition I intercepted them.'[2] (He had been studying pilot whales off the Hebrides in the previous month). Then there were his four voyages to the island of Newfoundland (1902, 1903, 1905 and 1906), from at least one of which (1902) he travelled on to Labrador and Ontario.

He was as tough and wiry as ever, though he seems to have had some misgivings as to whether his old physical fitness would last much longer. He wrote to Frank Wallace during the summer of 1907 that 'I managed to win the local tennis tournament last week which was not bad for forty-two. *Eheu fugaces*, etc! I wish I was your age again. One cannot grumble though, as I have had a good time.'[3]

PLATE 7   Raoul Millais: *Fighting Stallions*, 1985.

PLATE 8 *Nijinsky*, 1980 (top) and *Gordon Richards on Abernant*, 1950
by Raoul Millais.

Frank Wallace, 1905.

His hunter-naturalist instinct probably came through to him at least as much from Effie's side of the family as from his father's. Certainly his maternal grandfather had been a keen field sportsman and his uncle, Melville Gray, was a regular big-game hunter. Anyhow it was partly talks which he had enjoyed with his uncle – after Melville Gray returned from a hunting expedition on Vancouver island – that prompted Johnny to make a major tour of north America in 1908.

Journeying from Alaska through the Yukon towards southern Canada he fell seriously ill. He told Frank Wallace later how he journeyed 'up Telegraph Creek with a shocking cold, and that day the bad weather began, twelve days of continuous snow and rain. I trudged on to Deane Lake, seventy-eight miles, each day my cold going down onto my chest and then to my lungs. Fever began, yet I struggled on to the high ground (5,000 feet) where the caribou are. Here I had a regular pleuro-pneumonia for two days, and on a second night in a blizzard I thought I was going to die. The Indians took no notice of me. The next day the snow cleared a little and I got on my horse and descended to

Deane Lake, where I lay two days more and got my lungs better . . .'[4] Soon he was stalking grizzly bears and moose, as he recounts incidentally in praising his guide. 'I think the finest piece of woodcraft I have seen performed was done by my Liard river Indian, Albert, one day at Cassiar, British Columbia. . . .' The Indian (although he had not seen the animal in question) informed him that just ahead in the forest he would find a magnificent bull moose lying down, presenting an easy target. Johnny duly stalked and shot the animal, which had 'a massive head of 60 inches.' Then he asked the Indian: 'Now, Albert I want to know how you knew that moose was going to lie down?' Albert took him back a hundred yards and pointed to a small tree. 'See that bush? That extra good moose feed. If moose hungry he stay long time feeding.' The Indian picked up a chewed twig, held it towards Johnny, then let it go. 'No. Moose take one bite and drop it so – so moose full and he lie down.'[5] After that, sick Johnny took things a little easier himself.

The wapiti was a favourite quarry. 'It possesses horns of such magnificence,' he exulted, 'that they are without exception among other ruminants, except amongst the old Polish red deer of the past.'[6] He went on by rail to Winnipeg where some forty prize wapiti heads were displayed for him. He also '. . . examined in Winnipeg six unusually fine musk-ox heads,' and went on to mourn the near elimination of that species from over-hunting by Eskimos and pelt-trappers. From the train, between Medicine Hat and Macleod, central Manitoba, he saw several herds of pronghorn antelope, which prompted another conservationist's lament ('. . . But snow storms and wire fences are rapidly reducing their numbers and they will soon be extinct north of the Canadian Pacific railway'[7].)

He went on to Montreal and thence to New York and Washington where he was the guest at the White House of Theodore Roosevelt, whom he had first met earlier that year as a fellow-guest of Lord Lonsdale's in Cumberland. ('What, *Breath of the Veldt* Millais?'

Theodore Roosevelt and his son Kermit in East Africa.

98

exclaimed Roosevelt on being introduced). The President made a great impression on Johnny who, with his habitual single-minded vigour, determined to make an in-depth study of the American Negro; and Roosevelt '. . . gave me from memory an almost complete bibliography of the works discussing the slavery question in the United States from the books of Anthony Benezet in 1762 to those of Olmsted in 1861 . . .

'His active brain was a complete bibliography of a thousand subjects, and at a moment's notice he could give you chapter and verse to which to refer in regard to any point at issue. No man living could have produced two such diverse volumes as *Presidential Addresses and State Papers* and *Through the Brazilian Wilderness*, and if we add to this his experience as a soldier and exposition of his *New Bible*, we can obtain some slight grasp of his mental and physical activities . . . Personally he was a man of charming disposition, full of thought for others, ever alive to better the lot of the unfortunate, and possessed of that kindly sympathy which we always associate with really great men.'[8]

Johnny was also astonished at the breadth of the great man's knowledge of both American and African fauna, but remarked that he was inclined to be dogmatic and 'somewhat inconsistent'. They were to meet again after the publication of Roosevelt's *African Game Trails* (by which time – 1910 – Taft had succeeded him as President). 'He gave me a lecture of about twenty minutes (with scarcely a pause to take breath) on the superiority of pictures done on the spot by a zoological artist over all forms of instantaneous photography. As last when I managed to get a word in, it was impossible to refrain from saying "if these are your opinions why did you not take an artist with you instead of a photographer?"

' "Well, you have got me there." he admitted, laughing. "I could not have found the right man, and if I had it is doubtful if he would have come." '

In Johnny's opinion Carl Rungius was the best living artist of mammals in north America. So he asked 'What was the matter with Rungius? Did you ask him? There was no answer to this, for had Roosevelt taken Rungius to Africa with him,' Johnny continues 'we should have had a magnificent pictorial record of the larger mammals of Africa, which would have made his book one of permanent interest, and then we should have been spared that dreadful series of bad portraits of the author standing in fatuous attitudes over mangled corpses of deceased hartebeests, lions and zebras. Roosevelt probably knew this himself, but his book was written for the man in the street, so he perhaps felt that those horrible portraits were expected of him, but it only reminds us of Corney Grain's

Choirboy whose voice o'er-topped the rest
Though very inartistic, the public liked the best . . .'[9]

Having seen the three leviathan volumes of his *Mammals of Great Britain and Ireland*, followed closely by *Newfoundland and Its Untrodden Ways* through his publishers, *The Natural History of British Game Birds*, the twelfth book to come from his pen, was out for the autumn of 1909. Fred Selous wrote a few months before, 'My dear Johnny, I hope that by now you have quite recovered from the effects of the pleurisy you caught in British Columbia. Are you going anywhere this year, I wonder?'[10] The answer was predictable. J.G. Millais rarely vegetated in Sussex in the autumn. The 1909 season was the one in which he first went stalking as the guest of Prince Henry of Lichtenstein, who rented the great hunting lodge of Tartarow, in Galicia (western Ukraine), from the Austrian government, together with the sporting rights of some 4–500,000 acres of the Carpathian mountains.

Johnny was a leading consultant to the British Museum and the Natural History Museum, in South Kensington, among several other scientific institutions, so he called first at Berlin ('where I had some work to do in the museum and zoological gardens.') He arrived in Austria's capital on 12 September and paused to note that 'having once

John Guille Millais: *Courtship of the Scaup Duck*, from *British Diving Ducks*.

seen Vienna it is a matter of surprise that more English do not visit this queen of cities . . . Wealth and taste here are happily married and the result is a never-failing joy to the artistic . . .'[11] And so on to the Carpathians, where, he told Frank Wallace 'You have to work very hard. Out at three every morning, and up to the forest – sometimes five or six thousand feet, going very rough in places and felt boots essential.'[12]

The following summer he was busy, not only with his writing but in helping to organise in London the first public exhibition of his paintings. Then in September, 1910, he was invited to Tartarow again. As the international exhibition of deer heads was held in Vienna that year, he spent five days studying and sketching them, and also making an elaborate chart showing where the best horns were to be found, together with minute statistics under appropriate headings: length, circumference above the beam, spread, points, weight of horn and frontlets, weight of stag, locality and owner. His accolade from among the home contributions went to the fallow of Petworth Park, but he was generally disappointed by the British exhibit which, 'though well arranged by Mr Fairholme, was scarcely representative.'[13] He also detected a number of frauds, '. . . copies of stags' heads in iron, plaster of paris and wood [which] are so perfectly executed as to deceive most experts until they are handled, [then] the weight and composition of the skull give a clue to the material.'[14]

He went on from Galicia in 1910, to stalk in Hungary, Poland and (with the bird artist George Lodge) in Norway, from which country he recounts an amusing experience near Namsus with his hunter and the man's black elk hound. 'My hunter, Kristian Fiskum is the best in the valley . . . not only a first-class man at the dog-work, but a real good fellow, indefatigable, keen and self-reliant – three of the most essential qualities in a good hunter – good-natured, too, modest and absolutely trustworthy . . . To my brother sportsmen, who think of hunting in Upper Namdalen, I would say by all means secure his services, if you can, you cannot do better . . .

'His dog, Bismarck, was worthy of the name he bore, a really great dog. Elk dogs, educated like him to the utmost limit of their capacity, are gifted beyond any other in the art of speaking without words. A raising of the nose and tossing it from side to side, a quick snuffle in a footprint, a sudden cocking of the ears, a whispered whine, an indifferent yawn, or a straining throat rattle, tells the hunter exactly what he wants to know as to the movement of the game in front . . .' Johnny and Kristian followed up a wounded bear, but the dog 'absolutely refused to have anything to do with the business. However, Kristian . . . talked gently to Bismarck, he cajoled, he flattered, he caressed, he bamboozled, and finally succeeded in awakening a lively interest where formerly there was none at all, making the dog understand that here was an animal which he had certainly never seen before, but which, nevertheless, his master earnestly desired him to follow.

'It was a really fine performance on the hunter's part. The elk hound presently began to sniff the tracks and led us along slowly – oh! so slowly – all the time with his ears back and occasional backward glances at his master as much as to say "Well, I'm doing this under protest, and, if I did not love you very much, I would not do it at all". By and by he began to cock his ears, a good sign, and the pace increased to a fast walk. Everything was going on swimmingly when we suddenly came on a fresh cow-elk track, whereupon Bismarck woke and immediately rushed along it, only to be immediately switched off by his master. He just gave us one look as if to say "well of all the idiots!" and grumpily resumed the bear spoor . . .'[15]

With zoological work to complete in Copenhagen, in 1911, Johnny was easily lured back to Norway – hunting, he tells us, 'on to Jotenheim, round the magnificent Gallopegen, the [country's] highest mountain.' 1912 found him back in the Carpathians with Prince Henry of Lichtenstein, so more prize heads fell to his rifle to help fill the spacious, tall-ceilinged museum at Compton's Brow. With its fine parquet floor this often served as a reception room and ballroom, and sometimes, too, a playroom for the three children. Geoffroy was sixteen now, Raoul eleven and Rosamund, nine.

Raoul remembers an impressive and diverse stream of visitors coming and going, naturalists, painters, politicians and horticulturalists. Rudyard Kipling, Frank Wallace and, of course, Johnny's closest friend, Fred Selous, who lived at Worplesdon, were frequent visitors. 'We always looked forward to Selous's arrival,' says Raoul. 'I remember he had the most piercing blue eyes and a wonderful sense of humour and told us marvellous stories on adventure in Africa.' Hilaire Belloc, from the nearby village of Shipley, dined regularly once a month. 'A dozen bottles of beer were provided which he drank rapidly. He and father both had very loud voices and would roar with laughter and shout until two in the morning. I may add that father was a teetotaller, but he did smoke a pipe – as his own father did – non-stop. They both suffered from terrible migraines, an affliction which I inherited.

'You may wonder whether mother got bored often with mainly just us children for company, father being way so much. Not a bit of it. She was a keen horsewoman, a subscriber to the Crawley and Horsham hunt and a regular follower of their hounds. She was a knowledgeable and assiduous gardener, and a good water-colourist, too. She was also very social, and took us, unwillingly, to numerous parties. The worst were the garden parties.'

Raoul (who represents the third generation in this family saga) recounts many unhappier traumas than the boredom of garden parties. There was the nanny who often locked him for more than half a day in an attic cupboard when he became too much of a handful. She grossly over-dosed him on calomel, causing excruciating stomach pains. When she beat him full strength about the head for crying in agony from those, she was promptly dismissed in melodramatic circumstances by Mrs Millais. Then there was a sadistic German governess who made him write out by the hour promises beginning 'I must not . . .' She was persuaded to leave after Raoul's mischievous elder brother, Geoffroy, sent the woman reeling down a precipitous flight of stairs with the help of a sharp push in the back.

In an earlier experience with the nanny who was sent packing Raoul's relationship with his father reached a turning-point. He vividly recalls flying at a milkman who continued remorselessly to flog his pony after it had fallen on its knees on an icy hill. Screaming so loud he alerted the whole neighbourhood Raoul, having seized the man's whip, pummelled him in the face, giving him a bloody nose. The nanny dragged him away 'promising me the fires of hell. My father was told, but instead of getting angry, he gave the nanny a serious ticking off, and taking me on his lap, said "well done – if I'd been there I'd have done the same". I think now that was the first time I realised I loved him. For many years I saw little of him but he became for me a guiding light – though perhaps only a pinpoint of light, as he was so often far away in the remote corners of the world . . .'

The fates of John Bunyan (a rabbit presented to Raoul and Rosamund when they were respectively six and four) caused deeper anguish. Shortly afterwards John Bunyan fell from the great altitude of the nursery window and was picked up, not only concussed but with his jaw and both forepaws broken. Johnny Millais produced brandy and a fountain-pen filler and showed the children how to make splints. The rabbit spent the next fortnight in Rosamund's bed, making a complete recovery. He walked everywhere with the children along with Flapper, their labrador, with which he became an inseparable friend. When he got into the habit of leaping up from under the sofa whenever visitors arrived, thumping his hind legs and hooting at them, Fanny told the children to build

Fanny.

Rosamund and Raoul.

him a hutch, which they did – out of a tea chest – and decorated it with Beatrix Potter prints. Notwithstanding the strongest chicken-wire, however, John Bunyan always bit his way out – to play his favourite game, which was to get under the dining room table and scratch everyone's legs, a cause of some embarrassment when guests were there.

Fanny Millais then relented, allowing him to sleep under the piano, on top of Flapper, to the absolute contentment of both animals. He would spend the day in the rambling rhododendron-filled garden, but returned to the house whenever he was called. John Bunyan was the children's constant companion for nearly three years. Then disaster. One day when the rabbit disappeared for a long time Flapper tugged at Johnny's sleeve, went a few paces into the garden, then looked back, anxiously barking, and repeating the performance several times. Flapper led Johnny and the children into the wildest part of the garden and there they found the rabbit with his head cruelly swollen and much of his skin torn away. He had been attacked by a cat. The vet administered pills and antiseptic and John Bunyan was laid gently in the dog basket under the piano where Flapper licked him incessantly for two days. When the rabbit died Flapper was inconsolable for weeks. 'It was,' says Raoul, 'as though a member of the family had died.'

The time had come for Raoul to go to prep school. On his first day there the ruling gang forced carbolic soap into his mouth, making him swallow it, then tied him to a tree and used him, at close range, for target practice with their catapults. It was only after

John Guille Millais: *Pairing Time*, from *The Natural History of British Game Birds*.

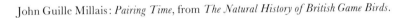

he had been held under water in the swimming pool for so long he surfaced unconscious, that the school authorities brought the culprits to book and sacked them.

'When I was twelve years old,' Raoul recalls, 'my father – who, not unnaturally had previously taken very little notice of me – decided to take me to Scotland with my great uncle Melville [Effie's brother] who had leased a deer forest in a remote part of Perthshire, and so began my initiation into the art and joys of stalking . . .' In 1913 Raoul was a member of the team that won the inter-preparatory school rifle competition at Bisley, and he went on to become one of the best shots – both game and rifle – of his generation.

His father had scarcely been home a week from Melville Gray's lease in Perthshire in 1913 when he boarded a ship bound for East Africa and was soon filling his diary – rather blandly to begin with: 'Since October 6th when we left Kijabe on the Uganda railway we had been going hard, mostly over a waterless and somewhat gameless country . . .' But before the First World War, East Africa still had plenty of big game to show for herself without recourse to strictly wardened and enclosed reserves, and within a week the rhythm of the diary buoyed up. '. . . As we left camp [by the Mara river] we immediately encountered a great herd of Thompson's gazelle, numbering at least two hundred . . . I made for a high ant-hill close by from which I could secure a view of the [other] game in front.

'What a wonderful sight it was! We have often read of the marvellous assemblage of animals in the Free State plains once seen by the hunter but now gone, and some people seem to think that all that was best has vanished forever . . . Could some pessimists see as we did during the next month the great herds of game found between the Amala [Mara] river and the old German border they would have had cause to alter their dismal views. Here was Africa untouched and still as prolific in wild life as it was a hundred years ago. Man the destroyer had not yet made his mark. There were no natives, except a few wandering Masai who never touched the game and perhaps only once a year some wandering hunter came for a month or two and shot a few heads. It was just Africa as we who love the wilds and the game had wished to see it. Everything was as we had hoped, and for once our dreams came true . . .'[16] Alas, the pessimists' predictions came true sooner than a bad dream might have told him. But Johnny had less than two decades of life left; fortunately for him he was not there to witness the twilight of Africa's big game.

Already the lions, attempting to steer clear of man, were mostly hunting by night as Johnny observed: 'Few people know how completely nocturnal lions have become in nearly all parts of Africa. It is now possible to live in some lion-haunted districts, and yet never see a single one in broad daylight . . . [They] soon learn it is not safe to be abroad after sun up and make for the dense bush by the rivers or lie up in dongas, where they are seldom surprised or seen, unless stumbled upon by chance.'[17]

However, he stalked and shot three lions in the space of forty-eight hours and was in ecstasy. 'As we sat at night over the camp fire and heard the lions rumbling in all directions, it seemed as if we had for the moment reached the acme of human enjoyment. Just to be in Africa's wonderland – and in the very best of it – free from all the cares and worries of human civilisation, with the power to roam at will into the great lands beyond where no man passes, was in itself, to lovers of the wilderness, an experience many strive for and few experience. When we add to this the delights of big-game hunting – surely the finest sport in the world – in a land that is still quite unspoilt, and where anything may turn up from an elephant to a dik-dik, life could hold nothing better . . .'[18]

'It is one of the charms of East African hunting that when you have arrived in camp and possess so excellent a camp manager as Judd you have nothing to do but just to hunt and enjoy yourself. Some men object to the so-called "white" hunter, who, except [when accompanying] the complete novice, does little actual hunting, but when the arrangements of the safari are in the hands of such a thoroughly experienced man, the hunter is relieved of all camp worries and arrangements, and can come and to at will. Personally I prefer to hunt alone, with one black follower . . . I wandered into the bush accompanied by my gun-bearer, Mabruki, a silent and keen-eyed Wakamba savage, who in his youth had been a cannibal.[19]

'How wonderful,' he exults, 'is the African morning in the wild and the coming of day with all its manifold sights and sounds! This indeed is the place above all others in which it is good to be a naturalist and to appreciate the marvellous pageant of Nature as the dawn unfolds.' He goes on to demonstrate his wide ornithological knowledge, moving from the exotic to the commonplace and back. 'More humble, but none the less welcome, was the advent one morning in November of one of our own little willow warblers from England. It sang a subdued little song, something like the one it utters just before leaving our shores in September, and seemed as though it had brought a message of love from home. As I watched it I wondered if it had come from my garden in Sussex.'[20]

Delighting in the songbirds when at home he frequently visited Fred Selous in Surrey and they went rambling together. 'We often used to go out and look for nests in the commons, hedgerows and woods at Worplesdon and it was now a sorrow that he could no longer, owing to a slight deafness, recognise the notes of birds at a distance.'[21]

The fact that Selous was over sixty did little to curb his adventurousness. In 1913 he invited Johnny and another friend, Heatley Noble, to join him on an egg-collecting expedition to Iceland. Johnny, remembering his naturalist's way around the country from his travels there in the 1880s, was virtually the party's leader. They went further north to the island of Grimsey within the Arctic Circle, where they secured some eggs of the little auk, and they returned to England with another magnificent collection. In the following year *The Big Game of Africa and Europe* (the first volume in the series *The Gun at Home and Abroad*) written jointly by Selous, Abel Chapman and Johnny, was published in a de luxe edition and dedicated to George V. By this time, too, Johnny had also illustrated the Badminton Library volume on game shooting along with sporting works by Seebohm and Sir Ralph Payne-Gallwey.

The war clouds were looming, and soon he would, for the first time in more than twenty years, don a uniform in combatant earnest: this time a naval uniform.

10

STRIFE

Raoul both adored and feared his engaging, wild elder brother, Geoffroy. When the boys' treasured old working spaniel, Smut, died from a dose of poison and no replacement was found for him, Geoffroy made the younger brother dress up in protective gloves, leggings and hood, get down on all fours and flush the game like a good gun dog. Raoul, having been cut to ribbons in bramble thickets, was instructed to go through nearly impenetrable gorse whins; and Geoffroy, who had been waiting with his gun for the rabbits to break covert, could not understand why the boy then ran home in fright and defiance. On another occasion, following a heated argument – which ended with Raoul having the last word and trying to make a quick exit – there was a sudden piercing pain in his back like a heavy bee sting. 'Stop!' ordered Geoffroy. Raoul felt his brother's hand below his shoulder-blade while the dart which had penetrated to the hilt was removed. 'If you tell father about this,' warned Geoffroy, 'I'll kill you!'

The brothers had hours of fun ferreting. They took the little carnivores to school and to bed, and there were frequently one or two of them to be found in their pockets. They nearly lost their precious pack of ferrets one day when Geoffroy, with a broken leg in plaster of Paris, careered downhill in his wheelchair – and into a stream. Guns, cartridges, nets and ferrets were scattered everywhere. The boys were forbidden to shoot or fish on the Sabbath, so one Sunday, as an alternative to ferreting, they collected bumble bees in matchboxes, took some hair nets from their mother's dressing table and went field-mouse hunting on a sunny bank. In crawled the bees, buzzing furiously, out came the mice – into the nets. Having enjoyed this sport they let the mice go and returned the nets to whence they came. Next day Fanny, ignorant of the situation, told them to do something about the plague of mice in her dressing table: 'they've been eating holes in my hair nets,' she complained.

Geoffroy set his heart on a naval career but, after a few months as a cadet on HMS *Conway*, he changed his mind and was transferred to Repton school in Derbyshire. As soon as war was declared, however, he ran away from Repton and joined the Sussex Yeomanry as a trooper (at about the same time that Siegfried Sassoon went into the ranks of that regiment). By then Raoul was at Winchester, and not enjoying it much.

As a new 'man' (never boy at Winchester) he was beaten ten times – once with blood running through his pyjamas, by a sadistic prefect called Ashton, whose pretext was that he was the only prefect among the six in each house, who had not had the opportunity of 'punishing Millais'. The other 'men' in the dormitory then set upon Ashton, who thereafter steered clear of Raoul. Then there was the prefect who, at 'prep', goaded him continuously with his umbrella. When Raoul caught the man neatly on the jaw with his fist – he had been taught to box by an amateur champion friend of his father's – the other juniors set on the bully, who, reeling about room, cried 'By Christ, Millais, I'll get you for this!' But no prefect came near him, tauntingly, again.

Raoul.

Raoul was not much interested in the conventional school games. Like his father and grandfather before him he was a naturalist and preoccupied with sport of a different kind. From the hours he spent in the museum at Compton's Brow, and, occasionally, from what rubbed off in his father's company he could identify most of the big fauna of Africa, north America and Europe and he also had a useful knowledge of all the mammals and birds of Britain. From about the age of nine he was equally handy with a fishing rod, a snare, a catapault or a .22 rifle. At twelve he was dead-eyed with a Mannlicher. He was also, like his father, used to sleeping out in all kinds of weather.

At about the time he entered Winchester he shot his first royal. It was on the hill which his great-uncle, Melville Gray, took on the Athol estate. The ghillie had told Raoul there was a good chance of securing the beast at dawn if he spent the night in a certain sheep shelter. He was thrilled by the stag's roar, and after two freezing nights, armed with the .256 Mannlicher (for which his father had invented a special sight) he spotted the royal, stalked and shot it. Wounded, it raced over the march onto the Duchess of Fife's estate, Mar Lodge. Raoul ran after it and finished it off where, at last, it lay. A party of stalkers and ghillies from the 'foreign' estate came (apparently) menacingly towards him. However, in the nick of time he cut off the prize head and, under the massive weight, ran back over the march to his great-uncle's side of the hill. Such an adventurous lad was unlikely to be content with football as his only school winter activity outdoors.

The Winchester wartime food being dreadful, in true Millais tradition he spent many an afternoon out of bounds – just as Johnny had done at Marlborough – in search of fish and game, and missed (apparently unnoticed) many an important science lesson in the pursuit. His essential equipment consisted of a bicycle, a sawn-off .22 rifle, snares made of rabbit wire and the two bottom sections of a greenheart salmon rod.

He had the cooperation of the house butler, and the fish and fowl that he surreptitiously brought back were much appreciated by the other boys. And no wonder considering this memoir. 'The food in our house was virtually uneatable. One day a large hunk of salt pork appeared in the dining hall for luncheon. We all crowded round and saw to our horror that it was covered in dead bluebottles. We went back to our places at table and started banging our spoons on the boards and shouting "poison, poison!" The housemaster came in and was shown the offensive specimen. It was removed, but replaced by something closely resembling cricket boots with nails left in.'

Fred Selous was on his way to fight in Africa when Raoul was involved in those Winchester dramas. He had been turned down for service in France on account of his age. 'How cross he was,' Johnny remembered. 'But shortly afterwards I received a wire that he was coming over to lunch. He arrived radiant as a boy home from school, the reason being that he was to go to Africa with a contingent of 150 with the rank of lieutenant at the age of sixty-three!'

At forty-nine, Johnny himself would not normally have been called up; but, with his knowledge of languages and of Continental Europe and the fact that a first cousin of Fanny's, Admiral Reginald Hall, was the head of the Royal Naval Secret Service, a place was readily found for him in naval intelligence. In 1915, he was posted as British Vice-Consul to Hammerfest, in northern Norway, with the principal role of counter-espionage. 'We had evidence that in all towns, especially in the far Arctic regions, agents – German and Norwegian – were industriously at work spreading the paean of future German triumph,' he wrote, 'and vilifying the hated English and their command of the seas. Spies lurked in every village and movements of any travelling Englishman were watched with sleuth-hound thoroughness . . .'[1] He sailed for the Norwegian mainland on the Norwegian steamship *Bessheim*, via the Lofoden islands, with the rings of a lieutenant-commander

John Guille Millais: *At the end of the Covert*, from *The Natural History of British Game Birds*.

on the sleeves of his tunic, in August 1915. And there we will leave him for the moment – on the *Bessheim*, tacking and twisting to avoid the enemy submarines.

A few months before sailing Johnny heard from his old naturalist friend, the Duke of Bedford, who was busy at Woburn raising a battalion of the Bedfordshire Regiment, which had been in 'suspended animation'. Aware that Geoffroy had been recommended for a commission by the Sussex Yeomanry's commanding officer, the Duke wanted to know if Johnny could arrange for the boy to be sent to him in the rank of second lieutenant? Indeed he could. And while the training programme at Woburn was quite leisurely, Saturdays during the pheasant season were great fun. The Duchess, stone deaf, highly eccentric as her husband was and an enthusiastic game-shot, arranged for an army of beaters to drive the birds over herself and Second Lieutenant Millais every week.

But, drafts from the Bedfordshire already being entrained for the front, it was not long before Johnny heard again from the Duke. 'I have some disturbing news about Geoff. As you know we are devoted to him and look upon him almost as our son. He is a very headstrong boy and yesterday he came to see me. He was obviously in a great state of agitation and said that if he was left behind again when the next draft went to the war he would desert. I know he is under age, but what can I do? I am convinced he will do what he says . . .'[2] The 19-year-old subaltern was sent to France with the next draft.

By the time Geoffroy Millais had gained his reputation as a fearless and most inspiring leader of infantry soldiers, his father had craftily avoided arrest by a U-boat captain and was sailing to the Arctic coast of Norway to take up his duties as British vice-consul in Hammerfest, which was the centre of the Norwegian cod industry. Though officially neutral the Norwegians, as Johnny pointed out, were largely in sympathy at that stage of the war with the Germans who, among other advantages, had virtually monopolised the fishing business and still enjoyed a reputation among the people for invincibility. But for the moment his life was mostly routine and recreation. Northern Norway was in the grip of snow until May. 'The consular and naval work was not easy and occupied the greater part of the day, and it was only at night in summer time that I was able to go out into the mountains and get some exercise and relaxation in watching the various Arctic birds now arriving on their Spring migration.' The artist George Lodge was at Hammerfest at that time as his very welcome bird-watching companion.

Here is a random handful from Johnny's copious and affectionate observations. 'On May 25 came the first spring arrivals, flocks of snow buntings two hundred strong, the black-backed males resplendent in their new plumage. In a few days these beautiful little birds began to sing though there was no sign of the ice-break . . . Before the end of the month came little parties of shore larks and the large Greenland wheatear which uttered a jerky, scratchy song and gave a pretty aerial courtship . . . On June 8 I heard a new note to me and advancing amongst some scrub saw a female bluethroat. She was shortly joined by two brilliant males, their gorgeous throats shining like jewels in the sun and they went through a leaping courtship, something like . . . the common robin. From now onwards during the ensuing fortnight, with every day of increasing warmth, new species arrived and at once indulged in their individual efforts and songs characteristic of the nuptial display . . .

'On June 6 some Iceland gulls, a red-throated pipit and a party of bramble finches passed, going north, and numbers of willow warblers were noticed singing in the low stunted willow-bushes . . . One day in July, as I was painting on a hillside above the sea, I heard a yelping note and, looking down, I saw an old sea eagle closely followed by her brown young one. She carried a brilliant scarlet fish in her claws and kept lifting it as if to entice her offspring forward in its flight . . .[3]

Johnny the sailor.

'Such sunsets as those of northern Europe are not to be seen in any other part of the world. One evening [out painting] I dashed in one of these, using nearly every colour in the spectrum, and when I looked at it next morning it seemed as if I had upset the paint-box. But a local merchant who saw it said it was just right and bought it on the spot. Often I used to take out a boat, have a little saithe fishing, and then paint the breaking sea on the outer islands as backgrounds for my eagle pictures, but the fisherman, who regarded me as a harmless lunatic or a cunning fellow with deep designs on the coast, were mostly unsympathetic, and thought more of the elusive kroner than the claims of art or sport.'[4]

In August he went reindeer hunting on the island of Rolfso, forty miles north of Hammerfest, and, shortly after his return, began reporting the presence of German submarines. A considerable number of Norwegian vessels were sunk. 'They could,' said Johnny, 'easily have escaped disaster if their captains had not been so obstinate and had come for information . . . Sometimes it even looked as if they did not care as long as they got the insurance money for the ships.'

He goes on to relate one of his many consular dramas from that time. A somewhat drunken Norwegian sea captain demanded, in a great hurry, bunker coal in exchange for a consignment of sea salt which he had brought with him from Trondheim. That could only be provided, replied Johnny, if the salt was English, not German. The man told him it was English. From which firm? Johnny asked. When the captain named the

F.C. Selous.

112

firm, Johnny telegraphed the consul in Trondheim for confirmation. The response was prompt: that firm only dealt in German salt.

The captain, returning more drunk than before and very quarrelsome was taken to task for lying. 'I shall *make* you give me the coal!' he screamed at Johnny. A fight ensued. '. . . he seemed to lose control of himself and shouted "Now I will *make* you give me, you cursed Englishman!" at the same time diving his hands into his pockets as if searching for some weapon . . . So I hit him with all my might on the point of the jaw and saw him go down the stairs all in a heap . . . For a moment or two my antagonist lay still, and then got up slowly and passed out into the snow.'[5]

The U-boats disappeared completely on the night of 1 December '. . . so I settled up my affairs. And, the work for which I had been specially detailed being finished, I took the mail steamer and went south.' In Bergen to avoid being kidnapped by German spies, he was obliged to pose as a Scottish doctor with the name of Stuart. He sailed safely on to Newcastle, however, whence he reported to the Admiralty.

Sixty-three-year-old Captain Fred Selous, 25th Royal Fusiliers won the DSO helping to fight General von Lettow-Vorbeck's army in east Africa. On 4 January 1917, the old hunter-explorer was killed. The Fusiliers' leading company (under his command) made contact with the Germans at Beho-Beho that day. General Smuts described the action to Johnny: 'Heavy firing on both sides then commenced, and Selous at once deployed his company, attacked the Germans, who greatly outnumbered him, and drove them back into the bush. It was at this moment that Selous was struck dead by a shot in the head.'[6]

That loss by no means completed Fanny and Johnny Millais' Great War cup of sorrow. Their son, Geoffroy, was commanding a machine gun company on the Western Front during and after Johnny's Norwegian sojourn. He was court-martialled after his men shot and killed some retreating members of a Portuguese detachment, mistaking them – in their grey coats, in a thick fog – for Germans. And, although he was exonerated, it was widely felt that this was the reason for a strongly worded recommendation on his behalf for the Victoria Cross being refused. He also found time to keep two lurchers in the trenches and spent much of his spare daylight time coursing.

One of his sergeants, visiting the Millais' after the war, told them that Geoffroy was 'the finest officer I ever served under; the men would follow him anywhere . . . He often gave them his own rations when food was short. His favourite game was crawling up alone to German machine gun posts in the middle of the night armed with a pick-axe handle and two hand grenades and laying about them. He killed four of the bastards one night and came back with a luger and four helmets.' A machine-gun bullet took Geoffroy in the chest three days before the Armistice; he died the following day. 'The news of his death,' says his brother Raoul, 'hit me like a thunderbolt. I could not believe it. I thought he was immortal. But now I feel he would never have fitted into the post-war world.' In the holidays, however, Raoul had the solace of the Fielding family, 'who helped create the happiest days of my life – there were two exceptionally beautiful daughters and a son, Rudolph, who became another brother to me.'

There were other traumas, albeit of a less dynamic nature, to be faced towards the end of Raoul's Winchester career. When his housemaster told him he was to be a prefect he refused the accolade, recounting the unjust cruelties he had endured at the hands of prefects when he was a junior boy. The housemaster naively enquired why he had not reported the atrocities at the time and received an appropriately ironic reply. At the final examinations when his science papers were returned almost blank he was summoned by a furious housemaster. Since he was due to leave Winchester for good by the first train next day he thought he would have nothing to lose by owning up to his out-of-bounds shooting and fishing adventures over the past three years, which had necessitated missing nearly all science lessons. (And of course he had spent a very great deal of time sketching.)

Raoul went on to reason that his sporting forays had been absolutely vital to supplement the inadequate wartime rations. The housemaster (whose universal nickname was 'the Tec') was not only livid with rage at having failed to detect Raoul's lawless activites for such a long period, but also saw himself as being thus virtually accused of starving his boys. He therefore sent Raoul to the headmaster, who told him that he was 'unquestionably the worst man I have ever had under my jurisdiction in this college ... It is my duty, Miller [*sic*], to birch you. Have you anything to say?'

'Yes, sir,' replied Raoul, 'I am leaving on the first train tomorrow for good. Wouldn't it be a pity if I left with a bad impression at both ends?'

When the headmaster then disappeared in apparently apoplectic anger, Raoul thought he would be returning with the birch. (At the same time the memory returned to him most vividly of the time he had successfully catapulted two of the man's Rhode Island Reds for supper.) Instead of that the headmaster reappeared saying that he had 'given this matter a lot of serious consideration, and owing to the fact that during these hard times you have perhaps been lacking in parental discipline, I am prepared to overlook your insubordinate behaviour. But I feel the college will benefit greatly from your absence. Good *bye*!'

Remembering his own escapades at Marlborough, Johnny was in fits of laughter listening to Raoul's report of the dialogue. 'History repeating itself!' he remarked. 'But don't you be too smug. You may not always be so lucky. One day you may fall flat on your face when you least expect it.' What Johnny still failed to detect was the talent in his son's doodlings; he had not yet observed that, like himself at that age, here was an artist in embryo.

11

RAOUL IN JOHNNY'S FOOTSTEPS

Raoul cannot remember a time when he did not draw. He illustrated *Hiawatha* from end to end when he was seven. He sketched by the hour in Johnny's museum at Compton's Brow and, from the first time he went to Scotland, he started making little pictures of the birds and mammals he encountered there. He was ever conscious, ever inspired by the family tradition in art and the fact that Lodge and Thorburn – closely combining nature and art – were his godfathers. He should have received more encouragement in his efforts from his artist father, but restless Johnny was too much away from home, too much preoccupied with his research and writing and with his own drawing and painting to afford the time for interest in the naive artistic efforts of his younger son. Nevertheless when Raoul left Winchester, Johnny applauded the young man's wish to attend the Byam Shaw Art School.

First-year Byam Shaw students were made in Raoul's words 'to draw nothing but busts and casts', which he found rather boring. Every given opportunity saw him with his sketch-pad at the zoo, and, as visitors were only allowed in the lion house at feeding-time in those days, he was left to draw the big cats in peace. He tells how he jumped the barrier, scratched the ears of the tiger, Rajah, with whom he 'became a great friend' – until the keeper reported him to the zoo committee who then banned him; and how, two years, later, he 'crept in unobserved and received a great welcome from Rajah.'

In 1921 Raoul left the Byam Shaw to take his place at the Royal Academy Schools. His entry was by no means plain sailing. Instead of completing the required qualifying exam – figure drawing and other conventional tests – he sent in a collection of animal drawings from his zoo and other visits. The committee summoned him. Two of its older members who had known the great Sir John well, told him 'you seem to be just as unruly as your grandfather was in his youth!' But they let him in without further trial all the same. Lawrence Irving, John Skeaping and the Zinkeisen sisters, Doris and Anna, were among his fellow students.

Munnings, Orpen, Solomon and John were regular visitors. 'Augustus John used to visit our life class,' Raoul remembers, 'and to my embarrassment always came and sat beside or behind me for half an hour and never said a word except "good!", when he got up and left. I think he meant to be kind but he taught me nothng.'

Raoul visited the National and Tate galleries again and again. He made a special study of Turner, Rembrandt, Rubens, Velasquez and the Dutch masters. ('I found them all technically fascinating and read every book I could find on their methods.') He spent a summer in Kent under the tuition of that great teacher of animal art, Frank Calderon, whom he thought 'a charming and splendid teacher'. Horses were Calderon's first love, as they would be Raoul's.

Meanwhile his father had been concerned in recent years more with plants than with animals. By the time the Great War burst upon the Millais family Johnny had just about exhausted his aspiration to write reference books on mammals and birds. The two volumes of his *British Diving Ducks* came out in 1913 along with his *Deer and Deer Stalking. The Gun at Home and Abroad* series with the strong contributions from his pen, came out in 1914–15, and those were followed by his *Life of Frederick Courteney Selous DSO*, in 1918, and the reflective *Wanderings and Memories* in 1919. His reputation for immersing himself in a subject until his knowledge of it was complete had not dimmed. Following many years of trial and error in the garden at Compton's Brow, which ran down in sixteen acres to a valley of St Leonard's forest – coupled with wide-ranging and studious visits to other gardens – he put together his mighty tome, *Rhododendrons and their Hybrids*, which was published by Longmans Green in 1917.

'It has always been a joy to me to see a new garden; for, apart from the pleasure of noting the expression of other people's ideas put into practice, there is,' he noted in the preface, 'always something new to be learned. In consequence I have travelled around to nearly all the best gardens in the British Isles. Eleven years ago I commenced the culture of these plants in Sussex, so that I might study them from a practical point of view, and was so fortunate as to have the tutelage of my friend and neighbour, Sir Edmund Loder, who at all times has given me the benefit of his great knowledge of the genus . . . The love of flowers and trees is perhaps the purest and most satisfying of all earthly pleasures . . .

'In the formation of the garden and its surroundings the details should not be left to the gardener or the professional landscape gardener, unless the owner is totally deficient in appreciation of artistic beauty. It is much better that he who will always live there should create his own surroundings even if he does make the most colossal errors. In time, by the study of other gardens, he can correct most of the mistakes and will appreciate any success he may achieve in far greater proportions than if it had been created by others. The owner should introduce into his own garden his own individuality. Quite one-quarter of the small gardens of England are still composed of roses with a few bulbs with back-grounds of laurel and yew. But look at the result! There are months in which it is not possible to find flowers at all, when the floral beauty should in reality be continuous . . .' The reviewers were ecstatic: 'Mr Millais has done a great service to horticulture,' said the *Gardener's Chronicle* in one of them; 'For a combination of sumptuousness and good taste it would be hard to beat this work,' *The Queen* enthused in another, 'the book is one which makes anyone with a gardener's heart tingle with excitement.'

Johnny's second azalea and rhododendron book came out in 1924. He introduced it as follows: 'Since my last volume was published the popularity of these noble plants has advanced in leaps and bounds. Gardeners, seeing the possibility of enriching their gardens with lovely flowering shrubs from February to August, are turning more and more towards a genus that gives a maximum of beauty with a minimum of labour . . . It seems to me that all the mass of new material should be consolidated with fresh matter such as the behaviour of the various species under cultivation . . .'

Then there was criticism from a quarter he did not welcome, and his preface waxed philosophically caustic. 'Recently I met a youth from Cambridge – a twentieth-century product of the "New Clever" kind – and he said to me: "is it worthwhile to attempt the impossible? Your book will be obsolete as soon as it is written." He was young, but he made me feel humble; for what he said was true. But what a creed! Here was Youth and Pessimism combined – a terrible sign of the times. Fortunately all are not on a par with this Intellectual Hobo. Ours is an age of real progress, in spite of cowards such as these, who are all criticism and no work. We go on labouring towards our goal through

Lion at the Zoo, drawn by
Raoul Millais in 1920 while
he was a Byam Shaw
student.

a mist of failure, but live in the hope that our poor efforts are not in vain. One day will
come some twenty-first-century New Zealander who will sit in his "atomic" chair and
laugh at the imaginings of today. Soon we shall witness the birth of our "Atomic" era.
In that new day – let us hope – man will have learned both to understand and to love
his fellow-men. So, with our lovely flowers, may we reach the garden of our dreams and
greater earthly happiness.'[1]

He was awarded the Loder Rhododendron Cup in 1923 and the Victorian Medal of
Honour, by the Royal Horticultural Society, in 1927.

'No matter where a man lives,' Johnny was to say in his *Far Away Up the Nile*, 'if he has
once seen and smelt Africa, he will ever feel the Claw hooking him back to the Sun and
the Great Spaces.' By 1923 the lure of Africa was strong on him again. He had felt that
luring 'Claw' first as a boy in the 1870s, when his governess had read him Baldwin's *African
Hunting*. It pulled on him again, prompting him to leave the Army, sail to Cape Town
and equip himself as a trekker in 1892; and he felt its urgings repeated, with East Africa
in view, in 1913. Now, when he was fifty-eight, the magnet of the great sub-continent
was beckoning once more. He had been toiling hard on the arrangements for an exhibition
of his pictures and also on the second volume of his rhododendron studies. 'The nature
of the work had made me so tired and depressed,' he confessed, 'that a long holiday in
the sunshine was absolutely necessary.'

The idea of Sudan began through the encouragement of his friend, the colony's game
ranger, Captain Courtney Brocklehurst, and his wife, Lady Helen. Those who held sway

in the colony knew that a book from Johnny's pen would doubtless emerge from his adventures, a book that was likely to reflect the prosperity of Sudan under British rule, one that would highlight the efficiency, justice and benevolence of the officers of the administration. They were aware, too, that Johnny's books were very widely read. So he was to be the guest of the Sudan government, whose financial agent, Colonel George Schuster, promised him free passes on the railway and the steamers. Schuster asked him whether he wished to bring anyone along with him, ('a doctor or any person of that kind'). Johnny replied that the only company he wished for was that of his son, Raoul.

Having just graduated from the Royal Academy Schools and being poised on the threshold of his chosen career, Raoul looked forward with great relish to this trip with his father, which promised, among other excitements, to provide him with plenty of material on which to ply his gift and new found expertise. They sailed in *The City of Canterbury* on 1 December 1923, from Southampton, where Raoul had bought two mouth organs and Johnny a good stock of 'modern books to last for four months', of which reading matter he took an unusually jaundiced view. ('What strikes one today is the increasing number of works which are nothing more than camouflaged revolutionary propaganda or dirty novels. Their authors, who are invariably brilliant writers, always remind one of those people who live in a lovely garden and sit on the manure heap. Tolstoy, a great artist but a mediocre thinker, was really the first of these. His pernicious doctrines, veiled in language all could understand, made him the real author of the Russian Revolution . . .'[2])

He complains, too, of the ship's bore, who hailed him with ' 'morning old man, how's the browsing and sluicing today, are you feeling good? . . . Are you a relative of the famous Millais? Your son looks exactly like an artist if I may say so . . . Are you Bubbles? You're very like him. How did you pose for that soap advertisement? Did you sit in a bath and reach for soap? How many times did you sit or lie? Was it cold doing that? Weren't you awfully pleased at what Marie Corelli said about it, that Sir John had ruined his art by painting soap advertisements for Pears? . . . We're having an awfully jolly time, aren't we? Have you noticed what a wonderfully nice lot of people there are on this ship?'[3]

Having arrived at Port Sudan on 16 December, got through the tedium of the customs and established themselves at the hotel, father and son spent the next fortnight in an acclimatising hunting excursion in the Red Sea hills. They engaged the cook, Mohamed Tahir, who would serve throughout their Sudanese journey, a camel master and a bodyguard and professional hunter, a policeman of the Hadendowa tribe.

They fed on the ibex and the dorcas gazelle which they shot, and at the end of Christmas Day Johnny was writing in his diary: 'This has been a wonderful day and one of the most interesting of many days spent in the hunting fields during my life. The whole entourage and methods of these savages during their chase, the magnificent scenery, the glorious air on the high tops, the turns and twists of the game to escape its numerous enemies, were all spread before us, and though I do not pretend that ibex driving as a sport is to be compared with stalking the same animal, yet its human interest was most absorbing and delightful. In Rome you must do as the Romans do, and in all these parts of the Red Sea hills where the Hadendowas live they will not permit stalking, but insist on driving because they enjoy the sport and it brings to the clans more money.'

Back at Port Sudan, five days later, the Governor invited them to lunch to meet Prince Arthur, Duke of Connaught, Queen Victoria's third son – who, as a young man had covered himself in glory during the Egyptian campaign of 1882 and who was later Commander-in-Chief Ireland, C-in-C Mediterranean, Governor-General of Canada, Inspector-General of the Armed Forces and subsequently Governor-General of South Africa, from which country he was now returning, following a successful hunting trip.

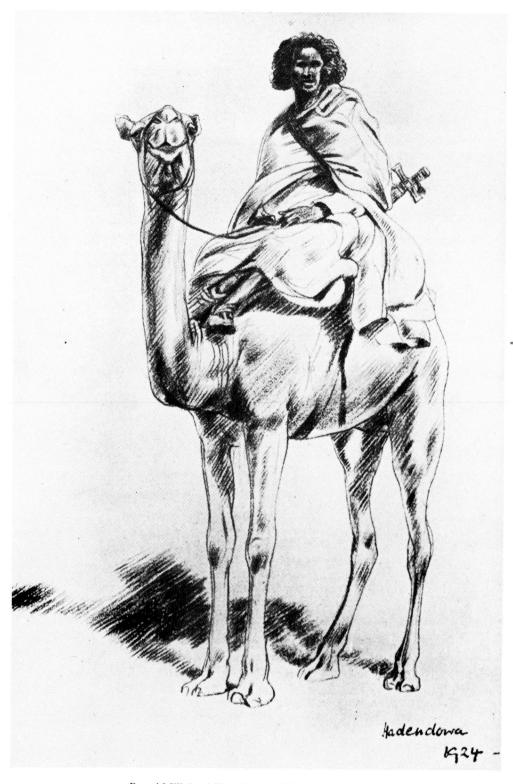

Raoul Millais: *A Hadendowa on his Racing Camel*, 1924.

The Princess (formerly Princess Louise Margaret of Prussia), says Johnny, 'had the good fortune to kill a splendid sable of fifty-two inches, probably the largest ever shot by a lady . . .'

'After lunch,' he goes on, 'the Prince said he desired to talk to me, so we retired to another room. I thought he wished to discuss the new game reserves in South Africa, near Cape Town, which I had suggested to – and had some correspondence upon with – General Smuts. But, after touching on this topic he went into a short account of his stewardship of South African affairs . . . Things are, it is to be feared, not going well there, and General Smuts, the one sheet-anchor of British supremacy, is a sick man who is soon likely to be ousted from his position by the pro-Boer General Hertzog [leader of the Nationalist-Labour Alliance, he defeated Smuts in 1924]. Moreover it is to be feared that new British settlers are few and will be swamped by the country vote, whilst nearly all English-born settlers are becoming intensely anti-British. The outlook is far from cheering and the new Governor-General is likely to have an even more unhappy time than had Prince Arthur, who was personally very popular with all sections of the community.'[4]

Johnny was, however, reassured regarding the situation in Sudan. 'Ever since British troops avenged Gordon and conquered the Khalifa [in the campaign that ended with the battle of Omdurman and the occupation of Khartoum, in 1898] a sure policy of consolidation and just government of the various native races has been in force . . . The last

John Guille Millais: *Bird Life on the Nile*.

120

to break out were the Dinkas, in 1922, and they, although a troublesome lot, are now, owing to skilful management on the part of the District Commissioners, coming to understand our strength and sense of justice, which must in time result in permanent peace and the possession of all they hold dear.'[5]

There was, however, an external threat. Egypt – having been granted her independence in 1922 and begun her constitutional monarchy with King Fuad just before the Millais trip began – laid her traditional claim to sovereignty over the Blue and White Niles, and thus the whole of the Sudan, with greater bombast than ever. It was a claim described by Johnny as 'absurd'.[6]

On 1 January he and Raoul and their servants entrained for Khartoum which they reached in thirty-six hours and where they were the guests, at the viceregal palace, of the Sirdar, Sir Lee Stack, (who was to be assassinated in Cairo by Egyptian nationalists in the following year). Johnny in admiring the palace is open about his political sympathy. 'Lord Kitchener in designing it evidently meant to impress the native mind as to the magnificence and power of our great Empire – along with the Gordon College and the Gordon statue – monuments to the fact that British power can rise, phoenix-like, from the ashes of a brutal past, and that the Mahdists in killing our pioneer soldier, did nothing to quench the strength and tenacity of a nation which never admits defeat.' He adds that 'some Labour members might say it is all a useless piece of miliary bombast – but then stay-at-home people do not understand the native mind . . . Nothing appeals to the savage so much as a display of splendour, aristocracy and general gorgeousness . . . To the coloured man equality and true democracy simply do not exist.'[7]

On 6 January they took the steamer up the Blue Nile and so, south, in to the White Nile, Johnny describing in his diary as they travelled, the comings and goings of the birds. By the 12th they reached Malakal where they dined with the officers of the 12th Sudanese Regiment and, on putting their names in the visitors' book, took note of Fred Selous's signature, inscribed there in 1911. After dinner, led by the commanding officer, Major Knapp, they took over instruments from the regimental bandsmen and 'let rip on a "coal black mammy" with voice and arm at full strength, and something is to be said for the conductor that at the end of two encores . . . he was still alive. On adjourning to the mess-room there were supper and more atmospheric moisture until midnight.'[8]

They listened to a wide variety of stories concerning Sudan's answer to the Loch Ness monster, the Lau, a mammoth breed of serpent said to inhabit the Nile swamps. Johnny compared the characteristics of the Shilluk, Nuer, Niam-Niam, Juer and Dinka tribes; and, foreshadowing Alan Morehead, he discoursed on the men who influenced life and history on the Blue and White Niles, from Alexander the Great and the Ptolemies to Speke, Burton, Gordon, Grant, Stanley, Baker, the sheiks and the slave traders.

His complaints of discomfort – complaints rarely voiced in his young adventurer-hunter days – speak unwittingly of his advancing years. His comment on the rest-house at Shambe where their overland journey commenced, was largely reserved for the *Anopholes* mosquitoes '. . . which came in great battalions and drove us to bed under the nets in quick time. The rest-house is said to contain a mosquito-proof room. It is correctly named, for mosquitoes enter in swarms, and the sleeping-chamber seems quite proof against them getting out again. These vicious little creatures were so cunning and swift in their movements, that often, when you put your hand outside the net for a cup of soup, several would dive in as you withdrew it . . .

'Then followed the usual hunt for the electric lamp with one hand and the other ready for use as a killer. You must creep all round the inside of the net to slay the intruder, or you will have no rest at night. In doing so a man gets so annoyed and intense in the pursuit of the last one that he generally upsets the soup in the bed. Raoul used to be overjoyed when this happened to me, but, when he upset his soup and I chuckled, he would remark that he saw nothing funny in spending the night on a small mountain of towels that bobbed up just where his back fitted.'

During the first night there the agony of the mosquitoes was compounded by the noise outside. 'Both donkeys were tied up with chains round the iron pillars of the rest-house and these they clanked at intervals when they were not roaring defiance at other gentlemen mokes of bellicose disposition. What was infinitely worse was the continuous screech and fighting of large fruit bats concealed in the thatched roof. This continued in an uninterrupted way from sunset until dawn. Also the natives started singing and dancing to a tom-tom about 100 yards away, and kept it up till midnight. At regular intervals pi-dogs howled in chorus, hippopotami grunted out on the lagoon, and shrieking spur-winged plover yelled in unison as they settled on the beach some twenty yards away. It was a perfect pandemonium, and, to make it worse, Raoul said next morning that he had had a lovely night and was feeling particularly fresh and good.'[9]

Now, with guide, cook and porters, mules and donkeys, they began their trek to a part of the interior where the natives had unusual culinary tastes. 'Their favourite dish is the small breed of dog . . . pot-bellied tykes of a type found in no other part of Africa . . . To the stranger it comes, and after regarding you for a few moments of careful inspection it considers whether you are worth knowing or not. Its funny little wrinkled forehead puckers as it looks at you, with head cocked on one side. It is friendly at all times, unlike the usual pi-dog, and regards man with a spirit of adoption if it likes him. Like its master, in the presence game, it is bold and savage, in spite of its diminutive size . . . The Niam-Niam, like all savages, has no sentimental interest in his dog, but keeps it purely for utilitarian purposes. He lavishes much care on it until it is really fat, and then it goes into his very hungry tum-tum . . . Lady Helen Brocklehurst has ventured on the experiment of introducing the breed to England.[10] If it stands our climate this new dog will be very popular.'[11]

They pushed into Dinka country, where Raoul went in pursuit of the antelope known as Mrs Gray's kob which he found in waist-high swamps, infested with electric eels. He stalked and shot one at 150 yards but in such adverse conditions that he 'was red from bites of mosquitoes, bloody from grass-cuts, and quite exhausted when he staggered into camp . . . He lay without moving for some minutes, but a sip of brandy and the smell of his delicious onions cooking made him sit up and take notice. Youth is buoyant,' adds Johnny, 'and in an hour he was quite himself again, and playing *Pagliacci* on the mouth-organ.'[12]

On 30 January Raoul got a buffalo, and Johnny wrote to Frank Wallace that 'Raoul is as good a hunter and shot as ever I saw. I gave him the first shot at a buffalo which he knocked down at 250 yards. [The buffalo] was inclined to be nasty so our noble followers took to the trees. Raoul and I stalked up to him and Raoul killed him dead with a spine shot. Afterwards I saw [Raoul] didn't want any looking after.'[13] Raoul also possessed the Millais youthful resilience and fortitude, which, in his father, was gradually ebbing. He endured considerable hardship on his hunting forays and, at one point, was close to unconsciousness from thirst. ('I thought I would have to shoot a hartebeeste or a waterbuck simply to drink the blood.')

On 1 February they were off at dawn, reaching two hours later a small Dinka camp in the forest, where Johnny was attacked by one of the severe migraines with which the family are afflicted. (Sir John Millais was a sufferer and so is Raoul.) Two days later Johnny wrote in his diary that 'we had to hold court on two porters. It appeared that one, Billy, the Bari, was struck on the back by Nathaniel, the Niam-Niam, as he passed on the way to water. Whereupon the Bari, using his ebony stick, hit the cannibal such

Raoul Millais: *Mrs Gray's Kob* and (*below*)
Giant Eland.

a welt in the stomach that it made a lump like a cricket ball. These two had been snarling at each other for some time, so on arrival at Rumbek we exchanged our four Bari porters for Niam-Niam men, and all was peace.'[14]

There they 'noticed tracks of the motor-cars which carried Lord Allenby and the Sirdar to Shambe . . . and swarms of Dinka chiefs [who were] all returning to their homes after the reception. Such an orgy of handshaking I never saw in my life. I felt quite sorry for the Prince of Wales, who has to do this kind of thing every day . . . One man, wearing a pair of trousers round his neck, approached Raoul at a turn of the path. It was a fearful moment. Should he don his breeks first and shake hands afterwards, or declare his savage nudity to a shocked world? He was a man of action and chose a middle course. As he ran forward, he got one leg into the trousers, and kept trying to run and insert the other limb into the trammels of civilization. Alas! it was a miserable failure, for he came a cropper right in front of the white chief, but lifted one feeble hand in friendship whilst in the other he held the recalcitrant pants in their proper position.'[15]

In discussing Dinka attitudes Johnny wrote that 'unless with their cattle or at war . . . they are lethargic and inefficient in every way.' That characteristic rendered the tribesmen more or less useless to the slave-traders; but the British District Commissioners got the better of them. One, Captain Kidd, told Johnny that when he wanted labour to build a garrison village and a road, at first the chiefs declined to provide it. Then they said they would try, but no work force turned up. So Kidd had the police confiscate a few head of cattle from each Dinka chief, whereupon the men were immediately forthcoming – and the cattle returned. 'Now the Dinka men came in regularly as required at the various stations, because they know Englishmen *do not bluff*. If my reader is a Communist or Labour member of Parliament,' ventured high-Tory Johnny, 'he will say that this is scandalous. But then he does not know or understand the native mind.'[16]

After dining with the Mamur, the headman of Rumbek, both father and son went down with dysentery. They journeyed on, however, now in search of eland and hartebeest. Raoul recovered after a few days, but Johnny's condition grew worse, though not quite bad enough to prevent him making diary entries. 'February 12 – started at 5 a.m. and had a long five hours march. There was no sign of game and I felt desperately ill. Raoul was very anxious about me and, like a good fellow, came many times in the night to attend me. It is a bad thing to be ill here without milk, which is the only cure for dysentery. Here we are, 1,000 miles from civilization and no doctor except the Syrian at Rumbek who, although a good fellow, knows about as much of medicine as I do. It was a bad look-out, and I feared I should break down before we reached the elands.'[17]

That did not stop him next morning from writing a diatribe against the Nile bees. 'French bees are excitable and Italian bees regular hot-heads and vicious to handle, but when you get to the Nile valley these insects are veritable little demons of anger. There are many instances of men being driven off their boats on the Nile, and more than one instance of men being killed or drowned in trying to evade the hostility of a big swarm. As they come and settle on you their voices break into a shrill angry scream, and it requires some nerve to remain quiescent as they crawl all over your head and neck. As Schweinfurth remarks, the charge of a buffalo or lion is less to be feared than a battle with African bees.'[18]

'I do not like the prospect of another day,' recorded Raoul on the same day, 'but it must be faced. Poor Dad was very sick all last night, and this morning I have given him more castor-oil, which cannot do harm and may do good.' But milk was what Johnny needed and milk was what they could not find.

On 15 February 'a shy, thin, long-legged Dinka' arrived at the camp, who turned out to be the 'one real hunter of Bahr-el-ghazal'. The following day, guided by this man,

Raoul Millais: *Buffalo looking Back*.

Raoul got his eland and, 'having removed the head and neck skin, we had a long hot walk back to camp. We had been going seven hours without a halt, and dad's delight at my success made African hunting the joy of existence.'[19] Raoul then turned his attention to buffalo and there was meat for all. He also took time off to cut some drawings of big game into the wall of a hut. (Up to as much as sixty years later he was to receive photographs of them from travellers. They told him the government had had them encased in glass.)

They retraced their steps on the 21st – Johnny on a litter – to Rembek, where Raoul secured fresh milk, and next morning Johnny's dysentery had gone. Within forty-eight hours, however, he contracted blackwater fever and '. . . I was in bed again with chattering teeth and shivering under four blankets.' The Syrian doctor filled him with quinine and four days later he was in pursuit of white-eared kob, only to be thwarted by bees which 'alighted on me in hundreds, swarming all over the exposed parts of my body, even looking for moisture round my lips. I had to keep shaking my head to keep them out of my eyes, and every moment I feared some irritable specimen would start an attack . . . There must have been at least a million bees since the swarm took several minutes to halt and pass, and no words can express my joy when I saw the end of the stream and the last of these little tormentors fade away.' He stalked on to secure his kob, '. . . but white ants got at it [the precious head] during the night and it was completely destroyed. The rapidity with which these pests work is amazing.'[20]

In the forest beyond, a tree awoke in him his gardener's aesthetic sensitivities. 'We suddenly came on the most lovely African tree in flower I have ever seen. It was a species of *Cassia*, with very long racemes of golden-yellow flowers . . . the whole looked like a golden-yellow wistaria in bloom. Luckily enough I was able to gather some long pods

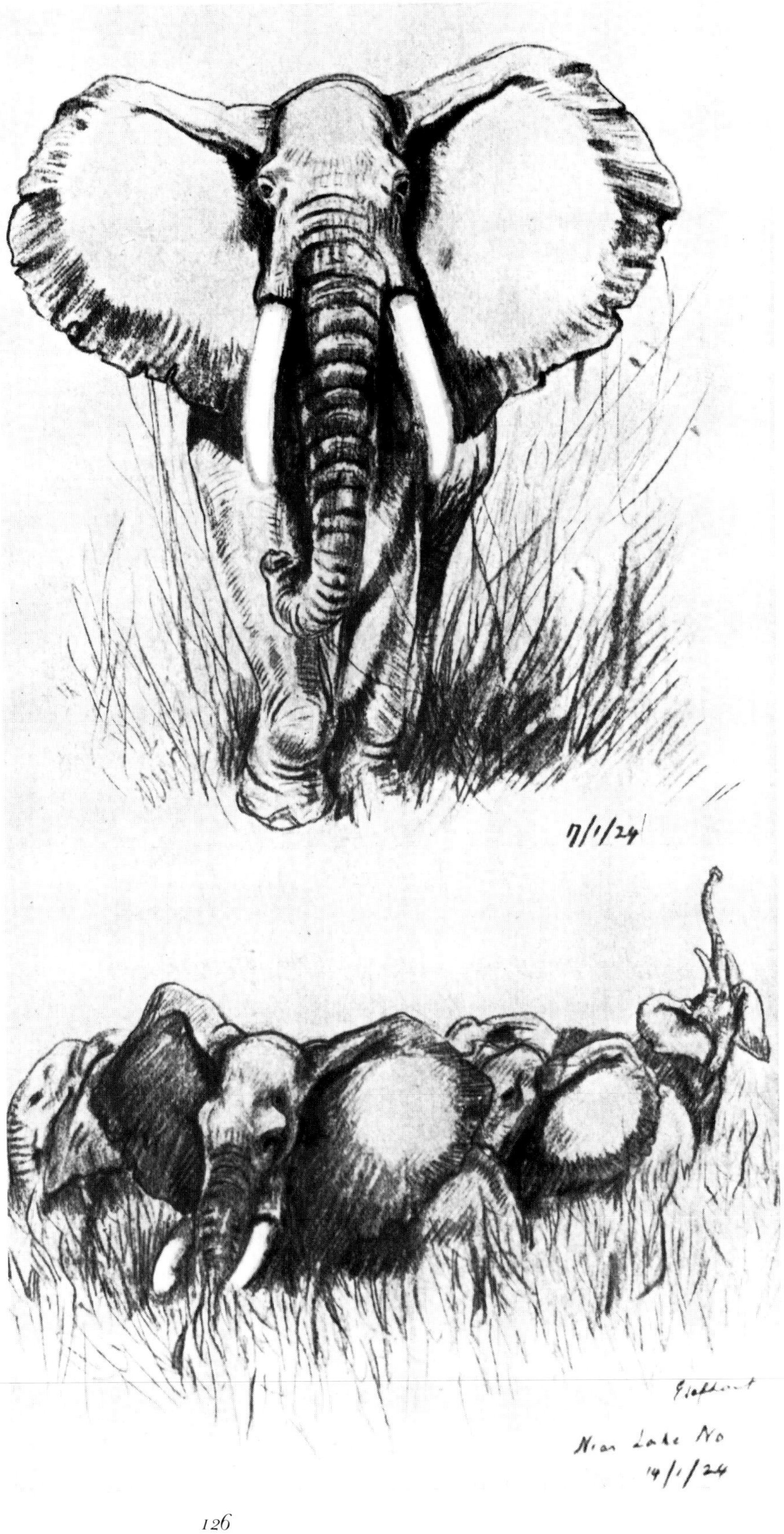

Raoul Millais: *Elephant*
Studies near Lake No.

7/1/24

Near Lake No
14/1/24

containing ripe seed of this tree, and have sent them, amongst other places, to Kew and the South African Botanic Gardens.'[21]

Never in Raoul's life did he learn so much from his father as he did during those Sudan weeks early in 1924. 'Father was not one to give advice directly, but one night over the camp fire he said "I suppose I have met people in all walks of life and I have remained on the outside looking in. I think my best two friends have been a duke and a shoe-maker in the Orkneys. Never judge a man because of his position or the circumstances in which he has been born. Never feel you are subservient to anyone and never feel you are superior to anyone. Never be impressed because a man has a handle to his name, whether inherited or bought or earned. Similarly never judge a man who has been born in a slum and has had little opportunity to improve his status. Judge him objectively, judge him as an individual human being." '

And so died the embers of another camp fire; so dawned another African day. Their next stop was at Gow on the west bank of the river Lao. There Captain Richards (commanding a company of the Equatorial Rifles) and the District Commissioner, Captain Kidd, and their servants looked after the Millais' beautifully. There was fishing and tennis and an exhibition dance by Achole tribesmen of which 'the wonder . . . was the performance of a perfect little Venus who knew all about jazz shakes and muscle ripples. She stood quite still, with her back towards us, and shivered the whole of the body muscles in a continuous quiver.' Johnny was informed that 'there are no women in the world who can do the stand-pat muscle ripple like the Achole women' and added that 'all other women I have seen doing it were mere amateurs.'

The following day, that alluring dancer, the wife of a corporal, was in trouble. An anonymous sergeant (who possessed no fewer than three wives of his own) put the corporal on guard duty and made love to her. At the subsequent court-martial the sergeant was reduced to the ranks. 'Captain Richards was much distressed about it, as it lost him one of his best men.'[22]

While Johnny's blackwater fever bouts kept him low, early March found Raoul after buffalo and tiang (a hartebeest-like antelope) of which he bagged three (which '. . . was just what I wanted as we were out of meat and the porters hungry.')

On 7 March they were ready to board the steamer for Khartoum at Shambe, where, 'just before dawn the sweet little white-throated swallows begin to sing on the veranda, and you hear the constant chink of the little bells on the feet of the women passing the house on the way to the river. The procession lasts for an hour, and every woman comes to the same spot to fill her gourd and gossip awhile. Then, as the light comes up the finest singer in this part of Africa, the large widow wagtail, pays you a visit and carols blithely like any canary in bursts of song. From 7 onwards to 11 a.m. there is a procession of village dogs to the water. They never venture in, and keep a sharp look-out for crocodiles.'[23]

Johnny's comment on the return river journey was reserved for condemnation of the reports he received on 'what big-game shooting should not be'. He tells how, at about that time, 'six foreigners hired one of the river steamers to shoot game on the Upper Nile. The cost of the entire outfit, including tent, fitments, provisions, and drink (an immense item) was £5,700 for two months . . . The greater part of the vessel was enclosed in mosquito-proof netting, and the whole ship was fitted up like a floating public-house.' The 'hunters' fired indiscriminately from the deck at any large mammals they saw and 'the result of the "big-game" expedition,' said Johnny, 'was one hundred odd heads of the various antelopes, mostly immatures. Needless to say these people will not be allowed in Sudan again . . . Captain Brocklehurst informed me that he found that some Italian ruffians had shot ten cow and immature elephants . . . He saw the dead carcases. Of course these misdeeds were not known until the offenders had left the country.'[24] Johnny elaborated on this theme in a letter to Frank Wallace. '. . . Lions shot from the deck of a steamer and a big herd of elephants driven by 200 natives on to a peninsula from which they could not escape. It makes me sick to hear this sort of thing called big-game hunting.'[25]

He was now in a very bad way again from the blackwater fever. ('Father just alive,' noted Raoul. 'Down to 8 stone. Normally 14 stone.') On board he made friends with a generous American who put his cool state room at his disposal, but it was necessary to carry him all the way from the dockside at Khartoum to a bed in the Civil Hospital. There, fortunately he had the services of Dr Hodson, 'the best doctor in all Africa – what he does not know of tropical diseases and their cure is not worth knowing. I shall always owe him a debt of gratitude for the rapidity and skill by which he cured me. It is a great misfortune for Khartoum and district that this excellent man and super-skilled practitioner has now finished his work there . . .'[26]

Johnny and Raoul sailed, homeward bound, from Port Sudan on 26 March 1924, in the *Llandstephan Castle*. On board they found 'several Sussex friends, Colonel S. Clarke, Colonel G. Godman and Dame Alice Godman and her two daughters who were on their way home from Uganda, where . . . Colonel Clarke had secured trophies of Uganda kob, white rhinoceros and other good things for his fine collection of African mammals. My old friend Lord Egerton got off at Port Sudan, and went to hunt on the Dinder, taking with him our late excellent cook, Mahomed.'[27]

Father and son berthed at Genoa, whence they took the sleeper to Paris. There, the Louvre being closed, they spent the afternoon at the Tuileries. This was followed by a dinner – 'that could not have been surpassed at the Ritz with a bottle of the best champagne, for 40 francs (14s 6d) – a cinema, and so to bed.' Taking a newspaper next morning Johnny read a headline *Mr Lloyd George on the failures of Mr Asquith*, and concluded that 'in the wilds it is a rest to do without newspapers, and when we encountered them again in Paris the futility and pettiness of life were manifest.'

Far Away up the Nile concludes with a word for 'those splendid young men [in Sudan] and the great work they are doing for England. Although most of the country will ever remain in its primitive state the day will come when Sudan will enter on its era of prosperity. This will be due' he thought, 'not to any skill on the part of Home Governments, or the futile Foreign Office, but to the wise men at the head of affairs, taught in the school of Cromer and Kitchener, and those noble lads, who, left to themselves, have made good in spite of difficulty.' Imperialist Johnny was writing at Compton's Brow. 'The cuckoo has come and I look out on my lovely garden and see hundreds of magnolia flowers flaunting white against the azure sky . . . Here, alas, men sleep only in selfish rest, neither thinking nor caring for our pioneers. Like *Danny Boy* [the Empire-builders] must go, but the drones will stay. Still, those who have suffered and left stout hearts to carry on KNOW and UNDERSTAND what is being done for England by men of courage and patriotism.'[28]

The big game of Africa was behind him for ever. He turned to his garden and began studying and researching for his final book, *Magnolias*. He had just launched, too, into his career as a sculptor.

12

RAOUL TAKES UP THE REINS

Johnny never returned to Africa, though he yearned for it. 'I expect you are longing for Africa and the sunshine as I often do,' he wrote to Frank Wallace. 'As one gets older one hates the coldness and darkness of winter more and more. I would not stop here from November to April if I had some "splosh". Those warm pellucid nights by the camp fire! How I long for them! But the royal exchequer being in an impoverished position I content myself with reading Baldwin's *African Hunting*, which I do every January. Anyway, it takes one back in imagination! . . .'[1] Like so many fathers he pictured in his son a projection of himself; in Raoul's vigour and hunter-instinct he saw a real prospect of another long lease for the Millais adventurer spirit. Through Raoul's surrogate, more than through Baldwin's prose, Johnny himself could adventure in southern climes again. He challenged his son to travel to Portuguese West Africa, to Angola, to bring back a head of the remote giant sable antelope. To conclude the bargain he gave him £250 for the trip. Though more condensed the hazards of that were to prove as dramatic as those of Sudan.

Raoul was the only Englishman aboard the German ship that sailed from Southampton that day in 1925. Everyone was whispering about the Portuguese counterfeit banknote men who embarked at Lisbon. As for those few German passengers who engaged him in conversation their theme was one long apologetic rationalisation of their nation's part in the 1914–18 war. At the Angolan port of Luanda he had a glimpse of 'the most horrifying prison' and at Lobito – a port over which the bubonic plague hung heavily – another of the slave market. At Lobito he signed up his boys for the expedition. His head boy was to be distinguished by a black velvet dinner jacket, a pair of army boots for a necklace and a yellow Dunlop tube box for a hat.

Their trek from the railhead to the sable country was heralded by a storm, of which Raoul gives a most graphic description. 'The Ironstone mountains rose from the plain like immense metal molehills. There had been ominous rumblings in the distance all afternoon and now they seemed to be louder and nearer. The air was deadly still as though the world was waiting for the crack of doom. Black darkness descended on us. I had three Chimbundra boys with me and I saw the naked fear in their eyes. We had been searching for kudu. The boys told me the kudu lived in the sparse vegetation growing between the great red-rusty iron rocks. And then it happened. There was a shaft of lightning, like a jagged white spear followed almost simultaneously by a deafening explosion. It felt as if we were in the centre of the stage. I quickly put my rifle on the ground and stepped away from it . . .

'The whole scene was lit by continuous flashes. White hot shafts bounced from rock to rock. They darted all around our feet; it did not seem possible we could survive. Now we were flat on our faces. The noise was deafening and the smell of hot metal overpowering. I thought of Dante's inferno; it seemed it would never end. Then came the rain – at first a few heavy drops, but soon it was as though we were under Niagara falls. Then a rushing spate of water descended, bringing with it an avalanche of rocks, and I just managed to grab my rifle before it was swept away. After what seemed an eternity, the storm appeared to be moving away; the blackness gradually dispersed, leaving us enshrouded in a vivid Prussian blue light. There was an overpowering smell of sulphur . . .'

Often he found the villages deserted, their inhabitants fleeing from visits by the dreaded Portuguese. Raoul was on the side of the Africans. When he had been in Sudan with his father, and here again in Angola, the inherent goodness of the natives convinced him that, overall, 'natural religion' and 'natural law' had served mankind considerably better than Christianity. ('The people . . . had a code of honour laid down by their tribes far superior to that which our so-called civilisation has today. They would never think of stealing or playing a dirty trick on their fellow-tribesmen . . . The missionaries, with the best of intentions and great self-sacrifice have done irreparable damage.')

None of the giant sable heads he saw during the first week were quite good enough, so he contented himself with shooting boar and waterbuck for food. At last, after a very long trek in gruelling heat he secured two sable bulls. As vividly he remembers parting with his only medicine, a bottle of aspirin. He gave it to a man lying in agony in a hut, apparently dying of gangrene. A tree had fallen on him and shattered his thigh.

It was on the journey back to the coast that the leading melodrama of the expedition took place. He found himself faced by a police sergeant accompanied by 'a rabble of six other men'. He was accused of poaching. In the ensuing argument one of his boys was struck on the head with a rifle butt. Raoul, towering six feet four over the assailant, seized his rifle and threw him in the river. The sergeant and his party scattered.

That, however, was not the end of the matter. The police instructed him to report to the District Commissioner. The Governor-General had ordered his arrest, the alleged offence being once again that he had taken game without a licence. But to the great annoyance of the DC Raoul produced a perfectly valid permit. Nevertheless he was ordered to pay a fine of the equivalent of £200. He refused. Well, £150? . . . £100? . . . £50? No, still he refused, and was at last freed, though with very ill grace. He was told by a railway engineer, the only Englishman then in the country, 'if they put you in gaol, for God's sake shoot your way out. You would never be seen again!'

He learned later from the Foreign Office that the whole trouble stemmed from his failure to bring the hunter's customary 'present' for the Portuguese authorities on arrival in the colony. Meanwhile he contracted both typhoid and dysentery and lay delirious in Lobito for fortnight before embarking for home.

He was astonished to find aboard the Union Castle ship that notorious gang of Portuguese forgers who had shared the second leg of the journey from Southampton with him. But their time in the sun was soon up. The police were waiting for them at Lisbon. As for Raoul, when his mother met him at Southampton he looked the very ghost of the fit young man who had set out 2½ months before. He spent the next ten days in the hospital for tropical diseases.

The following April he married his first wife, a Canadian girl, Clare Macdonell, (of the family of engineers of that name.) They set up house near Malmesbury in Wiltshire, in the middle of the Duke of Beaufort's hunt country, where Raoul – now, above all, an equestrian artist – embarked on his career as a portraitist of horsemen and women.

For the most nostalgic glimpses of the winter of Johnny's life we must turn to Frank Wallace compiling his reminiscences in *Happier Years* and *A Highland Gathering*, and referring to the pile of letters he had received from the older man over the years. First there was advice sought by, and given to, Wallace on art. In Johnny's estimation '. . . we are always at

Raoul in Angola with one of the giant sable antelope heads he secured.

Raoul's certificate to show that he crossed the Equator in the German ship *Walfisch*, bound for Angola in 1925.

school from the cradle to the grave. If we are good judges and subject to no illusions there is always so much still to be done and so little time in which to do it. If Methuselah had been an animal painter he might have been a successful one, but the ordinary life of one man is much too short. He has just learned a bit of his lesson and the great reaper steps in and claims him.'[2]

Wallace – himself one of the most distinguished animal artists of this century – went on to render his own appraisal of Johnny's work. '. . . One of the best draughtsmen of deer, both red and roe (and Wolf always said that the red stag was one of the most difficult of all animals to draw) was Johnny Millais. Some of his sketches in *British Deer and Their Horns* are as good as any attempted. This volume and *A Breath from the Veldt* contain some of his best work. He was not so good a colourist as a draughtsman, which is not uncommon, but in pen-and-ink work he was a master.'[3]

As his father had done in the reign of Queen Victoria and his son Raoul was to do in that of Queen Elizabeth, so Johnny condemned pretentiousness in art. But by the 1920s he doubted there was any voice in opposition to the post-war trend sufficiently powerful and influential to be heard. 'My father was a giant, both in work, brain-power and human charm,' he wrote to Wallace. 'His love for his fellow-creatures, Nature and art were all on the highest scale, and I often wish he were still alive today, if only to combat . . and he would do, as he had the courage . . the evil influences in modern art which dominate even for their little day certain schools of thought. I fear there is no one strong enough or bold enough to take his place.'[4]

Among numerous other activities Johnny continued his chairmanship of the Shikar Club, the big-game hunters' association, which he and Lord Lonsdale had founded thirty years before. Meanwhile, his departure into sculpture was giving him great pleasure and excitement, though funds were short for casting. 'The blackcock group is back and isn't so bad,' Wallace heard. 'I am having it cast in coloured synthetic stone – a new thing – which I fancy will be very attractive if it can be done as I hope. I thought that the reproduction of a sea trout that I did for the sea-eagle group wonderful, even better than bronze, such quality and finish. I think there is a future in this method. The big golden eagle group is in hand and will cost over £600, so I cannot put the sea eagle group in hand till I have some more luck and that in the present depressed state of all finance is not a very rosy outlook . . .'

And later: 'Have nearly finished my big group of sea eagles (six months work) and now am faced with sorrow and a longing for cash to put it in bronze. I think it is the best thing I have ever done, but then one just looks at it, stares and finds on completion one has fallen in the gutter as usual! Bad or good bronze at any rate lives for 50,000 years, and the judgement of posterity is – despite its futility to help the present – perhaps the only verdict. Some day the public taste may give up – and go and return to sanity. If I was a good ghost I would haunt that low imposter for insulting the memory of a decent workman.'[5]

Wallace hands down more charming vignettes from Johnny's last years, revealing him in many other dimensions. 'I remember him rushing up to me one day exclaiming "have you read *The Life of Benvenuto Cellini*? By Jove! It's the finest thing I've ever seen. What a scoundrel he was, but he was a great man. I should like to write my life . . ." Then with a twinkle in his eyes, those beautiful blue eyes which saw everything with photographic accuracy – ". . . to be published after my death." Benvenuto's life and *The Story of San Michele* he thought two of the most interesting books ever written.'

Johnny imagined he had a work of fiction in him, too. 'You seem to be the same as me about movies,' he confided to Wallace. 'There is much rubbish, but much good and dramatic stuff, which is absorbing when true to life. The Italian ones were splendid before the war, but I have seen no good ones since. I am thinking seriously of writing a novel, adaptable to the films when I get the time. It could be both interesting and, perhaps, remunerative . . .

'My new dining-room is nearly finished. The C girls taught me tonight to dance the foxtrot, so look out for me at the Hammersmith Palais de Danse as a high-kicker. I saw Pauline Frederick in *Madame X*. She is some actress, but too much sob stuff in it. *The Last Command* is about the best of anything I have ever seen. Quite magnificent. It gripped me in its true human intensity and power of suffering. I also thought *Seventh Heaven* very wonderful in its superb acting.'[6]

Wallace wrote of a first-class red deer he secured, and Johnny, always full of hunter's fellow-feeling, replied, 'I rejoice with you that you have at last killed a real Muckle Hart. It must be a beauty. I know no one who would appreciate it more. One sad thing is, like catching a 50-pound salmon, you are not likely to kill a better. I got five at Ardverikie in two days, one royal but no great shakes . . . Lord David Kennedy shot a magnificent head at Ardverikie [Ben Alder]. When he was dying almost the last thing he said to his daughter was "give that head in the dining room to Johnny Millais. He is the only man who ever admired it, or took any interest in it" . . .'[7] (It now hangs in Raoul's studio.)

Johnny was very near the end of the road himself when he wrote 'I am working hard at my last book *The Courtship of Birds*, a very difficult task. I don't know if any publisher will ever take it. So many illustrations. But I am keen on it, as the subject is new . . .' It was never published. He died on 24 March, 1931.[8] It was the blackwater fever of the Sudan that finally had the better of him.

Bertha Collin in her biography of her father, John Hornung (a close Horsham neighbour of the Millais'), described Johnny as 'a rather bohemian character,'[9] simply because he was an artist. The label was entirely inappropriate. Fundamentally, Johnny's lifestyle,

Raoul Millais: *Lord Mountgarret with the North York and Ainsty hounds.*

Raoul Millais: *George Earle*, of Baggrave Hall, Melton Mowbray, and (*below*) *Margery Earle*.

like that of his father, the PRA, was that of a conventional country gentleman. Raoul – notwithstanding his fine bearing, short hair, trim moustache and honest-to-goodness Anglo-Saxon presence – experienced the same pigeon-holing attitude almost from the moment he set forth on his career as a sporting artist.

'During the period between the wars,' he says, 'the British sporting fraternity – by which I mean those who spent their lives huntin', shootin', fishin' and racin', were apt to judge their fellow-men, not only by their appearance but also by what they did. For instance if a man occupied his time with those four sports and had been to a public school as well, they knew in exactly which pigeon-hole to place him. With a sigh of relief they decided there was no problem. But should he also paint, that was very disturbing. There must be something odd here and he should be welcomed with caution, if not suspicion. All my life I have at first been considered an enigma. To be a painter was, to them, almost as suspect as being on the stage.'

He goes on to relate a memory from the late '20s when he was commissioned to paint a certain Master of hounds surrounded by some favourites from the pack. Raoul was invited, at the same time, to have a day with the hunt in question. When it was announced that a horse called Badger was earmarked for him he heard one of the daughters of the house give a quick intake of breath and whisper 'oh no!'. Next morning Badger was duly produced and (Raoul goes on), 'while I was making mental notes for the picture I noticed two rather overfed purple-faced gentlemen, sitting on their horses behind me. "D'you hear Master's goin' to be painted? said the first. The second had indeed heard: "Yes, fellah called Raoul Millais. Frenchman I s'pose. Goes foxhuntin', they say." To which the other replied: "Oh dear, well he can't be a very good painter, can he?" The first purple face then took a closer look at Raoul's horse. "I say, isn't that old Badger? I hope that young fellah knows what he's in for." '

The upshot was that, while hounds gave their followers one of the best runs of the season, a five-mile point with a variety of daunting obstacles in between, Badger never put a foot wrong, and the artist stayed firmly in the saddle, greatly enjoying himself. At dinner that evening his host raised his glass towards Raoul: 'That horse usually bucks like an unbroken mustang; he's had everyone off since I bought him, but we've kept him because he's such a marvellous performer across country.' Raoul replied that it was just as well he didn't know, 'otherwise I'd almost certainly have communicated my anxiety to him, which would've started him off.'

Raoul clearly had a way with buckers; a few years later, he went through a similar experience with that great Quorn character, George Earle, of Baggrave Hall, Melton Mowbray, a renowned practical joker, whose equestrian portrait, together with that of his wife, Margery, Raoul travelled over to paint. Next morning, festooned in artist's equipment he rode out behind Earle to make some sketches at the chosen spot. It was a hot day and, while Earle led at a spanking trot, Raoul, thus accoutred, took his horse at a walk.

He noticed that Earle looked back once or twice, a question-mark on his face. This is how he concludes the story: 'At lunch Margery Earle said "I can't stand this any longer – Now own up, George!" My host looked a bit shamefaced as he explained: "I must apologise. I thought I'd have a bit of fun with you. That horse has never left the stable yard without bucking – There's no competition to ride him at exercise, I can tell you. I don't know what came over him this morning." ' Raoul had a caustic reply to that: 'Nor do I – I should get the vet to have a look at him, if I were you!'

He tells how he 'managed to persuade the tax man that to keep three horses, and pay a groom's wages and a hunt subscription were essential to my profession as a painter, which indeed they were. So the proceeds from my pictures made enough money to buy and keep horses.' In 1936 he held a one-man show of fifty of his pictures in London.

In three days it had sold out with enough orders to last him many years. That rewarding period with Frank Calderon – under whose tuition he had helped carry out autopsies on horses and cows, in order, like Stubbs to learn the animals' anatomy through and through – was paying off. Raoul achieved a three-dimensional rendering of the horses he painted every time, and the commissions he received took him all over foxhunting Britain and Ireland.

Among the many amusing incidents recalled from his Irish hunting visits was the occasion on which a black hireling was brought from Cork city to a United hunt meet for him, and the animal's boy attendant asking 'Wad ye kindly have him back by tree o'clock, the boss says, as we've an important funeral comin' up and he's wanted for the hearse.' Then there was the time when, looking for a good buy, Raoul was offered 'a veritable woolly bear of a horse' and was told it was 'the greatest lepper in the south of Ireland.' He tried him on a day's hunting and, after many an anxious moment at the obstacles, discovered from a follower who happened to be well acquainted with the animal that it had never jumped before.

A fine judge of a horse, he owned a succession of useful hunters. He especially recalls a grey he spotted, among others, on an Irish mountain which he bought for £120. 'I don't remember ever being so taken with a horse before or since, unless it was the first time I saw Nijinsky, over forty years later. He was a four-year-old, 17 hands . . . I got him home and found he had a mouth like silk and was a great natural jumper. Greyman carried me for three seasons without falling. I was offered very large sums of money for him, but no money could ever have bought him.

'There is a sad ending to this story. In the late summer after his third season I went out after breakfast to see if the horses were all right. There had been a severe thunderstorm during the night. To my horror I saw Greyman lying in the entrance of the shed in the corner of the field. He was stone dead. I'm afraid I unashamedly sat down and cried.

Raoul Millais: *The Countess of Feversham.*

PLATE 9   *Major Cuthbert Fitzherbert, Coldstream Guards, Pirbright, 1943.*
Nicholas Fitzherbert comments that this painting by Raoul Millais is
'a brilliant likeness of my father'.

PLATE 10
Summer Morning,
by Raoul Millais,
c.1960.

PLATE 11   *The Queen arriving at Ascot Racecourse*, 1977 (top) and
Mrs Corriat and her daughters, 1952, by Raoul Millais.

Raoul in the 1930s at his home, Farleaze, near Malmesbury.

Eventually the vet came. His verdict was "Ah yes, lightning." He took a knife and split the coat from ears to tail. Under the skin it was black as coal. "You see?" he said.'

Then there was Greyskin which Raoul purchased for £35 from a friend, Dick Howell, who had been declared bankrupt and was selling up. Greyskin had won twenty out of the twenty-two point-to-point races for which his friend had entered him; but Raoul, though warned that he had 'a mouth like steel', was advised to bridle him with nothing but a snaffle. In fact, he hunted Greyskin more or less successfully in a Balding gag, and 'although he frightened me to death, we had many happy days together.' That was until the horse put his foot in a rabbit-hole at full gallop and turned two somersaults. 'Greyskin of course was quite unscathed, while I was carted off on a gate. I was found to have broken a bone in my neck, cracked my shoulder and dislocated my spine. The doctor put me in a stiff plaster collar, sat me in a wheel chair and told me I'd never ride again.'

However, following some clever manipulation by a Bristol osteopath he was soon up and about, and by the following season was once more in the saddle. But by 1939 the neck had the better of him and his hunting days were over.

Notwithstanding his disability his last horses stayed with him until the war. These included Garland, the best cross-country performer of all, which Raoul bought from Oliver Dixon. 'No money in the world could ever have persuaded me to part with him. He was like a pet dog and seemed to understand every word I said to him. I used to talk to him on the way home from hunting and he would twitch back his ears and nod his head. He used to get very over-excited sometimes before hounds broke away, but a word or two would always stop him prancing about . . .

Raoul Millais: *The Cubitt Boys at Michelgrove*, c1938. The Hon. Jeremy Cubitt is on
the left, with the Hon. Harry Cubitt (now Lord Ashcombe) on the right.

'The War Agricultural Committee were taking over a lot of farmland in the country
and wrote asking me to remove my friends. There was a possibility, too, that they might
be commandeered for the war. I decided the kindest thing would be to have them put
down. As I went to the gate to say goodbye Garland threw up his head and came galloping
up to me. It was one of the most dreadful moments of my life.

'What made it all the worse was that a young horse coper occupying the adjoining
land quickly turned himself into a farmer, and with a "reserved occupation" kept a number
of horses for the duration of hostilities. I went to Cheltenham races in 1947, and he came
up to me as bold as brass with his hand out: "Hullo, sir, still got any of those nice horses
you used to have?" I stared hard at him for a moment without a word, and walked past
him, leaving his hand hanging in the air. I was rather ashamed of myself afterwards.
One should make allowances for people.'

Every winter there was a skiing diversion in Italy, Switzerland or Austria. It was still
the day of the long ski, with nearly all climbing on skins. He witnessed the bottom fall
of a funicular at Kitzbuhel; he saw a mighty avalanche carried over his hotel; and he
was there in 1938 when Mussolini's daughter, Edda, Countess Ciano, went to open a
new funicular and the wind rocked the cable car so hard it could not be brought into
the arrival platform for half an hour. In the Italian Dolomites on the same visit when
he and his brother-in-law were the only Englishmen in their hotel, he remembered a flood
of Germans coming over – only for the good food. They were accompanied by SS officers
who saw that their compatriots did not commit the crime of eating until Hitler's mealtime
broadcasts were over. Raoul remarks that his luggage and clothes were cut open and

searched by the Germans while he was out skiing. But there was no one else in the mountains and Raoul and his brother-in-law 'had the most marvellous ten days skiing.'

The greatest sporting joy of his life, however, was neither hunting nor skiing. It was – as it had been for both his father and grandfather – deerstalking. It was a pursuit which, despite his permanent injuries, he was able (along with skiing) to resume after the war.

Meanwhile he bluffed his way into the Army without a medical. He secured a commission in the Scots Guards and had a brief career with the Guards Training Battalion at Pirbright camp in Surrey. After three months on the drill square and undergoing instruction in the handling and firing of the various small arms, Captain Millais was appointed weapon training officer. 'I also taught young officers to ride motor-bikes,' he adds, 'and there were many casualties!'

Later Raoul commanded the Scots Guards company protecting Rudolf Hess. The defecting Nazi leader was incarcerated in a Victorian house at nearby Mytchett, strongly encircled with barbed wire – the relatively large strength of the guard being determined after the Poles had promised to go to Britain and kill him. Raoul says 'I got to know Hess well, and after some time he talked freely about the war, Germany, Russia, etc. He spoke very good English and seemed to be the most unlikely Nazi. He was also a terrible hypochondriac. He told me he thought the Duke of Hamilton was head of the youth movement here and he was trying to contact him. I did several drawings of him. After I left there – having reported what I had heard from Hess – I was told he'd twice tried to commit suicide by jumping over the balcony from the first floor where his rooms

Raoul Millais: *Rudolf Hess at Mytchett*, 1943.

Kettle Drummer of the 9th Royal Lancers, (detail). Raoul Millais' brother-in-law,
Lt Colonel Ronald Macdonell, a 9th Lancer, went on to command the
regiment during the Second World War and was killed in Italy.

were. Each time he landed on his feet and broke his ankle. Having spent so many hours
in his company I have always regretted I did not visit him afterwards in Spandau . . .'

In 1943 Raoul was given a month's leave by his regiment to paint King George VI's
winners, Big Game and Sun Chariot. He took the pictures up to Buckingham Palace.
'His Majesty came in smoking a pipe. I talked to him for half an hour and was greatly
impressed by his charm. I had been told he would stammer but he never did so once
during our meeting. Most of the time we discussed fishing, shooting and big game hunting.
He and the Queen were taken up the Nile some years after father and I journeyed there –
by my friend Courtney Brocklehurst, the game warden of Sudan. They seemed to know
all about us. In 1982 the Queen Mother asked my wife, Kay, and me to shoot. Afterwards
she showed us photographs which she and the King took on their Nile trip. She remembered the names of all the tribes in South Sudan and all the District Commissioners.'

13

AUTUMN

For some people autumn is primarily the time of ecstatic orange and copper hues, for some it is the year's wistful phase, a tranquil overture to the drama of winter; for others it is the season of mellow fruitfulness. For Donne 'no spring nor summer beauty hath such grace as I have seen in one autumnal face'. If that face was a Highland hillside in October with a herd of red deer grazing, the stags roaring, the same sentiment might be true of the Millais men, grandfather, father and son. All have been passionately keen stalkers. The ecstasy of Raoul's first royal, shot as a boy of twelve, has been described. His account of 'the hummel in the glen', a simple experience enjoyed shortly after that, perhaps exemplifies even better his love of those wild hills.

Up at first light in an endeavour to bag some grouse before breakfast, in addition to his habitual sketchpad and pencil, he carried a .22 rifle because the uncle with whom he was staying feared that, after mid-September, the sound of a shotgun would unduly disturb the deer and drive them over the march. 'There is,' Raoul recalls, 'a mysterious atmosphere about that time of day, when all the world is waking and the ground itself seems to come alive . . . The grouse were beginning to set up an incessant chatter and I heard the whistle of a flock of golden plover passing over . . .'

Having accounted for a brace of grouse, he says, 'I was preparing to retrace my steps when I saw three young stags coming out of the peat hags straight towards me, followed by an enormous beast with no horns. I had never seen a hummel before. Although he was lagging behind a little I guessed they would all pass within ten yards of me. The three little stags walked slowly across the road without seeing me, though it was clear they sensed some lurking danger. The hummel stopped dead and stared hard into my face. I was very young in those days and was sorely tempted to take a shot at him with my .22. I am glad to say I resisted the temptation. It is a great experience to come face to face with a wild animal. Time seems to stand still as if the moment is frozen. After more than seventy years the scene is engraved on my mind as if it happened yesterday.'

Raoul's second wife, Kay, was a close friend of Clare, Duchess of Sutherland, and after the Second World War for fifteen consecutive years the Millais' stayed at the Sutherlands' Scottish home, Dunrobin Castle, while Raoul enjoyed the stalking and game shooting rights on the Duke's extensive Sutherland forests. The Millais' were also at liberty to fish on the Duke's beat on the Brora and Helmsdale. Raoul, who first met the Sutherlands at their English home, Sutton Place, Guildford (later bought by Paul Getty) provides an interesting psychological sketch of the Duke and a contrasting one of the Duchess.

'I always felt there was a sadness in Geordie Sutherland's nature. He seemed to feel he lacked communication with people and that, because of his social position, he must keep himself aloof. This was taken by many people as arrogance, the result of a superiority complex, which was very far from the truth. He had a fine aristocratic appearance and was born with a golden spoon in his mouth. He was the heir to a vast inheritance which was considered to be the greatest slice of luck that can come to any man. But I think it is a handicap, and if it comes at an early age it cuts a man off from reality and often prevents friendships with real people.

'His wife, Clare, was the best thing that ever happened to him. She was known as "the Pocket Venus" which was an apt description, and her attractive voice could have charmed ducks off a pond. Apart from these assets she had a very determined character, great efficiency and exceptional organising ability. Also she had impeccable taste and was an interior decorator second to none. Sometimes there were large numbers of guests at Dunrobin and Sutton Place, sometimes only two or three. Owing to her genius both houses ran as on oiled wheels.

'Geordie's head stalker, Hugh Mackay, is still alive [April 1988] and we telephone each other regularly. Like most of the old school of stalkers he is a great gentleman.' Raoul goes on to describe a day's sport with Hugh. 'The rutting season was well advanced and a stag had been roaring since dawn just above the lodge. We had a good look at him and decided he was a big young beast with long horns and a head which was likely to improve with the years. Hugh and I had had long discussions as to whether it was certain that if a stag, with a poor head, got the hinds his progeny would necessarily grow worse heads than those of a beast with a fine head. Hugh was quite sure that this one with a good head must be far and away the best bet.

'The mist was rolling down the hill in great white sheets and seemed to be thickening as we went up the burnside. The wonderful smell of bog myrtle and thyme rose round us. It had been raining for several days and white cascades of water were spitting out of the steep hill face and bouncing across the rocks down to the burn, which was in heavy spate, the coffee-coloured water churning up mounds of froth and scum in the pools. At midday the mist still gave no sign of lifting and now it was raining again. We sat under the rocks and ate our sandwiches.

'Suddenly there was a roar from within the white blanket above us. It sounded very close. "It's nae use going up any higher," said Hugh, "we'd nae see ten yards in there. We should just wait here and watch if things improve." After a very long wait the mist cleared and 150 yards away we saw the stag rounding up the stragglers of his harem. "He's a royal," said Hugh, "we must leave him; aye, there are nae many stags aboot as good as that . . ." Suddenly a big stag came charging down the hill, scattering the hinds in all directions and crashing into the royal. The crack of their horns meeting echoed down the glen . . . The interloper had the short straight brow points which can do so much more damage than curled tines . . . The upshot was that the royal was smartly dismissed and the winner of the battle returned and began to round up the hinds for himself. "He's a big beast, I think he's a switch," said Hugh, "we'd better try a shot if he gives us a chance." '

Raoul takes up the narrative. 'At last the switch came down the slope towards us. "Tak him noo!" said Hugh . . . At first I thought I had missed. "You got him!" came Hugh's whisper. The stag walked away about twenty yards and toppled over dead. The hinds disappeared at a gallop into the mist. The stag was a very big beast in the prime of life with switch horns and small straight daggers for brow points. "He's best off the forest," remarked Hugh as he gralloched him. "We've done a good job today . . ." We were half-way home when I stopped and looked back. The mist had lifted a long way up the hill. We sat down and took out our glasses. There was the royal chasing up his hinds as if nothing had happened.'

Commenting on the immense strength of the red deer, Raoul relates how, on another occasion, at the end of an exhausting stalk he shot a big heavy stag which looked as though it lay stone dead. But when he and Mackay lifted it to move it into a more convenient

Raoul Millais: *Deer Studies*.

position for gralloching, without a second warning it jumped to its feet sending both men flying. But it only fled thirty yards before standing stock still, thus enabling Raoul to finish it off with a second shot.

His favourite hill on the Sutherland estate lay beside Loch Choire. One day, when the duke sent him up to stalk for an indefinite period there, the Choire head stalker – a jolly, red-faced and impeccably polite man, Murdo Macleod, who was in the habit of addressing guests as 'Himself' – greeted him in the gloaming with the enquiry 'Would

143

Raoul Millais: *Over the March.*

himself care to come and see the boys?' Raoul was completely mystified. 'Would himself kindly remain here behind this tree,' Macleod requested as they walked through the shrubbery towards his cottage. The evening was half drawn in now. 'He gave a low whistle and out of the cottage door came a figure in a long white dress carrying a bowl in each hand. It looked like a scene from Macbeth.

'She took a few steps then began to sing a melancholy song, which floated away into the forest. Out of the dark trees came two of the most beautiful stags I ever saw, a royal of perfect shape and a great wide 10-pointer. They were nervous and sensed there was something strange in the air, though Murdo and I stood like statues . . . The pale figure held out the bowls, while her sad song continued. When they had finished their supper they turned and wandered slowly away into the darkness of the trees . . .

'It appears that Murdo had found them as calves abandoned on the hill some years before and brought them home. His wife – who, poor lady, was not quite of this world – had brought them up on a bottle, and they became her "children". It was a most moving experience.' The other stalkers on the Sutherland estates enjoyed pulling Murdo's leg, and Raoul goes on to relate an incident in which Hugh Mackay, the Dunrobin stalker, pulled it rather too hard. Shortly after Raoul's introduction to 'the boys', he and Mackay were stalking at Loch Choire and, at the very end of a hitherto unsuccessful day, Raoul scored a right and left. 'We'll have some fun with Murdo when we get down the hill,' Mackay chuckled. 'I didn't realise what he was talking about,' says Raoul. 'We dragged the stags down to the pony path and left them in the bracken, Hugh chortling to himself all the way.

'Macleod, who had heard the shots, came briskly out of his cottage. "Bad news, I fear, Murdo," Mackay told him, pulling a long face and sighing. "We shot your 'boys'. It was all a terrible mistake." ' But when Raoul saw the colour drain from Macleod's face and the poor horrified man stumble towards the cottage, he could bear it no longer. He realised Macleod was heading to break the dreadful news to his wife. 'Murdo!' yelled Raoul, 'come back here, it was all a joke!' Whereupon Murdo turned slowly round and put in an angry rush at Mackay. The latter, however, had already made himself scarce.

From his huge fund of Highland anecdotes Raoul relates another from the day with an old stalker called Duncan who was afflicted with a game leg. After reaching the summit of the hill, following a long morning's climb, Raoul asked Duncan 'how's the leg?' To which Duncan replied, 'fine, fine, but it's nae sae guid doonhill.' After another hour's walk, they spotted a group of three stags, one of them on only three legs. They decided to try and get a shot at him. Separating itself from the others the three-legged one headed toward a steep-sided gulley which ended in what was known as the Black Loch. 'Aye, he'll be making for yon wood,' Duncan remarked. 'I've never been doon there, but they say it's an awfu' queer place.'

'I'll go down and try and cut him off,' replied Raoul. 'But you mustn't come, you couldn't make it on that leg.' So saying, Raoul began the perilous descent, slithering and sliding to reach the trees of the Black Loch into which he spotted the lame stag disappear. It was a dark place, of evil atmosphere, with dead birches propped against one another, great mounds topped with coarse grey grass and willows half alive in the black mire. 'The thicket gave a feeling of unreality and of menace . . . Suddenly I heard a twig crack. All around me there were stags rising from the ground. They didn't attempt to move away but stood staring at me as though I was a creature from another planet. Against the dark background they appeared to be almost white. All seemed to be in the last stages of emaciation . . . There must have been ten ghost-like apparitions staring at me, several just a few yards away.'

Raoul decided the kindest course would be to put these poor beasts – which had descended into the Black Loch, but could not get up again – out of their misery. He shot three. 'At first the others never moved and then they began to drift slowly away into the gloom and I could not bring myself to shoot any more. Inspecting the nearest body I found a bag of bones covered with what looked like hairy parchment. I could lift the whole carcass off the ground with ease . . .

'Duncan was waiting by the boat. "You look as if you've seen a ghost, sir," he said. I told him I'd seen ten. He listened attentively. "Aye, I've heard some strange tales of yon place," he said, "and I wud nae gang in there fer choice."

Raoul at Davos in the 1950s, with his sketch of skiers.

'I have stalked on many forests in Scotland and have shot a great many stags,' says Raoul. 'With very few exceptions I have found these mountain men, these professional Highland stalkers, to be among the finest examples of the human race.'

A year or two after the war Winston Churchill, very impressed by what he had seen of Raoul's equestrian paintings, invited him to paint a portrait of his great winner, Colonist. When he asked how much it would cost and Raoul said he would like to do it for nothing, Churchill wrote back: 'Dear Mr Millais, thank you; virtue, however, is its own reward, but art no!' Raoul then visited the great man at his home at Hyde Park Gardens, to find him, at 9.30 a.m. in bed with a glass of brandy in one hand, a cigar in the other, and 'attended by several people'. The following dialogue took place:

'Good morning, Mr Millais, you'll have a glass of brandy won't you?'

'No, thank you, Sir.'

'You'll have a cigar?'

'No thank you, Sir.'

'Are you ill?'

'No Sir, not at all, but I am not as strong as you.'

'Follow me!' instructed Churchill, getting out of bed and being helped into his dressing-gown and slippers. At the end of a passage, Raoul remembers being shown 'a terrible picture of a black horse in a brown loose-box,' and Churchill asking 'What do you think of that?'

'Not much, Sir.'

'You're quite right. I only showed it to you for size . . .' (Was it the work of the great man himself?)

Having started on Colonist, Raoul paid two visits to 10 Downing Street – Churchill was back in power by then – and found his client to be 'tremendously knowledgeable about painting and an extremely talented amateur painter himself.'

'You know what's the matter with my painting, don't you?' asked the Prime Minister.

'Yes, Sir, of course, you've never had the opportunity to learn to draw or go to an art school.'

'You are quite right,' said Churchill (though not looking at all pleased.) 'No-one has ever had the guts to say this to me before, but I know that's the trouble.'

The portrait of Colonist hangs over the drawing-room fireplace at Chartwell.

Among the other numerous celebrated racehorses Raoul went on to paint were Airborne, Tudor Minstrel, Court Martial, Nijinsky, Alycidon, Blue Peter and Blenheim. Another typical and most impressive Raoul Millais is his portrayal of Gordon Richards on the champion sprinter, Abernant. These were in the grand style, but he is also a master

Raoul Millais: *Holystone Fairy, Winner of the Barbican Plate, 1957.* The property of Major Nicholas Collin.

of the small oil picture which he paints with large brushes and woodcock pin feathers on thick unsized paper. One such picture in Jubilee year, 1977, was a presentation by the Ascot authorities to the Queen, of Her Majesty arriving at the course through the Golden Gates. (Raoul who refused the commission three times before finally succumbing, chuckles at the memory of spending one whole day painting the wrong gates.) Lord Abergavenny, the senior steward, asked him to be in attendance at the presentation ceremony. When the Queen turned to Raoul with 'I must find a very good place to hang this,' he suggested, in his self-effacing way, 'like a really dark passage at Sandringham, ma'am?'

Raoul moved into his present home, Westcote Manor, which lies on the side of a little Cotswold hamlet between Burford and Stow-on-the-Wold, in 1947. Originally a monastic dwelling, it was adjunct to Bruern abbey. The Millais spirit of adventure and creativeness welled up in Raoul the moment he first saw it. The army had occupied the building during the war and it was a wreck when he and his wife, Kay, bought it; but with the help of a German prisoner-of-war he re-built the ruined walls and added on. Most conveniently the ground contained a tall old tithe barn, which he promptly converted into a studio; the lovely 'old English' garden with its Italian figures was a hayfield when he moved in. The Millais' son Hesketh (Hexie) was born in 1952.

To Raoul, ruins never failed to present exciting challenges. In 1958 he and Kay bought another derelict place, Serafin, a property belonging to the Crichton-Stuart family, on a dominating mountain site close to the Mediterranen coast of Andalusia. Built by a prosperous pirate, Serafin, in 1720, it had mostly tumbled down or had at least fallen into a state of decay, all that was left being a wing, a tower, a donkey stable and a very primitive cottage. 'When,' says Raoul 'having negotiated the appalling so-called drive up to the property I got out of the car at the bedstead which served as a gate and heard the chorus of nightingales and golden orioles, that was it . . . My poor wife was almost in tears when she saw the house and no doubt regretted the day she married a lunatic, but she came to love it as much as we all did.'

His second son by his first marriage, Hugh (who was instrumental in finding the house), and his French wife, Suzy, did up the cottage and soon moved into it to give a hand resuscitating Serafin. Hugh is bilingual in Spanish and 'in fact', Raoul admits, 'this whole daunting project could never have been accomplished without him.' Led by Hugh the family scoured most of the secondhand shops and builders' yards of the town and villages of Andalusia for windows, doors, grilles and other artefacts. In an endeavour to offset the considerable expense of maintaining the property they started an avocado farm.

Raoul, the naturalist, was enchanted with the bird life of the place – apart from the ever-present beauty of the songbirds it lay on the raptors' direct migration route. The colour of the *flamenco*, the *corrida de toros*, the fruit groves, the market places and the fishing villages also delighted him and were excellent grist to the mill of his paintbox. There was to be a highly successful exhibition of his work at Marbella.

Smuggling was a major industry in Andalusia, much of the contraband going from Tangier to the rocky coast immediately below Serafin which had been built on a most strategic site by its founder, and at night the police-boats' machine gun fire was no uncommon sound. Dogs with panniers on their backs were trained to run the goods through the *sierras* to Ronda, their route passing very close to the house.

During the next twenty years the house was visited by innumerable friends and dozens of strangers. One one occasion, when the site was invaded by a film company, the director turned to Raoul with the words 'Mr Millais, I want you for my next picture. I've been looking all over Spain for you.' Raoul objected that he had never acted in his life. 'What

Raoul Millais: *The Three Matadors.*

sort of part did you have in mind?' he asked. 'Well,' began the director, 'there's this old beachcomber . . .' Politely and firmly Raoul turned down the offer.

One day during the 1960s the Millais' were invited, through an introduction of Hugh's, to a lunch party near Malaga. They arrived late to find some thirty guests seated at a long table in the open. 'I then noticed a grey-haired man at the end rise to his feet and beckon to me,' Raoul recalls. 'I went down and sat beside him in a place which he had kept empty. "I'm Ernest Hemingway," he announced, "may we have a nice long talk? I've read all your father's books – avidly from cover to cover. He has always been like a god to me. I admire him and Selous more than any of the other great hunters . . ."

'We talked for over an hour. Hemingway was a fascinating man, quiet and unassuming, quite unlike the aggressive bombastic character I had imagined. He had considerable knowledge of the big game of Africa and north America, and was, of course, a great *aficionado* of all the leading *toreros*. We discussed his towering book *Death in the Afternoon* (and, fortunately, I had read most of his other work.) Alas I never saw him again. He flew back to America soon after this and committed suicide, poor man . . .'

Hugh adds that Hemingway offered to buy and take to the United States the entire contents of Johnny Millais' Museum at Compton's Brow, which – with its 14,000 exhibits, including every known species of duck throughout the world and every African mammal and bird – comprised the largest and most comprehensive private natural history collection in the world. Owing to Hemingway's untimely death that never happened and the collection was broken up and distributed to many different museums and other collections. (The majority to the Perth museum, many to the Natural History Museum, South Kensington).

Fanny Millais, who married Johnny as long ago as 1897, was in her nineties by the heyday of Serafin. She had been at once a bold horsewoman, knowledgeable naturalist, gifted horticulturist and delicate water colourist. Raoul describes her as 'a most sweet and gentle character and one with rigid principles, but a woman who dealt with anything

Raoul Millais: *Fighting Bull Farm*.

unpleasant either by ignoring it or pushing it under the carpet.' One amusing tale he tells of her begins in the late 1940s when, already past seventy, she decided to take driving lessons. Her tutor, Mr Ireland, the head mechanic at the local Horsham garage, was a keen violinist who invariably played his instrument as she drove her Austin saloon. ('To calm his nerves,' says Raoul.) And while he gave his instructions – 'the brake, please, madam' or 'sound the 'ooter, if you will be so kind, madam' – the violin never left his chin.

Once when she braked hard into a cow occupying the middle of the road she managed to convince the farmer, with soft-voiced persuasion, that he was entirely at fault. The magistrates, to whom she was well known, let her off with a ten shillings fine when she rammed a bus going the wrong way up a one-way street in Petworth. Returning from a visit to Raoul at Westcote, then in her eighties, she got into a skid and somersaulted over a bank near Godalming. Afterwards she telephoned her son from home to say she had been 'quite warm and comfortable sitting on the roof. I had my cigarettes with me . . . Two charming lorry drivers came down the bank and towed me out. I'm going to write to their manager to tell him how kind they were, and ask him to increase their wages.'

She was eighty-seven when she was having trouble over PAYE in respect of her maid and gardener. By then *hors de combat* with rheumatism she was in the habit of holding court at Compton's Brow from her Elizabethan four-poster. Having ignored several applications from the authorities, (she described them as 'a great impertinence') she received a strongly worded request for an interview. At the end of the long monologue on the whys and wherefores of PAYE (of which she said she had never heard) by the two pin-striped men facing her at the end of the bed, she gave her maid, May, a resigned look with a heavy sigh. 'I suppose you're trying to tell me that I owe you some money,' she concluded. 'She reached across the bed for her cheque book,' says Raoul, 'at which gesture the two men accepted defeat and left.'

She died six years later, aged ninety-three. The house that Johnny built in 1900 was then sold, and the whole property with its lovely garden leading down to St Leonard's forest was soon obliterated by a housing estate, a suburb of Horsham. The only evidences of the former glory are the occasional outsize rhodendrons in relatively tiny plots, while 'Millais school' and 'Millais road' do a little more to keep remembrance.

Raoul is eighty-seven. Having sold Serafin in 1983 and having lost his wife, Kay, two years later, he is now permanently based at Westcote manor, its old grey stone walls overlooking the lovely garden that he and Kay created from a wilderness forty years ago, with, beyond, broad views across the Heythrop hunt country. The panelled rooms are decorated with a close array of *objèts d'art*, busts and bronze statutory, oil paintings, rococo carvings, piles of Raoul's sketches more loose than in albums, and a piano to remind him of his love of music and the talent that once was Kay's. There are also many pictures by Johnny and drawings by the great Sir John, one a remarkable study of human feet, drawn when he was seven.

Much of Raoul's day is spent a step or two across the yard, in the studio that was once a tithe barn. Its high walls are adorned with heads from the Compton Brow museum, including the royal he shot in Perthshire, aged twelve, and one of the giant antelopes he secured in Angola in 1925. Beneath them hangs a portrait of Johnny, dressed as a Seaforth Highlander, painted around 1890 by Sir John. He looks every inch the popular image of a soldier, as he would always look, with no hint to the casual observer of the artist-naturalist he was to become. Nor, for that matter, would most people guess that Raoul is a professional artist, for he is tall and lean and upright, with short hair and

Kay.

a spruced moustache on a singularly distinguished head while invariably dressed in the clothes of the conventional English countryman he is.

The studio is cluttered with cartridge papers and canvases, his miniature sketch of the Jubilee picture of the Queen and Prince Philip driving through the Golden Gates at Ascot, a repetition in oils of Churchill with Colonist, besides mementos of Raoul's Andalusian days, flamenco dancers and fighting bulls and more horses, horses, horses. There are, too, the elegant scenes he remembers from his Edwardian childhood, and which he loves to reproduce on a small scale in oils on unsized paper with brushes from the pin feathers of a woodcock, little pictures of decorative women with parasols squired by top-hatted gallants in open carriages, drawn by high-stepping steeds. And in the middle of it all stands regularly the lofty figure of the artist at work before the heavy vertical wooden easel that has been his since the Byam Shaw days nearly seven decades ago.

He has not painted for profit for many years; he no longer equates his pictures in terms of money, and has turned down many a brash five-figure offer from a Greek shipping magnate and American millionaire. He works only for the pleasure of his family and friends and himself. Nor will he exhibit again, though he does occasionally sell a picture to a gallery.

Regarding trends in modern art Raoul echoes much the same disgust that his father

Raoul, with Leo, at Westcote, 1988.

and grandfather expressed in their time. 'In art, as in every other walk of life when discipline is lost, disintegration is inevitable. For many years we have been going through a worse period of "free for all" than ever. When an art student, without talent or proper training, can be given a place in the schools and, with the aid of generous subsidies, throw paint or squeeze tubes onto expensive virgin canvases, without fear of criticism, he is expressing his "ego" and must not, apparently, be interfered with. Large sums of public money are handed out to so-called "original thinkers", who empty barrow loads of gravel or bricks onto the floor of the Tate Gallery . . .

'During my life I have watched with horror the art world being taken over by charlatans and con-men. I once watched a salesman in a gallery sell a piece of hardboard on which was hung a dirty shoe and a piece of string for £2,000 to an American dowager dripping with diamonds. When I asked him how he had the gall to do this he replied "Dear boy, it is my living and she has got millions. You must realise that the public are hypnotised by anything they don't understand. So why not remove their surplus wealth?" . . . In another corner of his showroom stood a cracked washbasin containing an old tennis ball. I said "What's that supposed to mean?" to which the salesman replied: "Dear boy, you must realise that man was the first to think of it . . ."

'I am not exaggerating, it is a typical attitude . . . Today we have the worship of the

153

Raoul Millais: *Arabs Fighting*.

mediocre,' Raoul says with another line of thought, contrasting with the previous sentiments: 'the priceless gift of initiative is too often stamped out. Safety first is our watchword. Let us all work as little as possible for as much as possible. Under the cloak of the old cliché, "the greatest good for the greatest number", there stalks the assassin of the individualist, the strangler of the man with the courage to live and feel independently. How will it all end? Man, in danger of losing his soul,' he thinks, 'is at last in fear of the deathly machine which he has created and turns to escapism for protection. Terrible . . .'

Following the Millais tradition Raoul, though not particularly interested in politics, is, by instinct, a high Tory. He admires Mrs Thatcher and recently her eyes brightened when she found herself sitting next to him at a lunch party. It turned out that Sir John is her favourite artist, and she can not only describe every one of his pictures on public view, but also remembers just where they all hang.

Raoul's voice is severely weakened from an operation following a throat infection, but the effort of talking never seems to tire him. When driving a car he wears a surgical collar to support his neck which he broke in the violent hunting accident in 1937. Nor does that inhibit his constant yearning for a life outdoors. This one time big-game hunter, deer-stalker, skier, *aficionado* of the *corrida* and foxhunter, remains an ardent trout and salmon fisherman. He still goes sporting in Scotland every year, and remains one of the finest game-shots in England.

An amusing raconteur, too, and infinitely charming he is asked to more covert shoots than he can reasonably accept. He still averages three days a week during the pheasant season. When his son, John, staged a family shoot at his home near Marlborough over the Christmas period, 1987, and organised some evening pigeon shooting for his sons and nephews, Raoul asked, 'Does that include me?' Of course it did. So on top of five hours at covertside he spent another two in a pigeon hide. Not bad for a man soon to enter his tenth decade.

'I have always been a fatalist,' he admits. 'Convinced that someone out there has his finger on the button and decides when and where one is to face the final black-out. I am sure that the more we try to avoid danger and take the safe option, the more likely we are to meet the man round the next corner waiting for us with a length of lead piping. This is not a question of courage, of which I have probably less than the next man. I say it on the conviction that somehow, somewhere, it has already been decided who shall survive and who shall not. Like everyone else who has led a very active life I have had my share of narrow escapes.' He has no aspiration now to perform feats of endurance or courage. But he does confess to thinking sometimes of 'painting a masterpiece at ninety.'

Meanwhile he has asked to conclude with this note: 'No man in a long lifetime has ever been more fortunate in his family and the accumulation of so many wonderful friends as I have, and from whom I have received so much undeserved kindness, hospitality and generosity – and very few enemies along the way. It is impossible adequately to thank all those who have been and still are, so good to me. They are responsible for making my life so enjoyable and they are far too numerous to mention by name, but I hope they realise how much I am indebted to them.'

Raoul's bookplate: a happy blend of nature, art, soldiering,
game-shooting, the stalking-ground and the hunting-field.

POSTSCRIPT

For several consecutive generations of a strongly talented family to inherit shared gifts, creative motivations and positive interests, even in moderate measure, is unusual. But in the Millais family the continuous thread is forcefully and transparently clear. I have not researched the pedigrees, biographies and characteristics of John Everett Millais' antecedents, but I am told by members of the family that, on his father's side, art and music figured very strongly in previous generations. Certainly a devotion to art, music, nature and field sports drove very powerfully through the union of John William Millais and Emily Evamy; their son, William, was an outstanding watercolourist, though overshadowed by his sporting companion and brother, the artistically superior John Everett.

It is surprising that Effie – being a pianist with a wonderful ear and musical sense, as well as having a great appreciation of the arts and an intense interest in nature – did not, by the prodigious John Everett, give birth to somewhat greater natural talent among her large brood. On the other hand their son Johnny, John Guille, seemed to combine their sense of adventure and sporting inclinations with all their artistic gifts, except music, while his prose was better than that of any of the Millais clan. And since his wife, Fanny, was a watercolourist, a naturalist and an artist gardener of repute it comes as no surprise that the blood stayed potent in the next generation, and in the next – through Raoul and Clare, who shared a host of interests.

The love of deerstalking, the British big-game hunting, is probably the strongest common motivation among the Millais men. John Everett, Johnny and Raoul were rifle shots of the highest calibre and all of them very skilful stalkers. Raoul's eldest son and his family,

Raoul's sons, John and (*left*) Hugh Millais going to shoot, aged twelve and ten.

Hugh Millais, aged fifteen, with his first salmon, caught on the Blackwater, Co. Waterford.

in particular, have also inherited a great love of the sport, along with game shooting and fishing.

Raoul's second son, Hugh, a Canadian citizen, linguist and graduate of the University of Mexico now living in London inherits the musical gift along with a buoyant pioneer and adventurous spirit, which doubtless comes from his mother's family, the Macdonell, engineers of Canadian Pacific Railway fame, as well as from the Millais genes. He has been a journalist, copywriter, property developer and advertising executive and has played roles in more than a dozen films. He lived, on and off, for more than twenty years in Spain. In his youth he bought an ocean-going schooner, sailed it from Montreal to Venezuela and took part in the great Bermuda race and other ocean challenges. (His grandfather would surely have looked on all that with the greatest approval). A guitar player since childhood he spent ten years in the Caribbean, earning his living as a calypso singer ('the only white professional calypso singer in the business', he assures me).

Hugh's elder son, Ian, a guitar player, too, graduate of Berklee College of Music and a published composer, was a member of Dave Lyttleton's (Humphrey's son's) band: while Joshua Millais, his brother – who in Hugh's words 'has a full understanding of all kinds of art form' – is a professional photographer.

It may be intriguing, let us hope so, to see how the talents bob up and the interests develop in the next generation.

APPENDIX A

Recollections of an old Friend by an old Friend
of Sir J. E. Millais (F. G. Stephens)[1]

The Sir John E. Millais of Presidential days was a very different person from the lad of thirteen whom, in the autumn of 1843, I encountered at the Royal Academy, when, with a host of other Probationers, that is students of the Academy on trial, I entered the Antique School and was greeted with shouts of 'Hallo! Millais! Here is another fellow in a collar!' These cries came from the older students assembled and drawing from the statues, busts and what not. Their occasion was myself, then just upon fifteen years old, who it was my mother's pleasure should wear on the shoulders of his shirt and jacket a white falling collar some four inches wide. It so happened that Millais' mother had a similar fancy, and that, being younger and much smaller than I, his collar had a goffered edging which, with his boyish features, light, long and curling hair, made him appear even younger than he was. Upon the cries ceasing there arose from the semi-circle of students, a lightly and elegantly made youngster wearing such a collar as I have described, a jacket gathered at the waist with a cloth belt and its clasp in front. With an assured air he crossed the room to where I was standing among the new arrivals; he walked round me, inspected me from head to foot, turned on his heel without a word, stepped back to his seat and went on with his drawing. It so happened that the ever-diligent Millais though much further advanced in the Academy and a student in the Life and Painting condescended from time to time to work among the tyros from the Antique such as I was. At that time he was exceedingly like the portrait which was painted of him about the date in question, by, I think, Sir E. Landseer; but there was more 'devil', and less sentiment in the expression of his features. After being inspected I settled to my work and forgot all about that ordeal till I found Millais, who was then not more than five feet two inches tall, standing at my side and, with an air of infinite superiority, looking at my drawing, which he greeted in an undertone as 'Not at all bad!' With such humility as became me I asked his advice about it and he frankly gave me some good counsel. I ought to have said that long before this I had heard of his extraordinary technical skill in drawing and painting, and I reverenced him as the winner of that silver medal which, the first of his Academical honours, had fallen to his lot not long before, but he being a pupil of Sasso's School and I a student in the British Museum, or 'Museumite' so-called, I had not come across the P.R.A. to be.

Abounding in animal spirits and not without a certain playful impishness, being very light and small even for his age, Millais was the lively comrade, I had almost said plaything, of the bigger and older students some of whom had, even in 1843–4, reached full manhood. One of the latter was 'Jack Harris', a burly and robust personage, a leader in all the feats of strength which then obtained in the schools, and the same who sat to Millais in 1848–9 for his exact portrait as the elder brother who kicks the dog in the picture of 'Isabella' now at Liverpool. Profoundly contrasted as in every respect their characters were, Millais and Jack Harris were comrades and playfellows of the closest order at the Academy. For example, I remember how, because some workmen had left a tall ladder against the back of the School, nothing would do but on one occasion Harris must carry Millais clinging round his neck to the top of this ladder. It so happened that just at this moment the door of the room slowly opened while no less a person than the Keeper slowly entered and took up his duties by teaching the student nearest the entrance. Discipline and respect for Mr George Jones forbade Harris to come down the ladder and his safety forbade Millais from letting go his hold. Doubtfully the Keeper saw the dilemma, for, without noticing the culprits, he hastened his progress round the room and left as soon as might be, but not before Millais was tired of his lofty position.

My acquaintance with Millais, which was thus begun, ripened into a sort of friendship not amounting to intimacy during the next few years while I continued my duties and he passed from grade to grade winning the Gold Medal and exhibiting pictures at the Academy as well as, in 1847, contributing the very large 'Widow's Mite' to the great gathering in Westminster Hall. In October, 1848, an agreement was come to by Millais, Rossetti and Mr Holman Hunt which resulted in the setting up of the Pre-Raphaelite Brotherhood. My notions about art being pretty well known to incline towards what has since been called Pre-Raphaelitism I was, by the above-named three, asked to join them as one of the society which soon afterwards included Woolner and James Collinson, with W. M. Rossetti as secretary. As the last-named still dear friend of mine has truly said in his account of the matter the Pre-Raphaelite Brotherhood was then and for about five years later truly a Brotherhood, each member of which as fully rejoiced in the success of his comrades as if they were his own and gladly shared with them all the contumely and insults, the vile misrepresentations and impertinences the movement called forth from the lower and lesser depths. Of course the worst of these outrages fell upon Millais and Mr Hunt. Collinson had his share as an exhibitor, Rossetti had not then appeared, but he and all the others were abused vigorously. Even those who, since then, have carried out the essentials of Pre-Raphaelitism in the mood of its original inspiration, but upon different lines from those of the distinguished painters, did not then, nor till the whole hubbub died away, escape their share of the abuse. It was largely owing to this that Collinson seceded. My intimacy with Millais of course took a new form with this brotherly agreement, and it was probably in consequence of this that I sat to him for the head of the prince in the little picture of 'Ferdinand lured by Ariel' which, being painted in 1849–50, was at the Academy in 1850, and is the leading example of Pre-Raphaelitism according to Millais, (each Brother worked according to his own lights and the general view of the Brotherhood) at that time. Such being the case I may describe the manner of the artist in this particular instance. In the summer and autumn of 1849 he executed the whole of that wonderful background, the delightful figures of the elves and Ariel, and he sketched in the prince himself. The whole was done upon a pure white ground so as to obtain the greatest brilliancy of the pigments. Later on my turn came and in one lengthy sitting Millais drew my most unFerdinand-like features with a pencil upon white paper, making as it was a most exquisite drawing of the highest finish and exact fidelity. In these respects nothing could surpass this jewel of its kind. Something like it, but softer and not quite so sculpturesque, exists in the similar study Millais made for the head of Ophelia in pencil which I saw not long ago and which Sir W. Bowman lent to the Grosvenor Gallery in 1888. My portrait was completely modelled in all respects of form and light and shade so as to be a perfect study for the head thereof to be painted. The day after it was executed Millais repeated the study in a less finished manner upon the panel and, on the day following that I went again to the studio in Gower Street where 'Isabella' and similar pictures were painted. From ten o'clock till nearly five the sitting continued without a stop and with scarcely a word between the painter and his model, the clicking of his brushes when they were shifted in his palette, the sliding of his foot upon the easel, and an occasional sigh marked the hours while, strained to the utmost, Millais worked this extraordinarily fine face. At last he said 'There, old friend, it is done!' Thus it remains as perfectly pure and as brilliant as then fifty years ago, it now remains unchanged. For me, still leaning on a stick and in the required posture, I had become quite unable to move, rise upright or stir a limb till, much as if I were a stiffened lay-figure Millais lifted me up and carried me bodily to the dining-room where some dinner and wine put me on my feet again. Later, the till then unpainted parts of the figure of Ferdinand were added from the model and a lay figure.

It was in the Gower Street studio that Millais was wont when time did not allow out-of-door exercise to perform surprising feats of agility and strength. He had since we first met at Trafalgar Square so greatly developed in tallness, bulk and manliness that no one was surprised at his progress in these respects. He was great in leaping and I well remember how in the studio he was wont to clear my arm outstretched from the shoulder, that is about five feet from the ground, at each spring; the studio measures 19.6 by 20 feet this giving him not more than 14 feet run. Many similar feats attested the strength and energy of the artist.

It was in the Gower Street studio that in 1853 the variously described meeting of the Pre-

Raphaelite Brotherhood then in London occurred in order that the artists present might send as souvenirs to Woolner then in Australia, their portraits, each drawn by another. Millais fell to me to be drawn and to him I fell as his subject. Unhappily for me I was at that time so seriously ill that it was with the greatest difficulty I could drag myself to Gower Street; more than that, it was but the day before the entire ruin of my family, then long impending and long struggled against in vain, was consummated. I was utterly unable to continue the sketch I began, I gave it up and Mr Holman Hunt, who had had D. G. Rossetti for his *vis à vis* and sitter, took my place and drew Millais' head. The head which Millais did of me is now in my possession, the gift of Woolner, to whom it was, with the others, sent to Sydney, whence he brought the whole of the portraits back to England. My portrait, which, by the way, is a good deal out of drawing, attests painfully enough to the state of ill-health and sore trouble in which I then was. This meeting was one of the latest 'functions' of the P.R.B. in its original state, Collinson had seceded and Woolner emigrated to the 'diggings' in search of the gold he did not find. Up to that time the old affectionate conditions still existed among the Brothers, but their end was near. Millais was shooting ahead, Mr Holman Hunt was surely, though slowly, following his path towards Fortune, D. G. Rossetti had retired within himself and made no sign before the world, W. Rossetti was rising in Her Majesty's Service and I was being continually drawn towards that literary work which brought me bread. None of the six had, however, departed from the spirit of the Pre-Raphaelite faith which was in him.

Millais was very much interested in the arrangement of his pictures at the first great collection which was made of them at the Grosvenor Gallery in 1886. On this occasion it was at first intended to hang them in chronological order beginning, for instance, with the portrait of Mr Wyatt of Oxford and the 'Isabella' of 1849 and ending with 'The Ruling Passion' in 1885. Part of this intention was carried out but when Millais saw that, however instructive the arrangement might be it resulted in that which was by no means decorative as a whole, he cried out with characteristic energy, denounced the very notion of such a scheme and insisted on the works being re-grouped, the earlier works, except 'A Huguenot', being relegated to the small room of the gallery and the larger ones disposed according to their coloration and their tone schemes on the walls of the chief room. It was while compiling the notes embodied in the catalogue of this exhibition, all the proofs of which he carefully corrected, that I told him how, according to Northcote, who had the fact from Richardson, to whom an old lady while sitting to him for her portrait related it, that when very young she had sat to Van Dyck. Richardson learnt from her that at that time, and while they were but recently painted, all the portraits she saw in Van Dyck's studio were very much lighter, brighter, and less mellow than they were even in Northcote's days, that is more than a hundred and a quarter years ago. Millais was deeply interested in this, and told me he should modify his practice accordingly. It was at this epoch that 'A Huguenot', which he had not seen for more than thirty years was brought to London in order to be exhibited again. The case it travelled in was opened in my presence and while Millais was in the gallery so that I called him to look at his masterpiece. He came and, having the panel released from the frame, he took it in his hands and studied the surface of the picture with the keenest interest and most searching attention, nothing could exceed the force of this regard; he called upon me to notice some characteristics of the handling and reminded me of various technical details in it which, as I had often seen him at work upon the panel in the Gower Street studio during 1859, were still present in my memory. He laughed with pleasure when, recognizing certain trial touches with a sable brush made upon the white margin of the panel (which the frame ordinarily concealed) he told me a ludicrous story connected with Miss Ryan, the girl model who sat to him. It was with evident pride and many happy memories that, putting the picture back again into its frame, he said 'Really, I did not paint so badly in those days old man!' He was especially delighted because the panel having been in the country since it left the Academy of 1859, it was then (1883) perfectly unchanged in all respects. 'I used,' he said, 'such a colour for this, and such for that, it was risky, perhaps, but then, you see, it is all right now!' I never saw him more deeply moved anent his own work than on this occasion.

APPENDIX B

'Recollections of J. E. Millais' by Mrs Richmond Ritchie
(daughter of W. M. Thackeray) in a letter to J. G. Millais[1]

Dear Mr Millais,

When I first saw your father I was a girl in the schoolroom, and even to my schoolroom-eyes he seemed scarcely more than a boy. Perhaps he looked younger than he really was. He was not so handsome then as he grew to be later, but he was very striking in appearance with wonderful thick bushy hair; he was gay, strong and he talked. He was *somebody* in short. We already knew some of his pictures. In those days it was our custom to admit ourselves to certain Private Views of our own. We used to get up very early, and with some girls who lived close by, go off to the Academy together and be at the doors when they first opened. On one occasion when we arrived, although it was so very early still, I remember there was already a little crowd assembled round a certain picture. We had to wait to see it till we could get to be in front of the people. I gazed, charmed and bewildered. Was it Faery-land or was it real? That shining glen, that floating radiant figure. I knew not what I saw, but the picture took hold of my imagination as pictures do, and after years and years, when I saw the Ophelia again it was not less beautiful than I remembered it. When as girls, we went abroad and could not see the Millais pictures, we used to read the papers and imagine them for ourselves, and I can remember being in Paris and trying to make a fancy sketch of the Naturalist – with all the brightest purples and greens in my paint box; it was an absurdity, but it shows what a present Fact those special pictures were for the girls of my generation.

Soon after your parents' marriage my father took us with him one day when he went to call upon them, somewhere near Montagu Square. I do not remember being shown any pictures on this occasion but there is one I can still see. Your mother was recovering from some illness, and she was extended straight in some beautiful glowing dress upon a sofa, with her hand resting upon a round gilt leather cushion which made a 'background of pale gold' to her face.

We saw most of your parents after my father's death, when my sister and I were living very near to Cromwell Place, and we used to meet your father in the street and go to see him sometimes in his studio, and now and then he came to our house. I can remember one little speech of his to some very charming and fastidious young women who were staying with us then – 'Ah,' said he – when they objected to someone or other – 'you young women are all alike; you expect a man to be as handsome as the Apollo Belvedere and as wise as Socrates and as rich as Croesus, and nothing short of perfection all round will content you.' And then in a sort of humourous way he began enumerating various attributes of various friends: A's hair and B's eyes and C's white teeth and D's amusing wit and etc. etc., 'only you expect to get them *all* together in one individual,' he said, and everyone burst out laughing. He had a way of illuminating people and brightening up commonplaces; he always spoke straight out and even adverse criticism didn't hurt, it was so kind and so true. I remember taking a picture to him once that an importunate friend was most anxious he should see. '*You* know better than to bring me such as thing as that!' said he, 'take it away,' and to this day I blush when I recall that work of art. The simplicity and the directness of his blame took away the sting of it, for it is not so much criticism that people resent generally as the spirit of censure in which it is given. With Sir John, as indeed with most real men, there was a feeling of confidence and trust in his judgement.

Once he took several of us – I am ashamed to say I only remember *myself* – to the National Gallery, and went round with him for he was not afraid to speak and to speak out loud. The Loiterer opened their eyes and ears; The Triumph of Bacchus became a glorified triumph indeed later as he stood before it praising and cheering, but the poor little Raphaels, St Cecilia and others, might well turn pale and hang their affected heads as that slashing sword of justice went by.

One day he was painting in his studio and he said 'I will give you a lesson in colour.' He was painting a lady in garden gloves with a rough basket of flowers on her arm; it was a delightful picture but the effect was perhaps rather dim. 'Now you will see what a little yellow will do,' he said and as he painted a bright yellow flower into the basket it was like a note of music suddenly striking up; the whole Composition lit up by magic.

Almost the last time I ever went to see him in that same studio, that beautiful picture of the old Scotch Garden stood upon the easel. I said how beautiful I thought it. 'Do you like it,' he answered rather sadly, 'I can tell you that a bit of my life has gone into that picture.' It was on that same day, I think but I am not sure, that he showed me his daughter Mary's portrait. 'Here is something you must like very much,' he said, and then he went on with a father's fond pride to praise the sitter.

One thing and another comes into my mind as I try to think of it all – and among the rest I can remember Robert Browning's vivid description of his own great pleasure and gratitude when Sir John gave his advice to Pen Browning and urged him to take up painting as a profession. The young man had been with the Millais' up in Scotland and from what Mr Browning told us we gathered that they had all been out of doors painting together and Pen Browning had worked with the great master's paints and brushes.

I once saw an artist at work in a little wood near Knole – on a certain day in July when we all started on a happy expedition Mrs Millais had invited me to join. Her sister was there and the Trollopes and Mr Charles Clifford. We had found sunshine everywhere and a drag at Sevenoaks and we drove to Knole and to Igtham Moat. From Knole as we walked through the woods, we came upon this painter at work under the trees. Our host stopped for a moment – (Knole and all its lovely surroundings seemed to me to belong to your father for all that day and for ever since indeed.) 'Why,' said he to the painter, 'you have not got your lights right – look this is what you want,' and he took the brush out of his hand and made a line or two on the picture and then nodded to him and walked away. Mr Trollope laughed 'The man looks bewildered – he ought to know it is Millais!' said he, and he ran back and told him; then someone else laughed and said 'he ought to know it is Trollope' so a second message was conveyed to the unfortunate painter, and amused with everything and in good spirits we all walked on through the wood to where the carriage was waiting.

The last time I sat by your father at dinner was at the house of my husband's sister, Mrs Freshfield. It was a very great pleasure to me to find Sir John there and still more to find my place by his at dinner and he was in good spirits and talking delightfully. He told me a ghost story, and talked of books and pictures. He recommended a book for my boy and wrote the name down 'Robbery under Arms'. 'It is a delightful book,' he said, 'I couldn't lay it down. At first I thought it was going to be something marsupial, but read it straight through once I had begun.' Then we talked about a little drawing of my father he had once given me and of old friends and old times and pictures . . .

APPENDIX C

Obituary

The Times, 27 March 1931

MR J.G. MILLAIS
HUNTER, NATURALIST AND GARDENER

Mr J.G. Millais, F.Z.S., hunter, naturalist, and landscape gardener, died at Horsham on Tuesday, his sixty-sixth birthday.

The fourth son of Sir John Everett Millais, Bt., President of the Royal Academy, whose biography he published in 1899, John Guille Millais was a hunter and collector even before he was sent to Marlborough, where he had painful interviews with Mr Bell, the Master, for possessing a forbidden weapon called a 'tweaker'. At the age of thirteen he began to wander along the east and north-east coasts of Scotland in search of birds for his collection. Gamekeepers took to him, and he was friends in time with every fisherman and longshoreman between St Andrews and Arbroath, being known to them as 'Johnny with the long gun'.

'Many a day (he wrote in his reminiscences) I never reached my dry clothes and extra cartridges (which had been sent on) because I had seen some rare visitor at which a shot could not be obtained. Then it meant a night, and sometimes two, out in the open, until the specimen was bagged or lost.'

Millais did not kill for the sake of killing; his collection of some 3,000 birds that regularly visit these islands set up in his museum at his home at Compton's Brow, Horsham, is of obvious scientific value. The skill, patience, knowledge, endurance, and courage which it involved can hardly be estimated. Millais himself considered that big game shooting, of which he had plenty of experience, was not more dangerous than wild fowling in a punt in Northern firths. In 1924 he published 'Far Away up the Nile', a record of a big game shooting holiday which he took with his son, illustrated by admirable sketches made by both.

It was by no means his first visit to Africa; he travelled and shot big game in South and Central Africa as well as in Iceland, Western America, Canada, Newfoundland, where he mapped and explored about 100 square miles, Norway, Alaska, the Arctic regions, and the Carpathians. He was the biographer, in 1918, of that great hunter, F.C. Selous, and he was the author of many other books of sport and natural history, notably 'Game Birds and Shooting Sketches', 'A Breath from the Veldt', 'British Deer and their Horns', 'The Wild Fowler in Scotland', 'The Natural History of British Surface-Feeding Ducks', 'The Mammals of Great Britain and Ireland', in three volumes, 'Newfoundland and its Untrodden Ways', 'The Natural History of British Game Birds', 'British Diving Ducks', 'Deer and Deer Stalking', 'European Big Game', and 'American Big Game'. An article of his on the wild cat in Scotland in *The Times* of October 23, 1926, may be recalled. He also illustrated many books, including the Badminton volume on shooting, Seebohm's and Sir R. Payne-Gallwey's works, and the 'Encyclopaedia of Sport'. He was an excellent painter and animal sculptor, and had two exhibitions of his works in 1910 and 1921.

As a landscape gardener Millais advocated more space devoted to beds and woodland walks of flowering shrubs, and less to lawns and borders and beds for roses and herbaceous plants. He published a monumental treatise on rhododendrons and the various hybrids, as well as a book on magnolias. He received the Victoria medal of the Royal Horticultural Society and the Loder rhododendron cup.

From Marlborough Millais went up to Trinity College, Cambridge, and after three years in a Militia battalion joined the 1st Battalion of the Seaforth Highlanders in 1886. He retired in 1892, but rejoined for the Great War, and was lieutenant-commander, R.N.V.R. He was employed in an official position in Norway. His elder son, Geoffroy de Carteret Millais, died of wounds in 1918. He married, in 1894, Frances Margaret, daughter of Mr P.G. Skipworth; she survives him with one son, Mr H.R. le Jarderay Millais, and one daughter. Millais leaves a brother, Sir Geoffroy Millais, Bt., and two sisters, Lady Stuart of Wortley and Miss Mary Millais.

The funeral will be private, and it is requested that no flowers be sent.

APPENDIX D

The Millais Descent

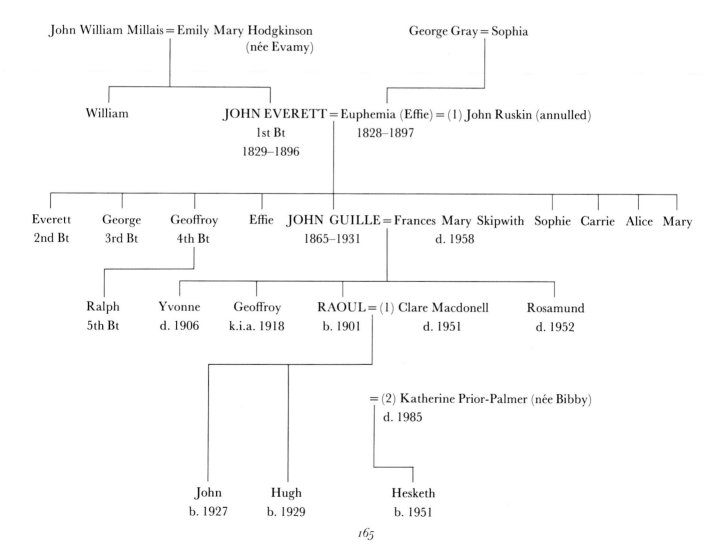

John William Millais = Emily Mary Hodgkinson (née Evamy)　　　　George Gray = Sophia

William

JOHN EVERETT = Euphemia (Effie) = (1) John Ruskin (annulled)
1st Bt 　　　　 1828–1897
1829–1896

Everett 2nd Bt　　George 3rd Bt　　Geoffroy 4th Bt　　Effie　　JOHN GUILLE = Frances Mary Skipwith　　Sophie　Carrie　Alice　Mary
　　　　　　　　　　　　　　　　　　　　　　　　　　1865–1931　　　d. 1958

Ralph 5th Bt　　Yvonne d. 1906　　Geoffroy k.i.a. 1918　　RAOUL = (1) Clare Macdonell　　Rosamund
　　　　　　　　　　　　　　　　　　　　　　b. 1901　　　d. 1951　　　d. 1952

= (2) Katherine Prior-Palmer (née Bibby)
d. 1985

John b. 1927　　Hugh b. 1929　　Hesketh b. 1951

165

Raoul Millais:
Flamenco.

SOURCES

Chapter 1   Child Medallist

1   J.G. Millais, *The Life and Letters of Sir John Everett Millais*, Vol I, pp 7–8

2   *Ibid*, p 12

3   *Ibid*, pp 16–17

4   Walpole Society, Vol 44, p 3

5   J.G.M., *Life*, I, p 49

6   *The Journal of Beatrix Potter*, p 31

7   M.H. Spielmann, *Millais and his Works*, p 21

8   From the original in the possession of Raoul Millais

9   J.G.M., *Life* I, p 179

10   *Ibid*, p 265

11   *Ibid*, pp 269–70

Chapter 2   Effie

1   Spielmann, p 24

2   Peter Quennell, *John Ruskin, The Portrait of a Prophet*, p 93

3   *Ibid*

4   Ruskin, *Works*, Vol 12, p XXIV

5   *Ibid*, p XXII

6   Admiral Sir William James, *The Order of Release*, p 220

7   Mary Lutyens, *Millais and the Ruskins*, p 193

8   James, p 204

9   Walpole Society, Vol 44, p 7

10   From *An Ill-Assorted Marriage*, an unpublished letter from Ruskin to F.J. Furnivall (British Museum. Cup 503 n.11)

11   Lutyens, p 141

12   Walpole, Vol 44, p 16

13   James, pp 242–43

14   *Ibid*, pp 246–48

15   Lutyens, pp 261–62

16   J.G.M., *Life*, I, p 288

17   Lutyens, pp 264–65

Chapter 3   A Greater Breadth of Treatment

1   J.G.M., *Life*, I, pp 267–68

2   *Ibid*, p 259

3   *Ibid*, p 295–96

4   *Ibid*, p 311

5   Potter, p 119

6   J.G.M., *Life*, I, p 342

7   *Ibid*, pp 342–45

8   *Ibid*, pp 345–49

9   A.L. Baldry, *Sir John Everett Millais, His Art and Influence*, p 94

10   J.G.M., *Life*, I, pp 367–71

11   *Ibid*, p 390

12   *Ibid*, p 391

13   J.G.M., *Life*, II, p 417

14   *Ibid*, I, p 417

15   *Ibid*, p. 421

16   *Ibid*, II, p 19

17   *Ibid*, p 13

18   Spielmann, p 35

19   J.G.M., *Life*, II, pp 26–30

20   *Ibid*, p 25

21   *Ibid*, p 66

22   *Ibid*, pp 147–48

Chapter 4   Johnny-with-the-Long-Gun

1   J.G.M., *Wanderings and Memories*, p 45

2   *Ibid*, p 20

3   *Ibid*, pp 20–21

4   *Ibid*

5   *Ibid*, p 2–3

6   *Ibid*, p 12

7   *Ibid*, p 15

8   J.G.M., *Life*, II, p 107

9   Baldry, pp 71–2

10   Potter, p 10

11   Spielmann, p 58

12   *Ibid*, p 125

13   J.G.M., *Wanderings*, p 105

14 J.G.M., *Life*, II, p 110

15 Potter, p 100

16 J.G.M., *Life*, II, pp 116–17

17 Spielmann, p 125

18 Arthur Fish, *John Everett Millais*, p 160

19 J.G.M., *Life*, II, p 137

20 *Ibid*, p 75

21 *Ibid*, p 140

22 *Ibid*, p 157

23 J.G.M., *Wanderings*, p 34

24 *Ibid*, p 31

25 *Ibid*, p 45

26 *Ibid*, p 47

27 Abel Chapman, J.G. Millais and F.C. Selous, *The Gun at Home and Abroad*, Vol II, p 374

28 J.G.M., *Wanderings*, p 90

29 *Ibid*, p 67

30 *Ibid*, p 81–2

31 *Ibid*, p 96

32 *Ibid*, p 97–103

33 Potter, p 97

34 Fish, p 139

35 Potter, p 154

36 J.G.M., *Life*, pp 223–24

37 Spielmann, p 40

38 *Ibid*, p 41

39 *Ibid*, p 41

40 Potter, p 47

41 Spielmann, p 67

42 J.G.M., *Life*, II, pp 223–24

43 *Ibid*, p 297

44 Potter, p 418

Chapter 5   *Adventures on the Veldt*

1 J.G.M., *A Breath from the Veldt*, p 1

2 J.G.M., *British Deer and their Horns*, p 84

3 J.G.M., *A Breath from the Veldt*, pp 47–48

4 *Ibid*, pp 77–81

5 *Ibid*, p 116

6 *Ibid*, p 140

7 *Ibid*, pp 165–66

8 *Ibid*, pp 162–65

9 *Ibid*, pp 318–21

10 *Ibid*, pp 325

11 *Ibid*, pp 330–32

12 *Ibid*, pp 15–16

Chapter 6   *The President's Last Trek*

1 J.G.M., *British Deer and Their Horns*, p 200

2 J.G.M., *Life*, II, p 300

3 Spielmann, p 20

4 J.G.M., *Life*, II, p 354

5 *Ibid*, p 332

6 *Ibid*, p 448–49

7 *Ibid*, p 330

8 *Daily News*, 14 Aug 1896

9 Potter, p 408

10 J.G.M., *Life*, II, p 258

11 *Ibid*, p 335

12 *Ibid*

13 Spielmann, pp 42–45

Chapter 7   *The Naturalist at Home*

1 Theodore Roosevelt, *African Game Trails*, p 502

2 J.G.M., *Wildfowler in Scotland*, p 51

3 *Ibid*, p 44

4 *Ibid*, pp 45–50

5 J.G.M., *Life of Frederick Courteney Selous* pp 235–50

6 J.G.M., *Natural History of British Surface-Feeding Ducks*, Preface.

7 J.G.M., *Newfoundland and its Untrodden Ways* pp 139–40

8 J.G.M., *Mammals*, II, pp 242–43

9 J.G.M., *Mammals*, I, p 161

10 *Ibid*, p 144

11 J.G.M., *Mammals*, II, p 232

12 *Ibid*, I, p 17

13 *Ibid*, p 65

14 *Ibid*, p 64

15 *Ibid*, p 85

16 *Ibid*, p 115

17 *Ibid*, III, p 54

18 *Ibid*, pp 216–17

19 *Ibid*, II, p 23

20 *Ibid*, p 129

21 *Ibid*, p 23

22 *The Gun at Home and Abroad*, *II*, pp 25–26

23 J.G.M., *Mammals*, I, IX

24 H. Hesketh Prichard, *Through the Heart of Patagonia*, Preface

25 J.G.M., *Mammals*, I, p 317

26 *Ibid*, p 321

27 *Ibid*, pp 332–33

28 *Ibid*, III, pp 59–63

29 J.G.M., *Wanderings*, p 106

30 J.G.M., *Newfoundland*, p 140

31 J.G.M., *Wanderings*, pp 145–51

Chapter 8   Newfoundland Discoverer

1 J.G.M., *Newfoundland*, p 4

2 *Ibid*, pp 14–15

3 *Ibid*, p 31

4 *Ibid*, p 33

5 *Ibid*, pp 39–40

6 *Ibid*, pp 75–76

7 *Ibid*, p 79

8 *Ibid*, p 88

9 *Ibid*, p 99

10 *Ibid*, p 116

11 *Ibid*, p 131

12 *Ibid*, p 174

13 *Ibid*, p 184

14 *Ibid*, pp 189–90

15 *Ibid*, p 203

16 *Ibid*, p 210

17 *Ibid*, p 214

18 *Ibid*, pp 229–30

19 *Ibid*, p 236

20 *Ibid*, p 259

21 J.G.M., *Wanderings*, p 120

22 J.G.M., *Newfoundland*, p 267

23 J.G.M., *Wanderings*, pp 121–23

24 J.G.M., *Newfoundland*, p 275

25 *Ibid*, p 235

26 *Ibid*, p 264

27 J.G.M., *Life of F.C. Selous*, p 258

28 H. Frank Wallace, *A Highland Gathering*, p 192

Chapter 9   Faraway Places and Family Life

1 *The Gun at Home and Abroad* : III, p 301

2 *Ibid*, II, p 241

3 Wallace, *A Highland Gathering*, p 174

4 *Ibid*, pp 176–77

5 *The Gun at Home and Abroad*, II, pp 243–44

6 *Ibid*, p 284

7 *Ibid*, p 386

8 J.G.M., *Wanderings*, pp 113–114 and footnote

9 *Ibid*, pp 112–13

10 J.G.M., *Life of F.C. Selous*, pp 272–73

11 *The Gun at Home and Abroad*, III, p 319

12 Wallace, *A Highland Gathering*, p 179

13 *The Gun at Home and Abroad*, III, p 340

14 *Ibid*, I, p 33

15 *Ibid*, III, pp 263–67

16 J.G.M., *Wanderings*, p 193

17 *Ibid*, p 197

18 *Ibid*, p 219

19 *Ibid*, p 192–93

20 *Ibid*, p 202

21 J.G.M., *Life of F.C. Selous*, p 286

Chapter 10   Strife

1 J.G.M., *Wanderings*, p 221–22

2 From a letter in Raoul Millais' possession

3 J.G.M., *Wanderings*, p 245–48

4 *Ibid*, p 258

5 *Ibid*, p 270–72

6 J.G.M., *Life of F.C. Selous*, pp 344–45

Chapter 11   Raoul in Johnny's Footsteps

1 J.G.M., *Essays, Rhododendron Gardens* (2nd series), Preface

2 J.G.M., *Far Away up the Nile*, p 4

3 *Ibid*, p 3

4 *Ibid*, pp 30–31

5 *Ibid*, p 32

6 *Ibid*, p 37, 39

7 *Ibid*, p 44

8 *Ibid*, p 60

9 *Ibid*, pp 99–100

10 The various attempts, starting in 1895, to establish the native dog of the Niam-Niam tribe in England all failed until the successful foundation of the breed (since known as the Basenji) by Mrs Burn and Miss Veronica Tudor-Williams in 1936–37.

11 *Ibid*, pp 112–13

12 *Ibid*, pp 125–26

13 Wallace, *A Highland Gathering*, p 188

14 J.G.M., *Nile*, p 149

15 *Ibid*, p 150

16 *Ibid*, pp 161–62

17 *Ibid*, pp 190–91

18 Schweinfurth, *The Heart of Africa*, p 75

19 J.G.M., *Nile*, pp 195–96

20 *Ibid*, pp 207–08

21 *Ibid*, pp 208–09

22 *Ibid*, pp 210–11

23 *Ibid*, p 220

24 *Ibid*, pp 222–23

25 Wallace, *A Highland Gathering*, p 188

26 J.G.M., *Nile* p 227

27 *Ibid*, p 228

28 *Ibid*, pp 231–32

Chapter 12   Raoul takes up the Reins

1 Wallace, *A Highland Gathering*, p 185

2 Wallace, *Happier Years*, p 200

3 *Ibid*, p 197

4 Wallace, *A Highland Gathering*, p 188

5 *Ibid*, pp 184–85

6 *Ibid*, p 192

7 *Ibid*, pp 188–89

8 The date is recorded in the reference books as March 31. But see Appendix 'C'

9 B.M. Collin, *J.P. Hornung, A Family Portrait*, p 54

Appendix A
1 From the original in the possession of Raoul Millais

Appendix B
1 From the original in the possession of Raoul Millais

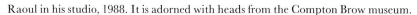

Raoul in his studio, 1988. It is adorned with heads from the Compton Brow museum.

BIBLIOGRAPHY

Anon. *Ruskin's Romance*, Reprinted from 'a New England newspaper'. BM copy No 1608/1609

Armstrong, W., 'Sir J.E. Millais Bt, RA. His Life and Work'. In the 1885 *Art Annual*. BM copy P.P. 1931 p.c. (2)

Baldry, A.L., *Sir John Everett Millais. His Art and Influence*. George Bell, 1899

Chapman, Abel, Millais, J.G. and Selous, F.C., *The Gun at Home and Abroad*, London and Counties Press, 1913–15: *Vol I British Deer and Ground Game, Dogs, Guns and Rifles, Vol II The Big Game of Asia and North America, Vol III The Big Game of Africa and Europe*

Fish, Arthur, *John Everett Millais*, Cassell, 1923

James, Admiral Sir William, *The Order of Release*, John Murray, 1948

Loveday, Arthur F., *Three Stages in the History of Rhodesia*. Including a brief Biography of F.C. Selous, Balkana, Cape Town, 1961

Lutyens, Mary, *Effie in Venice*, John Murray, 1965
    Millais and the Ruskins, John Murray, 1967
    Rainy Days at Brig O'Turk, Dalrymple Press, 1983

Millais, Everett, (J.G. Millais' brother), *The Theory and Practice of Rational Breeding*, In the *Fanciers' Gazette*, BM 7294 ccc 4
    Two Problems of Reproduction, Lecture reproduced in *Our Dogs*, 28 February 1895, BM 7206 dg 1–4

Millais, Geoffroy, *Sir John Everett Millais*, Academy Editions, 1979

Millais, J.G., *Game Birds and Shooting Sketches*, Henry Sotheran, 1892
    A Breath from the Veldt, 2nd Ed., Henry Sotheran, 1895
    British Deer and their Horns, Longmans, 1897
    The Life and Letters of Sir John Everett Millais, printed privately by Brendon and Son, Plymouth, 1899
    The Wildfowler in Scotland, Longmans, 1901
    The Natural History of British Surface-Feeding Ducks, Longmans, 1902
    The Mammals of Great Britain and Ireland, Longmans; Vol I, 1904; Vol II, 1905; Vol III, 1906
    Newfoundland and its Untrodden Ways, Longmans, 1907
    The Natural History of British Game Birds, Longmans, 1909
    British Diving Ducks, 2 vols, Longmans, 1913
    Deer and Deer Stalking, Longmans, 1913
    Rhododendrons and their Various Hybrids, Longmans, 1917
    Life of Frederick Courteney Selous DSO, Longmans, 1918
    Wanderings and Memories, Longmans, 1919
    Rhododendrons, 2nd series, Longmans, 1924
    Far Away up the Nile. Longmans, 1924
    Magnolias, Longmans, 1927

Potter, Beatrix, *The Journal of Beatrix Potter*, Frederick Warne, 1966

Prichard, H. Hesketh, *Through the Heart of Patagonia*, Heinemann, 1902

Quennell, Peter, *John Ruskin: The Portrait of a Prophet*, Collins, 1949

Roosevelt, Theodore, *African Game Trails (An Account of the African Wanderings of an American Hunter-Naturalist)*, John Murray, 1910

Ruskin, John, *An Ill-Assorted Marriage*. An unpublished letter, 1854, British Library, Cup 503 n.11

Selous, F.C. *A Hunter's Wanderings in Africa*, Bentley and Son, 1881
    Travel and Adventure in South-East Africa, Rowland Ward, 1882

Spielmann, M.H., *Millais and His Works*, William Blackwood, 1898

Trollope, Anthony *Autobiography*, Ed. OUP 1950

Wallace, H. Frank, *A Highland Gathering*, Eyre and Spottiswoode, 1932
    Happier Years, Eyre and Spottiswoode, 1944

Walpole Society, Vol 44, University Press, Glasgow, 1974

INDEX